GHOSTS
along the Mississippi River

ALAN BROWN

University Press of Mississippi / Jackson

www.upress.state.ms.us

The University Press of Mississippi is a member of
the Association of American University Presses.

Copyright © 2011 by University Press of Mississippi
All rights reserved
Manufactured in the United States of America

First printing 2011

∞

Library of Congress Cataloging-in-Publication Data

Brown, Alan, 1950 Jan. 12–
Ghosts along the Mississippi River / Alan Brown.
p. cm.
Includes bibliographical references and index.
ISBN 978-1-61703-143-4 (cloth : alk. paper) — ISBN 978-
1-61703-144-1 (pbk. : alk. paper) — ISBN 978-1-61703-145-8
(ebook) 1. Ghosts—Mississippi River Region. I. Title.
BF1472.U6B742 2011
133.10977—dc22   2011007985

British Library Cataloging-in-Publication Data available

*To my wife, Marilyn, who gave me the
idea for this book and accompanied me
to many of these haunted places*

Contents

Acknowledgments

I would like to thank Patti Pointer, Shirley Smollen, Michael Espanjer, and Lisa Marks for telling me their stories. As always, I am beholden to author Troy Taylor for the support he has given me over the years with my various projects. I am also indebted to the following ghost tours for helping me pinpoint each city's haunted sites: Haunted Ghost Walking Tour of Memphis, Annie Wiggins Ghost Tour of Galena, the History and Hauntings Ghost Tours of Alton, Vicksburg Historical Ghost Tours, Natchez Ghost Tours, New Orleans Ghost Tours, and Garden District Tours. Finally, I would like to thank the University of West Alabama's University Research Committee for providing me with the funding for my trips to these haunted cities.

Ghosts along the Mississippi River

Introduction

The Mississippi River is, and always has been, the most important river in the United States. Second only to the Missouri River in length, the Mississippi's drainage area covers 40 percent of the United States and forms the third-largest drainage basin in the world. From its beginnings in Minnesota, the Mississippi flows south along the borders of Wisconsin, Illinois, Kentucky, Tennessee, and Mississippi on the east and Minnesota, Iowa, Missouri, Arkansas, and Louisiana on the west. Its most important tributaries between Minneapolis and St. Louis are the Illinois, Chippewa, Black, Wisconsin, Saint Croix, Iowa, Des Moines, and Rock Rivers. The Ohio River feeds into the Mississippi River at Cairo, Illinois. By the time the river has completed its course down to New Orleans and the Gulf of Mexico, it has covered 2,348 miles.

A Spanish explorer named Hernando De Soto was the first white man to cast his eyes on the body of water the Indians called "The Father of Waters" in 1541. In their search for a water passage to China more than a hundred years later, Jacques Marquette and Louis Joliet traveled down the Wisconsin River to the point where it connects with the Mississippi, south of Prairie du Chien in 1673. When the pair reached the point where the Arkansas River and the Mississippi River join, they realized that the river would not take them to China, and they headed back. In 1679, LaSalle and his friend, Henri de Tonty, traveled down the Illinois River by canoe and made their way to the Mississippi. Father Hennepin went to St. Anthony Falls, and LaSalle traveled down river to the Gulf of Mexico. In 1782, LaSalle arrived at the mouth of the Mississippi River and claimed the entire Mississippi Valley for France, which ceded the region to Spain in 1763 but reclaimed it in 1800. Three years later, the United States acquired the Mississippi River as part of the Louisiana Purchase.

The Mississippi River was used as a means of travel and transportation long before the arrival of the white explorers. The Indian tribes that Lewis and Clark encountered when they passed through the Mississippi Valley in 1803—the Winnebago, the Fox, the Ojibway, the Sauk, the Chickasaw, the Choctaw, the Natchez, and the Alabama—had traveled up and down the river in canoes. The French fur traders navigated the river in crude bull boats. The early settlers used flatboats and keelboats to reach their destinations. The first paddle-wheel steamboat—the *New Orleans*—began chugging up and down the Ohio and Mississippi Rivers in 1811. In 1823, the *Virginia* became the first steamboat to travel the upper Mississippi River. Steamboat traffic on the Mississippi was temporarily halted during the Civil War. However, in 1863, the Mississippi River was used as an invasion route for the Union army after the capture of Vicksburg. After the Civil War, steamboats once again plied the Mississippi River, but they faced increased competition from the railroads. Still, by 1800, 4,800 steamboats were carrying passengers and freight on the Mississippi. Navigation on the Mississippi River improved greatly in the late 1800s and early 1900s as a result of the changes made by the army engineers, who removed the snags, dynamited boulders out of the channels, and built a series of dams. The lock-and-dam system in the upper Mississippi River authorized by Congress in the 1930s made possible the transportation of commodities like grain, petroleum, fertilizer, rock salt, and anhydrous ammonia.

Before the Civil War, most of the workers who loaded the boats and did the heavy work on board were Irishmen and Germans. After the Civil War, many of these jobs were taken over by newly freed slaves. Working on the river was often tedious and mind-numbing, so to pass the time, river men amused themselves by drinking, gambling, wenching, and spinning yarns. They talked about "her-girls," mermaid-like creatures who dragged a Greenville black man named Big Black down to the bottom of the river. On dark, cold nights, the workers frightened one another with tales of a black deckhand named Chattanooga who drowned in the Mississippi but whose ghost returned each night to take a cigar out of the icebox, light it, and blow smoke rings. White river men spoke of Sal Fink, the daughter of famed keelboat man Mike Fink, who snapped off all of the snags on the river and rode on the back of an alligator.

The Mississippi River has also inspired a number of well-known American authors. The first was Herman Melville, whose 1857 novel *The Confidence Man* is a savage indictment of the greed and commercialism of the mid-nineteenth century. The author who is most associated with the Mississippi is Mark Twain, who finally achieved his lifelong dream of becoming a steamboat pilot in 1860. In his book *Life on the Mississippi*, Twain described the river as an implacable force of nature that could never be tamed. F. Scott Fitzgerald, who was born in St. Paul, Minnesota, wrote of the gulf separating the affluent urban dwellers and the poor who lived along the river. T. S. Eliot, who spent his formative years in St. Louis, credited the Mississippi River as having a tremendous influence on his poetry. In "The Negro Speaks of Rivers," black poet Langston Hughes wrote of Abraham Lincoln's life-changing trip down the Mississippi River to the slave markets in New Orleans.

Literary expressions of the Mississippi River will always hold a special place in the imagination of American readers. Ironically, in recent years, many people have become fascinated with the river's oral narratives, especially those tales that deal with its link with the supernatural. Haunted buildings like the Lemp Mansion in St. Louis, Missouri, and the Mineral Springs Hotel in Alton, Illinois, are regularly featured in television shows like *Ghost Hunters* on the Syfy Channel and *A Haunting* on the Discovery Channel.

The large number of ghost stories associated with the Mississippi River begs the question, "Is there a connection between the river and the paranormal?" An examination of haunted places throughout the world reveals that water figures prominently into a large number of these tales. In Greek mythology, the River Styx transports spirits to the Underworld. Many tourists and tour guides have seen the ghost of a long-dead sailor aboard the battleship *Texas*, which is moored east of Houston, Texas. Alcatraz, the most haunted prison in the United States, was built on an island in San Francisco Bay.

Indeed, some of the country's most haunted cities, like Charleston, South Carolina; San Francisco, California; Savannah, Georgia; and Galveston, Texas, are located near large bodies of water.

The Discovery Channel television show *Ghost Lab* explored the connection between the Mississippi and the preponderance of paranormal activity along its shows. In an episode entitled "Nottoway Plantation and Metro Club," which aired on November 5, 2009, the Ghost Lab team traveled to Nottoway Plantation, which sits on the bank of the Mississippi River in White Castle, Louisiana. Working on the assumption that entities must draw energy from an external source in order to manifest, the directors of the group, Barry and Brian Klinge, interviewed Dr. Tony Ambler of the University of Texas. Ambler said that the large numbers of impurities in the Mississippi River are excellent conductors of electricity. The Kling brothers concluded that there must be a direct flow of energy from the Mississippi to Nottoway Plantation.

Of course, there could be other reasons why so many of these places are haunted. Many river towns, like Natchez and New Orleans, have a very violent history, due in part to the brawling deckhands and "rowdies" who entertained themselves in these port cities. The Civil War, which had a tremendous impact on river cities like Vicksburg, may also have produced many of the restless spirits who roam these old buildings. Paranormal investigators have placed a large number of these sightings in the category of residual hauntings, which resemble a film loop that replays over and over again.

It goes without saying that it is easy to overanalyze something as ephemeral as ghosts and the reason for their return. Ghost stories should be enjoyed, and valued, because they preserve the history and values of the people who pass them along. The ghost stories of the Mississippi River are so compelling that they, like the river itself, are likely to "just keep rollin' along."

Arkansas

HOLLY GROVE

Holly Grove is the land where the Europeans first crossed the Mississippi River in 1541. In the early 1800s, the earliest families settled in Baytown twenty miles south of Holly Grove. Most of them were from North and South Carolina, Georgia, Alabama, Virginia, Mississippi, Tennessee, and Kentucky. Most of the first settlers relocated from Baytown to Holly Grove because of floods and a malaria outbreak. Mr. and Mrs. J. M. Smith and Dr. A. K. Roberts named the town "Holly Grove" because of its three holly thickets, one in the center of town and two in the northwest part. Holly Grove was incorporated on July 25, 1876. Holly Grove is located in one of the best cotton-growing areas in the country. Rice and soybeans are also grown extensively.

CAPTAIN MULL'S HOUSE

One of the most fascinating of these early settlers lived in a house halfway between Holly Grove and Helena on what is now U.S. Highway 49. The house, which was built entirely by slaves, was originally owned by James Kerr. Slaves cut trees growing on James Kerr's property and hauled them by oxen to Indian Bay, where they were shipped by boat to Helena, Arkansas. Once the logs were fashioned into boards, they were transported by oxen once again to the Kerr house. A few years after the Civil War, James Kerr sold the house to a Mr. Allen of Helena. He, in turn, sold the house to a retired sea captain named Captain Mull in 1880.

Captain Mull's life changed forever after moving to Holly Grove. The story goes that he fell in love with an Indian girl. For a few short years,

he was happier than he had ever been sailing on the ocean. When his
wife died, Captain Mull was devastated. He was so reluctant to part
from her completely that he had her interred in a glass casket. Captain
Mull kept her casket in his house to keep her with him all of the time.
After Captain Mull died in 1935, the corpse of his wife was buried in
the local cemetery. For several years, the house stood abandoned. Before
long, people passing by the house claimed to have heard the sound of
someone playing the piano. The old house is now a private residence.

Glass coffins have always held a morbid fascination for loved ones.
For almost a century, thousands of people have walked past the glass
coffin of Revolutionary leader Vladimir Ilyich Lenin in Moscow. After
Michael Jackson died in 2009, there was talk of casketing his corpse
in a glass coffin so that he would always be accessible to his legions
of adoring fans. However, the sad tale of Captain Mull bears a closer
resemblance to the story of Snow White, a beautiful young woman who
was also placed in a glass coffin after death by the ones who loved her.

HELENA

Founded in 1820, Helena bills itself as the quintessential Mississippi
River Delta town with its Civil War history, southern mansions, and
blues legacy. During the Battle of Helena, Confederate forces tried
unsuccessfully to expel the Union army from the city to relieve pressure on Vicksburg, Mississippi. During the 1940s and 1950s, Helena
was home to a thriving blues community. Helena's blues legacy is per-
petuated through the annual King Biscuit Blues Festival, a three-day
festival held each October. The Delta Cultural Center preserves and
interprets the culture of Arkansas's Mississippi River Delta.

THE PHILLIPS COUNTY MUSEUM

Helena's public library was constructed in 1891 on Pecan Street. Because
there was no museum, artifacts from the county's past were placed on
bookshelves and inside file cabinets. By the 1920s, it became clear that

Phillips County needed a separate museum. A local woman named Mrs. Margaret Ready started taking up a collection to start a museum. She even sold bricks for ten cents apiece. Thanks to Mrs. Ready's crusading efforts, the museum opened its doors in 1929. An addition to the museum was constructed in the 1970s. The exhibits in the Phillips County Museum include the Thomas Edison collection, Native American artifacts, Civil War armaments, and letters from General Lafayette and General Robert E. Lee. However, the Phillips County Museum is best known because one of its exhibits is said to come alive at night.

The museum's most fascinating exhibit is a wax mannequin in a glass case on a second-floor balcony. The mannequin is fashioned in the likeness of Maybelle Thatcher, whose family was among the earliest settlers in the county. *In the 1870s, Maybelle fell in love with a boy named Ralph Mooney, who lived across the Mississippi River. Every night, he crossed the river on a ferryboat to visit her. On April 17, 1877, Ralph boarded the ferry. The moon was full, and the river appeared to be calm. Without warning, lightning flashed across the sky, and the thunderclouds boomed. Drops of rain the size of pennies began pummeling the small craft. The wind howled, and the waves became choppy. Suddenly, a huge wave swamped the ferry. All of the passengers drowned, including Ralph.*

When Maybelle heard the news the next day, she was devastated. For several days, she shut herself up in her room and lay on her bed, hardly touching the food that her mother brought up to her. One morning, several weeks following Ralph's death, Maybelle's mother entered her room and was about to set the tray on the nightstand when she noticed that the girl's eyes were wide open. After a few seconds, the poor woman realized the awful truth: her beloved daughter was dead. She scooped up the girl's lifeless body in her arms and wailed uncontrollably. People said that the girl died of a broken heart, for lack of a better explanation.

Harriett Collett, who has worked at the museum for ten years, categorizes Maybelle Thatcher's ghost as one of those restless spirits who has unfinished business. Legend has it that every night when the moon is full, the mannequin of Maybelle Thatcher leaves her glass enclosure and walks around the balcony of the museum, looking for her lost love. Ms. Collett says that she has never felt afraid to be in the Phillips County Museum alone: "I don't believe in ghosts. I know they are just stories." She adds, though, that she only works from 10 A.M. until 4 P.M. and has never stayed in the building long enough to test the validity of the stories.

Illinois

ALTON

In 1818, Rufus Easton founded Alton, Illinois, at the confluence of the Mississippi River and the Missouri River. The riverfront is dotted with huge grain silos, the sides of which bear marks indicating the levels the Mississippi River's floodwaters have reached over the years. In the nineteenth century, Illinois, a free state, became a refuge for slaves escaping from nearby Missouri, a slave state. On November 7, 1837, Elijah P. Lovejoy, the editor of an abolitionist newspaper, was murdered by a mob, which also threw his printing press in the Mississippi River. On October 15, 1858, Alton was the site of the seventh Lincoln-Douglas debate. The first penitentiary in Illinois was built in Alton. Between 1863 and 1864, thousands of Confederate prisoners died of smallpox inside the prison. Alton's most famous resident is Robert Pershing Wadlow, listed in the *Guiness Book of World Records* (2010–2011) as the world's tallest man. Wadlow was 8 feet 1.5 inches tall.

THE MANSION HOUSE

The first building in Alton to be designated a haunted site is the Mansion House on State Street. Built in 1834 by a Captain Botkin, the Mansion House served as a hotel for many years. Later, the house was converted into a Catholic boarding school, run by nuns of the Ursuline Order and the Daughters of Charity. In 1864, after an outbreak of smallpox in the Alton Penitentiary, President Abraham Lincoln asked three nuns from the Daughters of Charity in St. Louis to help curb the smallpox epidemic in Alton. The nuns treated hundreds of smallpox victims as the Mansion House, making it the first hospital in Alton's history. A number of Confederate prisoners also stricken with the disease were treated on Sunflower Island in the middle of the Mississippi River. After a few months, the disease abated, but not before hundreds of people died, including a number of victims being treated in the Mansion House. Many people who have occupied the building since then believe that the spirits of these smallpox victims are still walking the halls of the Mansion House. However, the ghost that is most likely responsible for the paranormal activity in the Mansion House is the spirit of a grizzled old soldier named Tom Boothby.

Tom Boothby was an Indian fighter who had participated in several of the Indian battles in the War of 1812. By the time he arrived in Alton in 1836, he was a very intimidating looking fellow, having lost an arm and an eye to an Indian's arrow. For two years, the injured veteran lived as a virtual hermit in a downstairs room in the left corner of the house. It is said that a young man brought Tom his meals every day, leaving them in front of his door. Tom was convinced that the ghosts of the Indians he had slain tormented him in his sleep. The other tenants were frequently awakened in the middle of the night by his shrill screams. When they knocked on the door and asked him to be quiet, he usually mumbled a short apology behind his closed door and returned to bed.

Soon, rumors spread that Tom Boothby had moved from town to town along the Mississippi River in an attempt to evade the spirits that pursued him. Most people dismissed him as being nothing more than a harmless, albeit annoying, lunatic. One night, the screams that routinely resounded through the Mansion House had a different tone. Tenants clearly heard cries of "Help" coming from his room. However, instead of coming to his aid, they simply ignored his screams, just as they had done so many nights before, and went back to sleep.

The next morning, the young man who brought Tom his meals every day picked up his empty tray and replaced it with a full one. He became alarmed the next morning when he discovered that Tom's tray had not been touched. The boy got the landlord, who walked back to Tom's room and unlocked the door. The pair stared in horror at Tom's body, sprawled sideways across the bed. His clothing was torn, as if he had been in a terrible struggle with an invisible foe. It soon became apparent that the old man had strangled himself some time during the night. The ghosts of the Indians who died by his hand had caught up to him at last—at least in his fevered imagination.

In *Haunted Alton*, author Troy Taylor says that before the Civil War when the Mansion House was used as a hotel, the proprietor usually rented out the downstairs apartment in the left corner of the building to guests who did not know about Tom Boothby's tragic end so that if they heard any screaming during the night, they would assume that it was coming from some other part of the house. Troy Taylor says that in October 2000 a couple who had just moved to Alton told him that they were hearing footsteps and shrieks during the night. When Troy told them the story of Tom Boothby, the couple decided to search for a new house.

On January 15, 2010, the Mansion House was gutted by a devastating fire. At the time, the historic building was being used as a four-family apartment. The fire started in the basement and spread upward.

THE McPIKE MANSION

The McPike Mansion, which, in its present state, resembles a classic haunted house, was designed by the architect Louis Pfeiffenberger for Henry Guest McPike. Pfeiffenberger is known today as the designer of a number of prominent buildings in Alton, such as St. Mary's Church, Lincoln and Garfield schools, and the Haskell Playhouse, which is a miniature replica of the Haskell home. Henry Guest McPike, whose Scottish ancestors served at Valley Forge with George Washington, arrived in Alton from Kentucky in 1847. He soon established himself as one of Alton's most enterprising businessmen, working as an insurance executive, real estate agent, and box manufacturer. During the Civil War, McPike was appointed deputy provost marshall of the district. After the war, he began to dabble in politics. After serving as a representative in the city council, he served as the mayor of Alton from 1887 to 1891.

During McPike's lifetime, his mansion was one of the most beautiful houses in the area. The sixteen-room Italianate-Victorian-style mansion, which has a vaulted wine cellar, certainly befitted a man of

McPike's stature. His "country estate" of fifteen acres, which McPike called "Mt. Lookout," was planted with a variety of flowers, shrubs, and vineyards. Henry and his wife raised five children in their Victorian home and were, by all accounts, very happy there. According to some records, Henry McPike's descendants continued to live in the old house well into the first half of the twentieth century. However, conflicting accounts claim that Paul A. Laichinger bought the house in 1908 and lived there until he died in 1930. Many people say that he rented out some of the rooms to tenants.

By the 1950s, the McPike Mansion's glory days were far in the past. The old, abandoned mansion had fallen prey to vandalism and to the ravages of time. Most of the expensive marble fireplaces and delicate woodwork were stolen years ago. With its broken windows and rotten wooden floors, the McPike Mansion stands as a sad, eyeless parody of its former self. In 1994, Sharyn and George Luedke bought the McPike Mansion at auction and set about restoring it with the intention of converting it into a bed and breakfast. Unfortunately, the old house is so dilapidated that the restoration process is proceeding very slowly. Ironically, the ghostly encounters that she and her husband have had in the McPike Mansion might prove to be the old house's salvation.

In an interview with Jim Longo, author of *Favorite Haunts*, Sharyn Luedke said that she did not even know that the McPike Mansion was haunted until a lady at the auction began telling her some of the ghost tales that had been circulating around Alton for years. Concerned that she might come into contact with negative energy, Sharyn contacted a friend of hers, a former nun, who suggested that they perform a Native American purification ritual using sweet grass and sage. After Sharyn performed the smudging ceremony, two local psychics suggested that the house be "cleansed" as well. The first time Sharyn and one of the psychics walked through the house together, the psychic immediately felt cold in certain rooms and hallways. Sharyn tripped on a loose board, but before she fell to the floor, she felt something tug on her jacket.

During the spiritual cleansing of the house, which was conducted once a week for three weeks, Sharyn learned about two of the spirits that haunt the McPike Mansion. One of them was a negative spirit on the third floor who did not want to "cross over." The second spirit was the ghost of a lonely lady who sat in a rocking chair, looking out a window on the ground floor. The psychic said that the poor woman wanted to leave the house but, for some unknown reason, could not.

Sharyn had another encounter with the ghost of a former owner of the McPike Mansion six weeks after she purchased it. In *Haunted Alton*, Troy Taylor says that Sharyn was outside watering her plants when she saw a man standing in one of the windows. He appeared to be staring in her direction in the front yard. In the few moments that he materialized before vanishing completely, Sharyn noticed that the man was wearing a striped shirt and a tie. She is certain that this was the spirit of Paul Laichinger because she has a photograph of him wearing the same shirt and tie.

Paul Laichinger's ghost has manifested on a fairly regular basis since Sharyn's first sighting in 1994. During some of the picnics, band concerts, and campouts that were held on the property to raise funds for the restoration of the house, people have seen the figure of a man standing in a second-story window. Antoinette Easton's ghost tours made frequent stops at the McPike Mansion. She told Jim Longo that sometimes she asked Paul's ghost if he would make an appearance. As a rule, a third of the people on her tour claimed to see a shadowy form that stepped into the doorway and then stepped back into the darkness.

Another ghost that has been identified is the spirit of a servant. Sharyn learned of the presence of the ghost of a woman one day when a man knocked on the door with an armful of books. He told Sharyn that he had removed the books from the McPike Mansion seventeen years before to keep them safe. After the man left, Sharyn thumbed through one of the books and noticed the name "Sarah Wells" written inside of it. Since then, Sharyn has referred to this particular ghost as "Sarah." Sharyn said that one afternoon she was picking up bricks from the third floor when an entity that she identified as Sarah gave her a big hug. She and her husband have also detected the scent of lilac on the third floor. Lilac, which was a popular perfume in the nineteenth century, could have been Sarah's favorite scent.

Thanks to television programs like *Scariest Places on Earth*, the McPike Mansion has acquired a national reputation as a haunted house. To defray the costs of renovations, Sharyn offers private ghost tours of the estate to the hundreds of curiosity seekers who flock to the old house. For centuries, ghosts were viewed as entities that one should avoid. However, thanks to the exposure that the media has given paranormal phenomena in the twenty-first century, many Americans are now running toward haunted places instead of away from them.

FIRST UNITARIAN CHURCH OF ALTON

The Alton Unitarian Church had its inception in the mind of Dr. William Emerson, Alton's first doctor. In 1836, Dr. Emerson invited William Greenleaf Eliot, the founder of Eliot Seminary in St. Louis, to attend a special meeting in his office. Eliot, who is the grandfather of poet T. S. Eliot, traveled around the St. Louis area, giving speeches and meeting with small groups to generate interest in the founding of Unitarian churches. Many Christians viewed Unitarianism as a radical religion because it promoted the validity of all faiths. In Alton, freethinkers, like the abolitionist Elijah P. Lovejoy, were not welcome. In fact, the first minister of the Alton Unitarian Church, Charles Andrew Farley, was strongly "encouraged" by a group of angry locals to leave town. Farley did as he was told.

For eighteen years, members of the First Unitarian Church met in one another's homes for services. In 1854, the Unitarian Society purchased the property where St. Matthew's Catholic Church stood before it was gutted by fire. The church was constructed using the stone and the foundation of the ruins of St. Matthew's. The site on which the new Catholic church was built was known as "Christian Hill." The Unitarian Church, on the other hand, was located on what locals referred to as "Heathen Hill."

The first minister of the new Unitarian Church was William D'Arcy Haley. At first, Haley's liberal views regarding social change angered the more conservative members, especially his strong stand against slavery. He submitted his resignation but quickly withdrew it after the church members agreed not to censor anyone for speaking what he or she perceived to be the truth.

The First Unitarian Church thrived under its commitment of tolerance for different points of view. Dr. William Greenleaf Eliot became minister of Alton's First Unitarian Church during the Civil War. The Unitarian equivalent of high school—"Advance"—was established in the basement in 1866. Twelve years later, a brick parsonage was built.

The First Unitarian Church of Alton experienced two serious setbacks in the first half of the twentieth century. In 1905, the church burned down, but it was quickly rebuilt. The next blow to the church was the death of its minister, Phillip Mercer, in 1934. On November 21, Mercer's friend, James D. McKinney, became concerned because on Monday night the minister had not returned to the room he was renting from the McKinney family. At first, McKinney thought that Mercer had stayed in St. Louis to watch a concert. By late afternoon the next day, McKinney decided to see if Mercer had had an accident in the church and was unable to call anyone. At 5:15 P.M., McKinney walked through the church doors on the west side of the church and started to walk into the Sunday School room at the rear of the church when he saw the minister's feet dangling off the floor in front of the door. McKinney ran out of the church and headed across the street to the police station. He then returned to the church with a policeman, Patrolman Waller. They discovered Mercer's body hanging from the transom. A piece of sash cord was tied around his neck. His neck appeared to be broken. Evidently, the minister had stepped on a nearby chair, tied the cord around his neck, and hanged himself. Deputy Coroner Klunk determined that Mercer had been dead approximately twenty-four hours before McKinney discovered his body.

The reason for Phillip Mercer's apparent suicide remains a mystery to this day. Little is known about his personal life, other than the fact that he was engaged to be married to a woman named Dorothy Cole from Minneapolis. Several members of the church said that in the last days he had become very concerned about his weight. He confided to a friend that he had lost fifteen pounds in just a few weeks. The physician Mercer consulted told him that all he needed was rest. Most of the members of the congregation concluded that Mercer had suffered from a nervous breakdown just prior to his suicide.

In the years following Phillip Mercer's suicide, a number of ghostly occurrences have been reported at Alton's First Unitarian Church. Peg Flatch from the First Unitarian Church told Troy Taylor that, over the years, many people have encountered strange smells and heard weird sounds inside the church. Some have heard disembodied footsteps. Others have walked through a doorway into the basement and felt pressure on their back. Peg herself had a bizarre experience in the fall of 1997. She drove over to the Unitarian Church to drop off several items. The door was unlocked, so she walked inside the double doors on Alby Street. She was standing at the kitchen sink when she felt an unpleasant sensation coming from the back of the sanctuary. Suddenly, she heard a group of people talking at the bottom of the basement steps. Relieved that she was not alone, she walked to the top of the stairs and called down to them. At that instant, the talking stopped. As a chill crept over her, Peg bolted out of the Alby Street door.

Carol Wolf, a minister at First Unitarian Church, has also had some very unsettling experiences there. Carol said that she had heard about the ghost stories because she accepted the position as minister. One day, when she was alone in the church, she walked into the sanctuary and proclaimed, "I am the minister now. Please don't bother me." The entire time she served as minister at the church, the only place where she had ever felt uncomfortable was the basement. "I can't go in the basement alone," she said. "It's like something doesn't want me down there."

Throughout most of the twenty-first century, the First Unitarian Church has been a regular stop on Troy Taylor's Haunted Alton Tours. During this decade, a number of tourists who walked through the Unitarian Church reported having their hair pulled and their arms pinched. Some people have felt that they were being watched from something hovering around the chandelier. A shadowy figure has been seen walking past one of the stained-glass windows in the sanctuary. Many people who did not know the details of Phillip Mercer's suicide have accurately identified the exact spot where he hanged himself, even though the area has been changed. One young lady was in the basement when she heard a shrill scream and the sound of footsteps running on the first floor. When she told her sister, who was upstairs, what she had heard, her sister said that she had not heard a thing. Another couple was standing in the basement when the woman's husband became so nauseous that he had to run to the bathroom. This writer visited the First Unitarian Church late one Saturday night in June 2004.

Like most of the people on the tour, I took pictures in the sanctuary. When I examined the photographs the next day, I discovered an orb floating above the pews in the rear of the sanctuary. Other people have photographed orbs in the First Unitarian Church as well.

In *The Ghost Hunter's Guidebook*, author Troy Taylor says that churches are ideal places to find ghosts because of the spent human emotion that remains there. Places where a suicide has taken place are also likely to be haunted, according to parapsychologists. In the case of Phillip Mercer, one wonders if perhaps his spirit lingers because of some unfinished business that has not yet come to light.

THE MINERAL SPRINGS HOTEL

Ironically, building a hotel was not the original intention of the Luers brothers when they began excavating what became the foundation of the Mineral Springs Hotel. August and Herman Luers were meat packers from Germany. August founded his meat-packing plant in Alton in 1881. His brother Herman, a butcher from St. Louis, joined August in Alton in 1893. In 1909, the brothers decided to build an ice-making and meat-storage plant on Broadway. The third sublevel was built as a meat-curing facility. However, as they excavated further, the brothers discovered artesian spring water. A chemist tested the water and concluded that the water had curative powers. At that moment, they realized that the site was better suited for a hotel and spa than it was for an ice-storage plant. In October 1913, construction began on the hotel's swimming pool. A holding tank for the water that filled the pool was housed in the third sublevel, where the wooden hooks used to hang meat are still visible. On the first floor, patrons could drink in the bar area, dance in the ballroom, or eat in the dining room. The guest rooms were on the second floor. Guests marveled at the hotel's lavish furnishings, which included plaster cornices, terrazzo floors, and marble staircases. The exterior of the building was constructed in the Italian villa style.

Between the opening of the Mineral Springs in September 1914 and the outbreak of World War II, the hotel was a resounding success. People flocked to the hotel primarily because of the water's alleged healing qualities. The Mineral Springs hired a man named "Doc" Furlong, who offered hydrotherapy baths to patrons who suffered from a variety of ailments. Not long after the hotel opened, the Luers brothers began bottling and selling the hotel's famous mineral water, which was advertised as being as effective as the water found at Hot Springs, Arkansas. People were attracted to the swimming pool, where they took swimming lessons, participated in the water polo clubs, and simply relaxed.

August Luers added several new rooms in 1925 but sold the building in 1926. Business dropped off so dramatically at the outbreak of World War II that the pool was drained as a cost-cutting measure. In the 1950s, the hotel began to deteriorate from neglect. The Mineral Springs struggled on for the next couple of decades as just a shabby shadow of its former self until it finally closed in 1971. Then in 1978, the Mineral Springs received a new lease on life when Roger Schuberts redesigned the old hotel as a mall with restaurants and shops. A few years later, real estate developer Bob Love reinvented the Mineral Springs Hotel as an antique mall. By the 1990s, the old Mineral Springs Hotel became known as a place where one could find precious antiques and maybe even a ghost or two.

Real estate agent Michael Love, the son of hotel owner Bob Love, said that something very strange occurred during a tour he was giving of the hotel in October 2001. Mike was telling the group about puddles of water that mysteriously appeared on the floor in a specific area of the hotel. Suddenly, two young ladies screamed and pointed to a puddle of water on the floor. Another woman who was holding a video camera filmed the entire incident.

Another haunted place in the Mineral Springs Hotel is the swimming pool in the basement. For many years, countless social gatherings like wedding receptions were held poolside. The story goes that during one of these parties, an altercation broke out between a married couple. Apparently, the woman thought her husband was paying too much attention to an attractive young lady standing by the pool. Screaming obscenities, the wife removed one of her high-heeled shoes and struck her husband in the head with it. With blood streaming from the hole in his forehead, the man stumbled backward and fell into the deep end of the pool, where he drowned. After the hotel closed down, the ghost of a tall, melancholy man in a black coat and tie has been seen standing by the pool. Today, the entire pool area has been closed off. Most of the people who go there now are paranormal researchers. A psychic identified the ghost as someone named "George." In 2001, a group that was videotaping in the pool area caught the image of a shadowy figure moving past the wall in the deep end of the pool. In 2004, another group of paranormal researchers found nothing really unusual in the pool area with the exception of the picture of an orb that hovered around a column. George's ghost is also said to have grabbed the arm and knocked the keys out of the hand of a barber who worked at a local barbershop. A second entity has been sighted at the pool. The ghost of a little girl who supposedly drowned during a swimming lesson has been seen at the pool and on other floors of the hotel as well.

A café on the main floor has also been the scene of haunted activity. In the 1920s and 1930s, the hotel's bar was located here. The story goes that an artist who was unable to pay his bar tab painted the large mural of Alton's riverfront on a wall between the dining room and the bar. Before he completed the painting, the artist died. In one variant of the legend, the painter hanged himself inside the hotel. For years, women have seen the forlorn ghost of the artist standing around the site of the old bar, looking disoriented. The ghost's wobbly stance has led some people to believe the ghost is drunk. Occasionally, the artist's ghost lets female patrons know he is there by touching their hair or tugging on their purses.

The most famous ghost in the Mineral Springs Hotel is the Jasmine Lady. Legend has it that she had married a wealthy man solely for his money. After her marriage, she rendezvoused with the man she truly loved at the Mineral Springs Hotel. One day, her husband followed her to the Mineral Springs and confronted her in her room at the top of the stairs. The terrified woman ran out of the room to the staircase leading to the lobby. In one version of the tale, the woman tumbled down the stairs and broke her neck. Another version has it that her irate husband caught up with her and pushed her down the stairs. Stricken with guilt, the husband returned to his wife's hotel room and hanged himself. Ever since, many people have smelled the pungent scent of her lavender perfume around the staircase. In fact, almost every time a ghost tour makes a stop inside the Mineral Springs Hotel, at least one person catches a whiff of lavender-scented perfume. Since 1992, her apparition has also been sighted many times around the staircase and in the sublevels of the hotel.

The ghosts of the Mineral Springs Hotel have manifested themselves in other ways as well. Disembodied footsteps, a pair of glowing eyes, objects that move by themselves, and cold spots have all been taken as signs that the ghosts are "in the house." Even now, some people who shop for antiques at the old Mineral Springs Hotel end up making contact with the past in a more intangible way than by simply buying an old chair or a piece of Roseville pottery.

THE WEAD BUILDING

The Spanish Flu epidemic of 1918 was the worst pandemic in the history of the United States. Unlike most diseases, the Spanish Flu struck the healthiest parts of the population: the twenty-to-forty age group. Soldiers fighting in World War I helped spread the disease as they were transported from port to port. Theaters, lodges, and dance halls were closed all over the United States. In Illinois, Chicago was hit particularly hard by the disease because it was the nation's largest rail hub. Influenza reached the city and spread from there to other parts of the state and the country. In Chicago alone, over 8,500 people died of the flu. The disease soon spread to Peoria, Kankakee, and Rockford, and by October 1918, it had affected every community in Illinois. In 1918, so many people in Alton contracted the flu that a temporary American Red Cross field hospital was set up on Broadway Street to treat them. By the end of December 1918, the worst of the Spanish Flu epidemic was over. However, some people believe that the spirits of the victims of the disease who perished in Alton linger on in the Wead Building, which was constructed on the site of the old field hospital in 1929.

Over the years, a number of businesses and offices have occupied the Wead Building. A law office, beauty salons, a dentist's office, a justice of the peace, and an antique store have all been housed there. In the late 1950s and early 1960s, my mother and I made regular trips to a pediatrician, Dr. McCormick, who had his office in the Wead Building. My fear of entering the Wead Building stemmed not from the prospect of encountering a ghost, but from the possibility that I might get a shot. In the autumn of 1997, the building was purchased by Brenda and Scott Baalman, who believed the location would be good for a coffee shop. A number of strange incidents occurred in the spring of 1998 as the couple renovated the old building. *One day, they were working in the building when they heard the distinct sound of someone sneezing. No one else was in the building at the time. A week later, Scott was working on the first floor when he felt someone pull on the back of his shirt. He quickly turned around, but he was all alone. One afternoon, Scott was sitting on the first floor, reading a newspaper, when he heard the distinctive sound of the pages of a book being flipped behind the bar. He got up and walked behind the bar, where he saw a gaseous, amorphous shape moving around. When Scott ordered it to stop moving, the entity vanished.*

The place where most of the weird events occurred was on the second floor, which was used for storage during renovations. Brenda was up there cleaning brushes one day when she felt as if someone was watching her. Other people reported hearing knocking sounds coming from inside the walls. A pile of magazines was strewn across the floor. People working on the first floor frequently heard footsteps right above them. One day, Brenda was on the second floor when she saw out of the corner of her eye a man in a striped shirt sitting in one of the small study rooms. When she turned her head to get a better look at the man, he was gone. In his book *Haunted Illinois*, author Troy Taylor says that right after the coffeehouse opened, Brenda was watching the monitor late one summer night just at closing time when she saw a man wearing a striped shirt walk through the front door, right past her husband and daughter Nicole, and climb up the stairs to the second floor. She also heard the footsteps of someone walking up there. Neither Scott nor Nicole saw anyone walk in the front door. Concerned that someone might have sneaked in, Brenda, Scott, and Nicole ran upstairs, but the second floor was completely empty.

For years, the Meridian Coffee Shop was a regular stop on the Haunted Alton Tours. One Saturday night in 2004, I was part of a tour group that walked through the coffee shop. The young lady who stood behind the counter said that she had not seen a ghost in the building but that she had often heard someone walking around the second floor when she knew no one was up there. The group then walked upstairs and took photographs in all of the rooms and hallways on the second floor. I took a photograph in the study room where Brenda saw the man in the striped shirt, and I caught the image of two orbs, a large one and a small one. Other people photographed orbs in the same room that night.

The Meridian Coffee House closed its doors in 2008. At the time of the writing of this book, a children's store called The Grape Vine was about to move in. Because many parapsychologists believe that children are much more sensitive to the presence of spirits than adults are, the sightings in the Wead Building are likely to continue for years to come.

THE FRANKLIN HOUSE

The Franklin House at 208 State Street is generally regarded as one of the most historically significant houses in the entire city. In 1836, the building was commissioned by the owners of the First National Bank of Alton. It housed the Alton Marine and Fire Insurance Company. After the company was incorporated by a special act of the Illinois Legislature, the local citizens who supported the business were responsible for expanding its services to include the deposit of funds and loans for small businesses. As time passed, this local insurance company developed into the National Bank & Trust Company. In the 1850s, the building became the Franklin House Hotel. At that time, the forty-two-room hotel was the finest hotel in the entire city. Its most famous guest was Abraham Lincoln. In 1858 Lincoln and Stephen A. Douglas held a series of debates in a campaign for one of Illinois's two United States Senate seats. Between July and October, 7 three-hour debates were held in each of the seven congressional districts. According to local lore, Lincoln stayed at the Franklin Hotel on October 16, 1858, for the last of the debates, which attracted over 6,000 people. While Lincoln was boarding at the Franklin House Hotel, he was joined by his wife, Mary, and his son, Robert Todd Lincoln. Although Lincoln's stay at the Franklin House has not been corroborated, he most certainly dined with Senator Lyman Trumbull at the Franklin House Hotel.

The Franklin House went through a variety of incarnations during the twentieth century. To capitalize on Lincoln's visit to the Franklin House, the owner changed its name to the Lincoln Hotel. As time passed, what was once Alton's finest hotel became a dilapidated wreck, a place that transients, not politicians, called home. In the 1980s, the new owners renovated the lower floors, which housed the tea room and gift shops. The upper floors remained vacant. In the 1990s, a restaurant, the Seafood Escape, took over the lower floors. Then in 2006, the Franklin House was converted into Lincoln Lofts, a chic urban apartment complex. At the same time that the developers were cleaning and repairing the old house, they did their best to maintain the historical integrity of the house. For example, the room where Lincoln is rumored to have spent the night is located in unit A, or "Abraham." Many people believe that one important piece of the building's history has been preserved in its ghost stories.

The primary ghost who haunts the Franklin House is the spirit of a little girl. *In the mid-nineteenth century, a traveling salesman who usually took his family with him as he hawked his wares in towns lining the Mississippi River stopped at the Franklin House Hotel. His seven-year-old daughter, Rachel, endeared herself to the hotel staff, who played with her while her father was away on business. The little girl was treated so well, in fact, that the hotel was like a second home to her. She particularly enjoyed playing in the lobby and on the staircase. One day, the little girl chased a ball out the front door into the street and was struck by a passing freight wagon. The child was killed instantly.*

For years, the ghost of the little girl was frequently encountered on the second and third floors of the old hotel. It is said that Rachel's ghost has tried to get people's attention by pulling on their clothing or by touching their hand. People have heard the sound of a dress rustling and the giggling of a small child. Many people have seen Rachel's ghost running down the hallway in the second floor. In his book *Haunted Alton*, Troy Taylor says that many guests refused to spend any time in the room on the top floor of the building where Rachel and her family stayed. People complained that the room never warmed up, even in the summer. Guests were also awakened in the middle of the night by strange sounds. Police officers passing by the former hotel frequently saw a light burning in the room, which was supposed to be deserted at the time. After the Franklin House was renovated, employees frequently discovered the door to Rachel's room was locked. By the time they retrieved a key and returned to the room, the door was standing wide open. A woman who worked in one of the gift shops in the building in the 1980s was so frightened by Rachel's ghost that she walked off the job and refused to return to work.

The little girl's ghost frequently made her presence known at the Seafood Escape. A small bell was attached to the top of the door to let servers know that a customer had arrived. On many occasions, servers who heard the bell ring ran into the dining room, only to find that no one was there. The staff also heard footsteps on the landing of the stairs and the sound of people walking and moving furniture in the upstairs rooms. Servers often reported to work in the morning and discovered chairs moved all over the dining room and change scattered on the floor. One server had a stack of dirty dishes knocked out of her arms by an unseen individual. Objects that mysteriously disappeared turned up in entirely different locations the next day.

The paranormal activity continued after the Franklin House was converted into an upscale apartment building. Some employees have seen the ghost of a little girl sitting with a man dressed in a Civil War–era uniform. They have also heard strange sounds, such as disembodied knocks, in the building. However, because the old building is reputed to be haunted by a little girl, most of the employees just chalk up the disturbances to the playful antics of a lonely child.

THE ALTON PENITENTIARY

Before the construction of the Alton Penitentiary, criminals were punished either by public flogging or by incarceration in rude log jails, which were easy to escape from. The resistance of voters in Illinois to higher taxes prevented the construction of an actual prison until 1827, when a grant of 40,000 acres of saline lands was made by Congress. A large portion of the profits made through the sale of these lands was appropriated for the establishment of a state penitentiary in Alton, the first penitentiary in the entire state. However, work on the new prison was delayed until the state appropriated an additional $10,000 for the project. In 1833, the stone prison, consisting of twenty-four cells, received its first inmates. The Alton Penitentiary was run on what was known as "the Auburn Plan." Prisoners worked together during the day and slept alone in individual cells at night. The prison was run by a "lessee," who furnished supplies and employed guards. Lessees, who possessed all of the powers of a prison warden, were supervised by a commissioner appointed by the state. The commissioner controlled all of the products of convict labor. Despite the fact that additions were made from time to time, the Alton Penitentiary proved to be too small to accommodate the growing number of inmates in the state. In 1857, the state authorized the construction of a new prison in Joliet. In 1860, the last convicts were transferred from Alton to Joliet.

By 1861, the two St. Louis prisons had become severely over-crowded. On December 31, 1861, Lieutenant Colonel James B. McPherson was dispatched to Alton to assess the Alton Penitentiary's suitability as a military prison. McPherson reported to Major General Henry Halleck that the Alton Penitentiary could house as many as 1,750 prisoners, provided that it was renovated at a cost of $2,415. On February 9, 1862, the military prison at Alton received its first prisoners. Members of the Thirteenth U.S. Infantry served as guards, under the command of Colonel Sidney Burbank.

Between 1862 and 1865, over 11,764 Confederate prisoners did time at the former Alton Penitentiary. A much smaller portion of the prison population consisted of civilians, most of whom were imprisoned in Alton for treasonable actions. A few others, classified by the state as bushwhackers or guerrillas, were imprisoned for burning bridges and sabotaging railroads. At times, the prison held as many as 2,000 prisoners. Life in the military prison was unbearable. Prisoners suffered from searing heat in the summer and freezing temperatures in the winter. Most of the prisoners were badly clothed and poorly fed. Dysentery was the most infectious of the diseases that ran rampant in the prison, but typhoid, measles, and pneumonia also claimed the lives of hundreds of prisoners. In the winter of 1862 and the spring of 1863, when an outbreak of smallpox raged through the prison, several thousand prisoners were living in a facility designed for 1,300. Most of the infected prisoners were taken to a quarantine hospital on Sunflower Island in the middle of the Mississippi River. Over three hundred of the prisoners who succumbed to the disease are buried on Sunflower Island, which was submerged after the construction of the Alton Locks and Dam in 1938. The names of 1,534 Confederate prisoners who died during their incarceration are listed on the monument that stands at the site of the old prison.

After the last prisoners were transferred to prisons in St. Louis, the Alton prison closed on July 7, 1865. The walls were dismantled between 1870 and 1875. Most of the stone blocks that were not used to construct the Arch Railroad Bridge were carted away in wagons by private citizens and used in the foundations of many homes in the city. The site of the prison was transformed into a playground called "Uncle Remus Park." In 1973, the only remaining section of the prison's walls was moved to its present location on William Street. A parking lot now occupies the original location of the Alton Penitentiary.

Not surprisingly, the suffering endured by the Confederate soldiers has left an indelible imprint on the spot where the old prison once stood. In *Haunted Alton*, Troy Taylor tells the story of a man who played in Uncle Remus Park as a child in the late 1960s. He said that some of his friends had told him about hearing strange sounds in the park, but the boy did not allow the uneasiness that crept over him as he heard these weird tales to prevent him from playing there. One bright sunny day, he and his sister were walking through the playground by themselves when they heard the sound of someone crying by the remnants of the prison wall. Thinking that one of their little friends had been injured, they looked behind the wall. No one was there, but the crying persisted. Terrified, the children ran home as fast as they could.

In the 1990s, a man who was cutting across the parking lot had an equally frightening experience. He paused briefly to kneel down and tie his shoe. When he stood back up, he was surprised to see a bearded man standing just three feet away from him. The bare-footed man was wearing heavy pants and a ragged shirt. He thought that the pathetic-looking figure was a homeless person—until he disappeared.

Many experts in the paranormal believe that the psychic residue remaining after the destruction of the prison extends far beyond its original location. They point to the large number of homes erected with the stone blocks of the prison that are now said to be haunted. Could this be the reason why Alton, Illinois, is one of the most haunted cities along the Mississippi River?

CAIRO

Cairo is located at the confluence of the Mississippi and Ohio Rivers. It was founded by the Cairo City & Canal Company in 1837 and incorporated in 1858. Cairo soon achieved prominence as an important steamboat port. Many of its beautiful Victorian homes are listed in the National Register of Historic Places. During the Civil War, Cairo served as a training center for the Union army. Fort Defiance, now a state park, was a Union Civil War fort commanded by General Ulysses S. Grant. The decline in Cairo's economy and population paralleled the decline in river trade in the 1900s.

THE CAIRO PUBLIC LIBRARY

The Safford Memorial Building, which houses the Cairo Public Library, was presented to the City of Cairo on July 19, 1884, by Mrs. Alfred B. Safford as a memorial to her husband, who died in July 1877. The Cairo Woman's Club and Library Association contributed fifteen hundred books to the library in exchange for a room that the organization would use for its meetings. Today, the old red-brick building retains many of its early 1880s characteristics. The ornate shelves that were originally in the Woman's Club reading room are now used for periodicals in the adult reading room. The leaded stained-glass windows are original. On the first landing of the stairs sits a rare Tiffany clock. Some of the furnishings were donated from other places, such as the chandelier, which originally hung in the Cairo Opera House. A number of additions have been made to the library over the years, including the new stack room in 1962 and a Special Collections room in 1984. In addition, the second-floor storeroom was remodeled to make it more suitable for the storing of historical materials. One aspect of the library that has not changed over the years is Toby, its resident ghost.

For years, librarians have had strange experiences in the library that cannot be easily explained away. Longtime librarian Louise Ogg told author Jim Longo that one day when she first started working at the library, she was alone during the lunch hour when she heard an odd noise coming from the reading room. It sounded like the creaking sound of an old rocking chair. When she left her desk and went into the reading room, the rocking stopped. She returned to her desk, and the strange rocking sound started back up again. Before long, other people began hearing the sound as well.

A few weeks later, Louise and another woman were in the library during the lunch hour when a strange light appeared from behind the front desk. "It was a white light that really looked ghostly," Louise said. "It wasn't a reflection from a car or anything like that. It was nothing we recognized. It just rose up from behind the desk, slowly passed the office, and disappeared into the book stacks."

Library director Monica Smith has also had encounters with the ghost. "Many times, I come back and find the lights on that we turned off in that room." When she works in the library at night, she occasionally hears someone walking around upstairs, even when she is certain that no one is there. "I definitely think there is a presence there," Monica said.

For lack of a better explanation, the librarians have speculated that the spirit responsible for the strange occurrences in the library is the ghost of a loyal library patron who is unable to stay away from the place where he had spent so many pleasant hours. Louise Ogg said that a young lady who worked at the library years ago nicknamed the ghost Toby so that they could blame a specific person every time something unusual happened, like the cards in the card catalog being out of place or the door in the back room shutting by itself. To cope with the chills that occasionally run up their spines, the librarians joke that Toby himself is "overdue," like the books that he might have hoarded at home.

MOUND CITY NATIONAL CEMETERY

In 1861, the federal government converted a brick building in Cairo into a military hospital. The building was large enough to accommodate between 1,000 and 1,500 patients. It was operated under the auspices of the Order of Holy Cross at Notre Dame, South Bend, Indiana. Mother Angela supervised the nuns who cared for the wounded soldiers. The first patients arrived after the battle of Belmont, Kentucky, on November 7, 1861. Many more wounded soldiers arrived following the campaign at Fort Donelson on February 13–16, 1862, and the Battle of Shiloh on April 6–7, 1862. In 1864, the patients who succumbed to their wounds and to disease were interred at the newly established Mound City National Cemetery, which was one of twelve national cemeteries authorized by President Abraham Lincoln on July 17, 1862. By 1869, the number of burials at the Mound City National Cemetery totaled 4,808. Over 2,000 of these burials were re-interments from isolated locations along the Mississippi River. In 1874, a monument acknowledging the wartime sacrifice of soldiers and sailors from Illinois was erected at a cost of $25,000. After the Civil War, the number of interments at the Mound City National Cemetery rose to more than 9,000. Most of the burials are veterans and their families from the Mexican War, the Civil War, the Spanish-American War, World Wars I and II, the Korean conflict, Vietnam, and the Persian Gulf War. The identities of many of the over 2,637 Union and Confederate soldiers and sailors buried here are unknown. Approximately fifty women are buried here as well. Most of them were nurses at the nearby military hospital. According to the legend, the spirits of one of these women haunts Mound City National Cemetery.

The female spirit who walks among the tombstones at Mound City National Cemetery is said to have been the wife of Brigadier General John B. Turchin, known by the soldiers under his command as the "Mad Cossack" because of his service in the Army of the Russian Tsar. Troy Taylor, author of *The Big Book of Illinois Ghost Stories*, says that during the Civil War, General Turchin brought his wife along with him to the battlefields. After her husband died, his wife frequently visited his grave in the Mound City National Cemetery. People familiar with the life of General Turchin believe that she is the ghost who has been sighted in the section where her husband is buried. The romantically inclined citizens of Cairo like to think that the Mound City National Cemetery's ghost story is proof that true love is indeed eternal.

MAGNOLIA MANOR

One of the most beautiful of all the Victorian homes in Cairo's Million-aire's Row on Washington Avenue is a fourteen-room Italianate-style mansion called Magnolia Manor. It was built between 1869 and 1872 of red brick fired in Cairo by Charles A. Galigher, who made a fortune during the Civil War supplying hardtack to the Union army. After the war, Galigher established a large ice factory in Cairo. Between 1872 and 1877, Mrs. Galigher stayed in a bedroom in an alcove of the first-floor drawing room because of illness. After she recovered, Mrs. Galigher spent most of her time decorating her house. She hired a local arti-san named McEwen to create the plaster frieze throughout the house. Some of the luxurious furnishings that reflect her elegant taste include fireplaces made of Italian Carrara marble, bronze light fixtures with shades of frosted glass, and solid cherry stair railings and spindles. The mansion even has a stage in the east end of the drawing room. The southeast bedroom is called General Grant's room because Grant, a friend of Charles Galigher, stayed there in April 1880 while en route home to Galena after a world tour. Galigher and his family played ten-nis on the courts on the south lawn. The cost of the house and the fur-nishings totaled $75,000. The Galigher family lived in the house until 1914 when a lumber dealer named Peter T. Langan purchased it. Fol-lowing Langan's death, Colonel and Mrs. Fain W. King bought the old house. In 1952, the Galighers' house passed into the hands of the Cairo Historical Association, which operates it as a museum. According to local legend, the ghosts of the original occupants still consider the old home to be their private residence.

In *The Big Book of Illinois Ghost Stories*, author Troy Taylor recounts some of the tales that have been circulating around Cario since it opened its doors as a museum in 1952. Guests to the museum have seen apparitions dressed in nineteenth-century attire that seemed so real that they mistook them for reenactors. People have also heard whispering and footsteps in the old house. A guest swore that she heard the footsteps of someone following her down the stairs. When she stepped aside to let the person by, she was shocked to find that no one was there. Staff members and volunteers who have spent a lot of time in the house claim to have seen the ghost of a little dark-haired boy between three and four years old. He is usually described as wearing dark pants, a white shirt, and suspenders. As soon as people notice him, he runs off. Staff members have seen doors open by themselves. A volunteer said that it felt as if someone was pushing against her on the other side of the door. The identity of the playful ghost is unknown.

Today, Magnolia Manor stands as a reminder of Cairo's prosperity following the Civil War. The loving care with which the old house has been preserved has enabled tourists to sample the lifestyle of Cario's wealthiest residents. The ghost stories people tell about the house suggest that the restorers have inadvertently brought to life more than memories of a by-gone era.

GALENA

The first inhabitants of Galena were the Fax and Sac Indian tribes. The first white settlers, the French, moved in during the late seventeenth century. American settlers arrived in the early nineteenth century. The city is named for "galena," the natural form of lead sulfide. By 1845, Galena was producing nearly 27,000 tons of lead ore. As a result of a decline in the demand for lead, Galena's population dropped from 14,000 in the 1850s to 3,396 in the early twenty-first century. Galena's big tourist attraction is the home where Ulysses S. Grant lived in 1860–1861.

THE GALENA–JO DAVIESS COUNTY
HISTORICAL SOCIETY AND MUSEUM

In the 1850s, Daniel A. Barrows, one of Galena's most prosperous businessmen, made a fortune as the owner of a lumberyard and a candy store. In 1856, his home and confectionary business burned down in the worst fire in Galena's history. In 1857, Daniel rebuilt his candy store on Main Street at a cost of $8,700. In 1858, architect William Dennison began work on a spacious home for Daniel A. Barrows at 211 South Bench Street, the site of his former residence. In 1859, Daniel, his wife, their son, their five daughters, his mother, and a servant moved into their new three-story home. Barrows's fortunes declined after the Civil War. The lumber business that he had founded in the 1850s foundered because he could no longer float his logs down the silt-clogged Galena River. His attempts to recoup his fortune by dabbling in whiskey distilling and flour milling failed to live up to his expectations. In 1883, Barrows defaulted on his mortgages and was forced to sell his home at Bench Street. In 1885, John Ross, who was also in the lumber business, purchased Barrows's former home. After Ross died in 1928, his daughter Loll sold the house to the Wildey Lodge of the International Order of the Odd Fellows. The lodge made extensive renovations on the old family home. The kitchen, dining room, and porches were replaced by a 40' x 80' addition. The lodge's budget was so depleted by the $40,000 cost of remodeling the building that the Oddfellows were forced to sell it to the City of Galena in 1938. That same year, city hall took over the first floor; a museum was housed on the second floor. In 1967, city hall was moved, and the Galena Historical Association took control of the entire building. The Galena Museum Association pays no rent on its ninety-nine-year lease with the city but is responsible for maintaining the grounds and the building itself. Today, the museum's 6,000 feet of exhibit space is taken up with 10,000 artifacts collected since 1938 and, perhaps, a ghost or two.

The ghosts in the museum waited fifty years to make an appearance. In 1988, an unseen hand played a chord on a piano when an employee walked through the room. Before long, reports of disembodied footsteps became commonplace. In 1989, an employee captured the sounds on a computer. In 1990, an employee was walking down the stairs when he heard someone walking behind him. Knowing that he was alone, he stopped walking. When the footsteps continued right in front of him and down the stairs, the hair rose up on his arms. In 1991, the resident ghost, or ghosts, became the focal point of a VIP reception held in the museum. A waiter was walking across the floor when his tray started vibrating, causing several glasses of champagne to fall to the floor. A few minutes later, a second waiter had just placed a number of champagne glasses on his tray, and they also spilled to the floor. Halfway through the reception, a tray full of champagne glasses sitting on a counter began rattling ominously. A waiter dashed over to the counter and grabbed the tray, but not before most of the glasses crashed to the floor.

The disturbances in the museum have continued into the twenty-first century. Recently, a woman entered the long hall in the two-story back room that the Odd Fellows added. She said that she had just walked through the door of one of the exhibit rooms when she saw a person to her left out of the corner of her eye. In a matter of moments, he ducked behind an exhibit partition. Knowing that she was the only tourist in the room at the time, she realized that she was in the presence of something unearthly. Sensing that the apparition was giving her "dirty looks" for trespassing in his room, she left immediately.

Museums seem to be ideal places to find ghosts. Many museums are located in historic buildings that have been renovated. Changing a structure, as many enthusiasts in the paranormal know, can awaken dormant spirits. It is also possible that spirits have attached themselves to the artifacts that were moved to the museum in 1938. Consequently, discovering the identity of the mischievous spirit in the museum will be difficult, if not impossible.

TURNER HALL

Turner Hall was built in the late nineteenth century by an association of German gymnasts called the Turnvereins. The organization was founded in 1811 by a German educator named Ludwig Jahn, who believed that physical exercise should be incorporated into all school curricula. After the Revolution of 1848, thousands of Turnverein members were forced to leave Germany because they sided with the factions who unsuccessfully revolted against the monarchy. In 1848, the Turnverein members who immigrated to America founded the American Turners in Cincinnati, Ohio. In 1851, the Turnverein in Galena was

founded for the purpose of developing "scientific gymnastics." However, the young German Americans were more interested in socializ-
ing than in exercising. Over the next few years, exercises became just
another form of social amusement for the Turners.

The society disbanded during the Civil War but reorganized on
April 6, 1872. So many people joined the Turners that their meeting
place, Wierich Hall, became too small. Because most of the citizens of
Galena were in favor of the construction of a large civic building, the
Turner Society formed a building committee, which purchased land
for the hall on April 1, 1874, for $1,050. In June 1874, a cornerstone con-
taining a book of poems, a collection of coins, the bylaws of several
Galena organizations, several envelopes containing donated valuables,
a copy of the *Galena Weekly Gazette,* and a copy of the *Volksfreund.*
When Turner Hall was finally completed in 1875 at a cost of $15,000,
it was considered one of the finest civic halls in the United Sates. Two
U.S. presidents spoke here: William McKinley on April 27, 1893, and
Theodore Roosevelt on April 27, 1900. Around the turn of the century, the Turner Society sold the building to the Turner Opera House
Association. For the next fifteen years, vaudeville performances, plays,
musical events, and banquets were held here. In 1926, the Eagles purchased Turner Hall for $10,000. In May 1926, the hall was officially
dedicated as a combined opera house, dance hall, and general hall.
However, ten weeks later, a fire gutted the Turner Opera House. The
damage was estimated at $12,000. The hall was rebuilt in the fall and
winter of 1926. It reopened on January 10, 1927. Sometime between
1935 and 1938, the City of Galena purchased the hall from the Eagles for
community events.

Turner Hall fell into decline over the next several decades, due at
least in part to the popularity of motion pictures. In 1960, the Galena
Art Theatre was formed to stage plays and to raise funds for the renovation of the old hall. The formation of the Save Turner Hall Fund
in 1970 also contributed to the city's restoration efforts. Thanks to
financial support provided by the City of Galena over the past few
decades, the necessary improvements have been made to preserve
and maintain the old building. Today, Turner Hall is used for concerts, plays, weddings, and many other events. It was not long before

workmen and volunteers became personally acquainted with the history of Turner Hall.

In his book *Ghosts of Galena*, Daniel Watson included a number of interviews he conducted with volunteers at Turner Hall. One day in the early 1990s, two volunteers were standing backstage against a brick wall when they felt as if they were enveloped in a cold cloud. The women immediately moved away from the wall. Just then, a loose stone from the loft above landed in the area where the women had just been standing. A few weeks later, one of the women and three other volunteers were working on the sets late one night when they saw a shadowy figure walk past the dressing room. They searched the backstage area for the intruder but found no one.

One night, a male volunteer who was the last to leave the building was walking around, turning off the lights. He had just turned the light off in the third-floor attic when he saw somebody out of the corner of his eye. Concerned that he might have turned the light off on somebody, the volunteer clicked the switch back on and walked through the entire attic. No one was there.

One of the most frightening incidents was experienced by a local pastor in 1991. He and his daughter were inside Turner Hall working on the "Ground Hog Dance," a fund-raiser for the hall. Within a couple of hours, almost all of the preparations for the dance were in place, and the pastor told the other two volunteers to go home. Right after the two girls left, the pastor and his daughter heard a loud voice coming from the north balcony. Someone sitting in a specific section of the balcony was saying something unintelligible in a very loud voice. Twenty seconds later, the talking stopped. Trying not to show any fear, the pastor walked up the stairs to the balcony and looked around, but no one was there. He and his daughter decided that they had done enough work for the night and decided to go home. They were walking out the door when they heard the angry voice once again. The pair quickly walked out the door and searched around the outside of the hall, but they were unable to locate the source of the eerie voice.

Local historians have identified the ghost of Turner Hall as the spirit of Charles Scheerer, who served many years as treasurer of the Turner Society and as the business manager of the hall. In 1910, he died

inside the building of a heart attack. At the time, Scheerer was com-
pleting his third term as mayor. Scheerer's dedication to the building
he loved so much seems to have outlived him.

In many ways, the ghost haunting Turner Hall is a playful spirit.
The ghost has been blamed for turning lights off and on and for hiding objects. Chances are that his spirit simply wants people to know
that he is around. This possibility does not really lessen the feelings of
unease that usually accompany his appearances, however.

THE DESOTO HOUSE HOTEL

The DeSoto House Hotel is the oldest continually operating hotel in
Illinois. It is also a remnant of Galena's golden age. In the 1850s, Galena
was a boomtown. The lead mines nearby brought thousands of dollars into the coffers of merchants and banks. Galena soon became one
of the most important landings on the Mississippi River. Steamboats
delivered goods and passengers to the burgeoning river port city on
a daily basis. In 1855, the DeSoto House Hotel was constructed on the
corner of Main and Grand Streets to accommodate the thousands of
guests who poured into Galena annually. When the 225-room, six-story
hotel opened its doors on April 9, 1955, it more than lived up to its bill-
ing as a true "luxury" hotel with its one-hundred-seat dining hall and
carving room, as well as a gentleman's reading room and several ladies'
parlors. However, Galena's boom days came to an end in the 1870s.
Increased costs were making the lead mines unprofitable. Also, the
town's primary investors put all their money in steamboat companies
and ignored the railroads, which eventually replaced steamboats as the
primary vehicle of transportation in the second half of the nineteenth
century. Eventually, the tons of silt dumped into the Galena River by
the mining companies made navigation up and down it impossible.
When the railroad built its terminus at East Dubuque, Iowa, Galena
lost its significance as a hub of commerce.

The DeSoto's fortunes rose and fell with those of Galena. In the late
1850s, both Abraham Lincoln and his rival for the U.S. Senate, Stephen
A. Douglass, gave speeches there. In the 1860s and 1870s, notables such
as Ulysses Simpson Grant, William Jennings Bryant, and Dorothea Dix
stayed there as well. Despite the hotel's prosperity, it seemed to many

people to be destined for destruction. In 1859, a fire raged through the hotel, causing thousands of dollars of damage. Then in 1869, the boiler of a dye works that had leased space in the hotel exploded, hurtling the main boiler across the street into a grocery store. In 1880, the owner of the DeSoto House Hotel removed the top two floors because the dwindling number of guests made them unnecessary.

In the 1980s, Mayor Frank Einsweiler endorsed an ambitious tourist campaign in an effort to bolster the economy of the region. The DeSoto House Hotel played a pivotal role in the mayor's plan. In 1986, the old hotel was completely renovated at a cost of $7.8 million. The first floor of the hotel is lined with shops and boutiques. The Courtyard Restaurant is located on the ground floor of the four-story atrium. The hotel's pub, the Green Street Tavern & Restaurant, occupies the site of the Galena Express Office. Fifty-five guest rooms can be found on the second and third floors. Some employees and guests of the DeSoto believe that the remodeling projected resurrected more than just the splendor of the DeSoto House Hotel.

For years, guests staying on the second and third floors of the DeSoto Hotel have reported seeing spectral forms strolling through the hallways and standing at the foot of their beds. Some people have seen ghosts walk through walls at the exact spot where a door once existed. Longtime employee Scott Wolfe told John B. Kachuba, author of Ghosthunting Illinois, *the story of a mother and daughter who were in their room late one evening around bedtime. The mother was lying awake in bed, and her daughter was sitting in a chair. All at once, the girl saw a woman in a hoop skirt standing in front of a window. After the figure vanished a few seconds later, she told her mother what she had seen. In a shaking voice, her mother said that she had seen it, too. Having a chance encounter with a ghost while staying at a haunted hotel seems to be one amenity that rarely finds its way into the promotional materials.*

GRAFTON

James Mason arrived in 1832 in what was then a wet and swampy area, although people had been living in the area as early as 1812. By 1836, Grafton was a burgeoning town with warehouses, businesses, and a wharf. Prescott Whittemore, who arrived in Grafton in 1838, named the town after his hometown in New Hampshire. Thanks to a flood in 1844, Grafton became accessible to steamboat traffic. The steamboats brought commerce and violence to the little river town. By the 1850s, the population had grown to 10,000 people. As a result of the end of the steamboat era in the 1930s and the closing of the last railroad line through Grafton in 1948, the town's fortunes and population declined dramatically. Grafton was revived when the Great River Road was extended from Alton in the late 1960s.

THE RUEBEL HOTEL

In the 1880s, Grafton was a "rough" place, populated by Irish and German quarry workers who drank and fought in the little town's twenty-six saloons. The finest saloon could be found in the Ruebel Hotel, which catered to the riverboat travelers and steamboat operators who poured into Grafton every day. The hotel, which was built in 1884 by Michael Ruebel, had thirty-two rooms and a bathhouse in the back. Guests could rent a room for $1.00 per day, or they could stay an entire week for $8.00. This rate included three meals a day. The hotel burned in 1912, but it was rebuilt the same year with two additions: a restaurant on the first floor and a dance hall on the second floor. During World War II, the dance hall was converted into quarters for thirty Coast Guard men.

Grafton—and the Ruebel Hotel—did not fare well in the second half of the twentieth century. The town had been experiencing a slow decline ever since the end of the steamboat era in the 1930s. Grafton received another crushing blow in 1948 when the last of the three railroad lines that had passed through the little town stopped service. In 1996, the Ruebel Hotel was resurrected when it was purchased and completely restored by the Jeff Lorton family, who soon realized that they had come into possession of something else besides an old hotel.

The hotel had just been open a few months in 1997 when three guests informed Jeff Lorton that they had communicated with the ghost of a little girl who identified herself as "Amanda." Down through the years, guests have claimed to see a little girl standing at the top of the stairway to the second floor or in the upstairs hallway. Several guests have taken photographs of orbs in different parts of the hotel in recent years. In a newspaper interview, Jeff Lorton told the reporter, "As many years as this place has been around, I'm sure that someone has died here, but none of us has seen anything. I figure if I don't bother them, they won't bother me."

Today, the Ruebel Hotel is still a colorful place to stay in Grafton, but with modern amenities. Guests can sample a wide variety of fine wines, beers, and spirits in the saloon from a restored bar from the 1904 World's Fair. Visitors can sleep in the same rooms where the rowdy quarry workers once stayed, albeit in new beds. With a nod to the twenty-first century, the owners also offer refrigerators, hair dryers, free wireless Internet, and 26-inch flat-screen televisions with satellite in every room. The Ruebel Restaurant offers the kind of fine cuisine that patrons from the nineteenth century could not have imagined. The Ruebel Hotel has also attempted to exploit the public's growing interest in the paranormal by recounting the story of Abigail on its Web site.

QUINCY

Quincy, known as the "Gem City," was founded on top of limestone bluffs by John Wood from Moravia, New York. In 1819, he became the first settler in the village known simply as "The Bluffs." In 1825, Quincy, named in honor of John Quincy Adams, became the Adams County seat. Most of the earliest settlers moved to Quincy from New England. In the 1840s, hundreds of German immigrants made Quincy their home. In the winter of 1839–1840, the citizens of Quincy offered sanctuary to five thousand Mormons who were on their way west from Missouri. Steamboat traffic in the 1850s transformed Quincy into a bustling river town. In 1858, Quincy became the site for one of the U.S. Senate debates by Stephen A. Douglas and Abraham Lincoln. Dr. Eells's House was station stop number one on the Underground Railroad from Quincy to Chicago. The construction of a railroad bridge across the Mississippi River made Quincy the second-largest city in Illinois in the 1870s. In the twentieth century, Quincy suffered serious damage in the Mississippi River floods of 1993 and 2008.

BURTON CAVE NATURE PRESERVE

The Burton Cave Nature Preserve is located in Adams County, just southeast of Quincy. It is an eighty-five-acre tract of upland forest, floodplain forest, and pine plantation. The Nature Preserve is also home to Burton Cave, a water-formed cavern composed of 330 million-year-old limestone. The arched entrance of the cave, which is seven feet by thirty feet, overlooks Burton Creek fifty feet below. Five species of bats live in Burton Cave, primarily because of the area's thick canopy of trees and a nearby source of water. A host of blind invertebrates never leave the cave. Scientists are particularly interested in a troglobitic insect found only in a few other caves in Illinois. Folklorists and ghost hunters are interested in Burton Cave for an entirely different reason.

Burton's Cave holds a strange fascination for the residents of Adams County, primarily because of a bizarre story about the site that has been passed down for generations. *In the 1880s, a group of young people rode out to this picturesque site with the intention of having a picnic beneath the trees overlooking Burton Cave. They had just spread a blanket on the ground when one member of the party pointed up to Burton's Cave. The others stared in horror at a black-robed figure standing in the entrance to the cave. His hands were buried in the folds of his robe; his head was covered by a hood. After a few seconds, the weird figure vanished. The watchers rushed up the hill and stood outside the mouth of the cave. The group cautiously walked in the direction of a faint glow coming from deep inside the recesses of the cave. Minutes stretched into hours as they peered in the darkness, not knowing what lay ahead of them. The dim light led them to a small room, in the middle of which was a makeshift altar. Lying on the altar was a woman in a white dress. To all appearances, the woman was dead. Lighted candles had been placed around her head and feet. Terrified, the group quickly groped their way out of the cave. They headed straight to the sheriff's office and led him back to the cave. When they returned to the cave, they were unable to find any trace of the woman, the altar, the candles, or the sinister robed figure.*

For over a century, curiosity seekers have flocked to Burton's Cave in the hope of seeing the black-robed figure. Unfortunately, the durability of legend of the phantom of Burton's Cave can be at least partially responsible for the vandalism that has marred its beauty. Today, Burton's Cave is protected by a bat gate installed in the late 1990s to protect its endangered bat population. If the legend is indeed based on fact, as most legends are, then the bat gate might protect would-be intruders as well.

GHOST HOLLOW ROAD

Ghost Hollow Road is located south of Quincy between Twenty-fourth Street and I-172. This serene-looking, rolling stretch of road takes the traveler past well-kept homes and through farmland. According to legend, Ghost Hollow Road also leads the driver on a journey to the other side.

Ghost stories about Ghost Hollow Road have circulated for many years. People tell of a mysterious mansion that appears and disappears in the woods. Supposedly, the old house burned down years ago. Legend has it that a more substantial house is located down a gravel road leading off Ghost Hollow Road in an area known as Ghazza Grotto. Intruders have found pentagrams and animal carcasses inside the house, leading them to believe that Satan worship has taken place. People who have parked outside the house say that they have found handprints on their car after they have driven home. They also say that strange, glowing balls of green light chased their cars as they drove off.

A female specter dressed in nineteenth-century clothing has been seen walking down Ghost Hollow Road. In the late twentieth century, a young woman who was having trouble sleeping decided to get in her car and drive down Ghost Hollow Road in search of a legendary graveyard. She had not driven far before she found what she thought was an old sign leading to the graveyard. The woman got out of her car to take a closer look. The sign was not helpful, so she returned to her car. When she opened the door, she saw a young woman in her twenties walking toward her on the other side of the road. She noticed that the woman had blonde hair and dark circles under her eyes. The strange figure seemed to smirk as she walked by. After a few seconds, the woman realized how unlikely it would be for a woman to be walking by herself down a lonely road. When she turned around to take another look, the figure was gone.

The graveyard that the driver was looking for is probably as apocryphal as the stories people tell about the road itself. According to legend, the graveyard, which is very old, exudes an eerie aura with its crumbling crypts and broken tombstones. In the center of the graveyard is supposed to be a black tomb inscribed with a single Latin word above the door. Passersby can tell when they are near the graveyard because they can hear the sounds of whispering and singing off in the distance.

Each year, hundreds of people look for ghostly encounters down Ghost Hollow Road. If they disturb the peace of the people living in the vicinity or if they damage private property, they are more likely to encounter the local police.

QUINCY UNIVERSITY

Quincy University was founded in 1860 by a small group of Franciscan friars who had left Germany two years earlier to offer a liberal arts education in the Catholic Franciscan tradition. They originally named the institution St. Francis Solanus College after one of the order's Hispanic missionaries. The college was formally chartered in 1873. When the university's name was changed once again in 1917 to Quincy College and Seminary, its primary mission became the training of Franciscan priests. The college became coed in 1932 when women were admitted for the first time. After World War II, not only did enrollment increase, but so did the number of friar and lay faculty. In 1970, the college eliminated the seminary portion of the school and shortened its name to Quincy College in 1970. Today, Quincy University offers a master of business administration degree, a master of science in education degree, and a master of theological studies degree, as well as undergraduate degrees in thirty-two fields and an associate of science degree in aviation. If the legends students, staff, and faculty have been telling for years are true, students also learn about the paranormal.

Quincy University has several haunted buildings, one of which is Solano Hall, named after St. Francis of Solanus. The building was erected on the site of St. Aloysius Orphanage. The old orphanage was destroyed by a devastating fire in which several children perished. The orphans who survived the fire were housed in the new building. After the orphanage closed down, Quincy University converted the building into a dormitory for football players. Today, the building houses the school of music. According to campus lore, the building is haunted by the ghost of the children who died when St. Aloysius Orphanage burned down. People have seen the ghosts of children running down the hallways. They have also heard childish laughter in the darkened corridors. The sounds of running feet and the screams of children have been so loud that people walking around outside have heard them.

MacHugh Theater, which is located in Francis Hall, is also haunted. Before the building was transformed into a theater in the 1980s, it was used as a gymnasium. It is haunted by the ghosts of a theater professor named Hugh "Fitz" Fitzgerald, who campaigned to have the theater re-started after it was temporarily replaced by a television station. He died in 1998, but "Fitz" was so attached to the theater that he had worked so hard to resurrect that his spirit remains inside the building. Students and faculty members working late at night inside the MacHugh Theater have seen his ghost in the light booth, from which he watches the plays, just as he did when he was alive.

The type of ghost that haunts Padua Residence Hall, the freshman boys' dormitory, can be found in campus dormitories across the United States. By the time they have completed their first semester, freshmen have heard about the homesick student who committed suicide inside Padua Residence Hall by jumping out the fourth-floor window. Students trying to sleep have been awakened by the sounds of footsteps, whimpering, and screaming in the hallways. A few students claimed to have walked through cold spots in different parts of the building. The story goes that the ghost became so active that the fourth floor was closed down for a while.

Willer Hall, a coed dorm for juniors and seniors, is said to be even more haunted. A young lady reported to Ghostvillage.com that she lived in Willer Hall between August 1996 and May 1997. At the time, Willer Hall was a comparatively new building, having been erected in the 1970s, so it did not have the long tradition of hauntings that other buildings on campus have. In fact, there is no account, either in the official campus record or in campus legends, of anyone's having died there. She said that when she first moved into her room, she felt as if someone were staring at her, usually between 5:00 and 6:00 P.M. She found out later that her roommate had the same uneasy feeling. She also said that she saw what she described as a "large pane of light" hanging from the ceiling on four different occasions, again, between 5:00 and 6:00 P.M. The apparition vanished after fifteen or twenty seconds. The girl was in the bathroom when her boyfriend saw the pane of light. Later, her roommate admitted that she, too, had seen the light, but she did not say anything about it because she thought her imagination was working overtime. Girls living on other floors also saw the strange light in their rooms. One girl said that before she went to bed, she left several books scattered all over her desk. When she awoke the next morning, the books were neatly stacked in a pile. The resident assistant, who had lived on the first-floor suite with several other girls, said that they were watching television in the living room when all of them saw the upper torso of a man pass down the hallway and into one of the girls' rooms.

In a way, Quincy University is no different from any other residential university in the United States. Students routinely entertain one another and indoctrinate in-coming freshmen by telling them ghost stories. Ghost stories, it seems, are as much a part of campus life as parties, all-nighters, and fraternities and sororities.

PRAIRIE DU ROCHER

Prairie du Rocher is one of the oldest surviving communities in the United States that began as a French settlement. Pierre Dugue de Boisbriand constructed the first Fort de Chartres in 1718. His nephew, St. Therese Langlois, founded Prairie du Rocher in 1722 on a piece of land donated by the Royal Indian Company. In the early years, settlers grew wheat and corn, which they sold in the markets in New Orleans. After the soil became worn out in the mid-eighteenth century, a large portion of the town's population founded Ste. Genevieve in Missouri in 1750. George Rogers Clark captured Prairie du Rocher in the Revolutionary War. During the Mississippi River Flood of 1993, the Army Corps of Engineers saved Prairie du Rocher by digging a hole connecting the Mississippi River near Fort de Chartres. Today, Prairie du Rocher is a quiet farming town with a rich history.

FORT DE CHARTRES

The first settlers in southwestern Illinois were the French. In 1720, the French built Illinois's first fort. Fort de Chartres was originally an outfitting outpost to assist with the French colonization of this part of Illinois. In 1736, a contingent of soldiers from the fort initiated a disastrous campaign against the Chickasaws. A priest and the commanders of Fort de Chartres and a French post on the Wabash River were captured by the Chickasaws and burned at the stake. By the time an Irish mercenary named Richard MacCarty took command of Fort de Chartres, it had already fallen into ruin. Using slave labor and limestone from a nearby quarry, MacCarty rebuilt the fort at a cost of $3 million. The new fort was large enough to house four hundred soldiers. In 1753, MacCarty led an expedition from Fort de Chartres against the British in retaliation for the attack of a group of French explorers by General George Washington. After the French ceded Illinois to the British in 1763, it was two years before the British could take control of Fort de Chartres. Over the next decade, most of the French settlers left the area, rendering the fort obsolete. In 1772, the Mississippi River flooded the region and left seven feet of water inside the fort. When the river channel shifted, the west wall of the fort collapsed and was swept away. Not long thereafter, the garrison was transferred to Kaskaskia. Over the next century, the abandoned fort fell into ruin. When restoration efforts began in the 1950s, much of the fort had been reduced to rubble. Today, several buildings have been reconstructed on the original foundations. Visitors to the old fort learn about life on the Illinois frontier in the eighteenth century. They also learn about the fort's most famous ghost story, which has grown out of a real-life tragedy.

According to one legend, during the French occupation of Fort de Chartres, a civilian got into an argument with a soldier stationed in the fort. *Within a matter of minutes, the verbal altercation erupted into physical violence. Predictably, the battle-hardened soldier killed the local man. On the advice of the commander of the French government in Kaskaskia, the commander of Fort de Chartres decided to play down the incident. Under the cloak of darkness, soldiers buried the civilian in a local cemetery.*

In another version of the tale, the combatants were a French and a British officer. *In 1765, an argument broke out between the two men over the affections of a local girl. The men fought a duel with swords, and the British officer was killed. The French officer fled down river, and the British officer was secretly buried to keep friction between the French and the British settlers and soldiers in the area from escalating.*

For over a century, the murder was forgotten. Then on July 4, 1889, a woman named Mrs. Chris was sitting on the front porch of her home with her neighbor to escape the heat. Around midnight, the two women noticed a group of people coming their way from the direction of the old fort. Some of the people were on foot; most of them were riding in carriages. The women counted forty carriages in all. At the end of the procession was a low wagon carrying a casket. Not only did the women wonder why the funeral procession was headed toward the cemetery at night, but they were struck by the fact that the only noise they heard was the howling of the wind. The women sat on the porch a while longer, waiting for the mourners to return from the cemetery, but they never did. The women did not learn of the murder at Fort de Chartres until several years later.

The phantom funeral procession has been sighted several times since Mrs. Chris and her friend first saw them. The mourners only appear when July 4 falls on a Friday. The last time they were seen was in 1986. In 1997, the Fourth of July once again fell on a Friday, but no one saw the funeral procession, probably because so many cars were on the four-mile stretch of road between the fort and the cemetery. However, at midnight, all of the coyotes in the area began to howl. Is it possible that the animals saw something that human beings could not?

Iowa

DAVENPORT

Davenport is located on the border between Iowa and Illinois. During the signing of the treaty that ended the Blackhawk War in 1832, Sauk Indian chief Keokuk gave a large tract of land to Marguerite LeClaire, the wife of Antoine LeClaire, who served as translator during the proceedings. Following Keokuk's instructions, Antoine built a house, the Treaty House, on the exact spot where the treaty was signed. Antoine established Davenport on May 14, 1836, and named it after his friend Colonel George Davenport. The city was incorporated on January 25, 1839. In 1856, the construction of the first railroad bridge across the Mississippi River by the Rock Island Railroad connected Davenport and Rock Island. During the Civil War, five Union camps were set up in the city. In order to care for the hundreds of Iowa children orphaned after the Civil War, the Iowa Soldiers' Orphans' Home was established on November 16, 1865. Davenport experienced a building boom in the 1920s. Buildings like the Kahl Building and the Park Building soared into the sky. Businesses like Sears and JC Penney started up in downtown Davenport during this time. The city's economy, which plunged during the Great Depression of the 1930s, bounced back in the boom following World War II. However, local businesses suffered greatly during the economic downturn of the 1970s. In the 1980s, many people lost their jobs when the Caterpillar plant closed. In the 1990s, Davenport bounced back with the revitalization of the downtown area.

THE BLACKHAWK HOTEL

Davenport's Blackhawk Hotel on East Third Street was built in 1915. In the 1920s, the hotel was completely remodeled to coincide with the city's growing prosperity. Four stories were added to the building, as well as marble accents to the windows. Some of the guests who stayed at the hotel's four hundred luxurious rooms included celebrities such as Pearl Bailey, Carl Sandburg, Herbert Hoover, Carey Grant, Ronald Reagan, Jack Dempsey, and Richard Nixon. Guy Lombardo and Stan Keeton provided the music for some of Davenport's gala events in the Blackhawk's huge ballroom. The Blackhawk Hotel's fortunes declined at the same rate as the city's. In the 1970s, Davenport tried to pump new life into its deteriorating downtown by building a new civic center, the Rivercenter. The city's efforts to rebuild its urban center were not enough to neutralize the effects of the economic downturn brought about by Iowa's farming crisis. However, the Blackhawk's future seemed to brighten when a convention center was constructed nearby in the 1990s. The construction of the Figge Art Museum and the restoration of Modern Woodmen Park attracted the Isle of Capri to downtown Davenport. Renamed "The President Casino's Blackhawk Hotel," the old hotel fell even further into decline. It became a "low-rent" hotel for gamblers unable to afford the cost of staying at the Radisson, the only other hotel in downtown Davenport. By the end of the decade, a meth lab fire and burst water pipes in the winter had caused so much damage to the old hotel that the Isle of Capri was forced to close it down. The Blackhawk received a new lease on life, however, in August 2008 when the state of Iowa awarded Amrit and Amy Gill, owners of Restoration St. Louis, an $8.5 million tax credit to renovate a number of buildings, including the Blackhawk Hotel. The Gills plan to transform the Davenport Club on the eleventh floor into luxury apartments. Nothing has been said so far about the fate of the ghosts who remain in the Blackhawk Hotel.

At least three spirits are believed to haunt the Blackhawk Hotel. One is the ghost of a musician. *Many people have heard someone playing the piano in the ballroom when no one else is around. A female spirit has been sighted floating down the hallways in a blue dress. Her dignified demeanor has led some eyewitnesses to conclude that she is the ghost of one of Davenport's "high society" women who regularly attended the soirees held in the old hotel. The Blackhawk's most famous ghost is the spirit of a world-famous movie star. On November 29, 1986, actor Cary Grant died from a cerebral hemorrhage in a room on the eighth floor. Grant has been identified as the elderly, well-dressed man waiters have seen walking through the hotel.*

Since 1914, the Blackhawk Hotel has been "reborn" several times. It has survived through most of the twentieth century and well into the twenty-first century, despite neglect and the ravages of time. The same can be said of the Blackhawk's ghosts, who also seem to be enjoying a second life in the dark recesses of the hotel.

PHI KAPPA CHI FRATERNITY

Phi Kappa Chi chiropractic fraternity was founded in 1961 by Dr. David D. Palmer at 723 Main Street. In its mission statement, the fraternity emphasizes "Quality, Academics, and involvement in issues concerning the chiropractic community." The members of Phi Kappa Chi participate in intramural sports and travel to chiropractic seminars and alumni doctor's offices. The fraternity house is equipped with a cervical chair, a Gonstead pelvic bench, a Zenith full-spine drop-piece table, and, according to some of the brothers, a ghost.

The house where Phi Kappa Chi fraternity is located was built in 1920 by a local doctor very close to the medical center. Following his death, a number of different families lived in the house until 1968, when the fraternity members took up residence there. One of the ghosts haunting the old house is said to be the spirit of a homeless man who was brought to the house one cold winter night in 1922.

The doctor did what he could for the poor man, but he died in the upstairs front bedroom. Since 1968, the ghost of a large man has been seen walking through the front door, going up the stairs, and entering the upstairs front bedroom. He is always seen wearing a heavy winter coat with the collar pulled up. In *Ghosts along the Mississippi*, author Jim Longo says that the paranormal activity inside the house really escalated in 1978. Neighbors across the street reported seeing a man standing in an upstairs window, staring out into the distance. Some people described him as wearing a ship captain's hat. The same year, fraternity members complained about hearing someone walking around upstairs in rooms that were so packed full of boxes that no one could have passed through. Some of the young men have also heard footsteps climbing up and down the stairs. The "peck-peck-peck" of a typewriter has been heard in an empty room. Another frequently heard noise is the sound of a door being locked and unlocked. Sometimes, locked doors open themselves with a loud bang. Toilets flush by themselves. The mischievous spirit has even turned off all of the electric and wind-up alarm clocks during the night, causing the men to oversleep.

One cold January evening, a young man who was the first to return to the fraternity house went upstairs and padlocked the fraternity's old refrigerator, which had been left open to defrost. He also shut one of the bedroom doors and went downstairs to watch television. After a few minutes, he returned upstairs to go to the bathroom and was surprised to find the padlock sitting on top of the refrigerator and the bedroom door locked. He tried to contact his fraternity brothers by phone to see if someone was playing a joke on him, but was unsuccessful. His feelings of dread increased when he realized that no one else besides him was in the house.

The old adage "Home is where the heart is" usually applies to the strong bond that pulls us back to the place where we grew up. However, this old saying could explain the ghostly disturbances at the Phi Kappa Chi fraternity house. Is it not possible that the homeless man who died there feels a strong attachment to the house where someone did his best to save his life?

AMBROSE HALL

St. Ambrose University, a private, coeducational liberal arts university, is affiliated with the Catholic Diocese of Davenport. The first bishop of Davenport, the Most Reverend John McMullen, founded St. Ambrose in 1882 as a seminary and school of commerce for young men. Between 1882 and 1885, classes were taught in two rooms of the old St. Marguerite's School. St. Ambrose moved to its present location on Locust Street in July 1885 when the cornerstone was laid for Ambrose Hall in a secluded grove of oak trees. Students began classes in the new building on November 2, 1885, even though only two of the four stories had been finished. When construction was completed, Ambrose Hall had a kitchen on the first floor, a study hall and several bathrooms on the second floor, a library and faculty rooms on the third floor, and the original chapel and rooms for boarding students on the fourth floor. Ambrose Hall was expanded in 1893 with the addition of an east wing, which housed a small gymnasium, study rooms, and a laboratory. In 1902, Ambrose Hall barely avoided a potentially devastating fire when a quick-thinking crowd threw Father Flannagan's burning couch out of the window to keep the fire from spreading. Other buildings were added to the campus as enrollment at St. Ambrose University increased, including separate housing for priests. Today, the student union, the John R. Lewis Board Room, the financial aid office, the admissions office, the records and registration office, and a few classrooms and faculty offices can be found in Ambrose Hall, along with a ghost or two.

Most of the hauntings in Ambrose Hall seem to center around the fourth floor. In the late nineteenth and early twentieth centuries, priests who taught at the school lived in apartments on the fourth floor. Many faculty members and students believe that the ghost of at least one of these priests is still up there. In recent years, faculty members working late in their offices on the third floor have heard footsteps on the floor above them when no one was up there. Blinking lights have also been seen in the darkened hallways and rooms on the fourth floor. Students who have lived in Ambrose Hall may also have come into contact with the spectral priest. The August 13, 1987, edition of *The Ambrose Magazine* mentions the "tales of the ghosts of priests long dead and creatures who play games while they sleep at night" (10).

According to the Web site HauntedHouses.com, a group of paranormal researchers might have discovered the presence of another spirit in Ambrose Hall. In 2007, the Iowa Paranormal Advanced Research Team stationed two people in Room 403, two people near the main staircase, and two people in the west-side annex office. During the night, the group heard a number of knocking sounds in the math hallway, on the main staircase, and just outside the west-side annex office station. One of the members smelled incense in the eastern hallway and saw flickering lights in the western hallway. Most of the thirteen Electronic Voice Phenomena (EVPs) the group collected were greetings, such as "Hi." One of the voices, however, was a female voice that made a startling confession: her belief that Jesus was not alive. In another EVP, the voice whispered, "There is something wrong with me." The group concluded that they might have recorded the voice of a female student who had lost her faith and had possibly committed suicide in Ambrose Hall.

In *The Encyclopedia of Ghosts and Spirits*, author Rosemary Ellen Guiley says that in folklore, one of the reasons why ghosts return is to complete unfinished business. Priests, like librarians, are conscientious souls whose dedication to their profession sometimes extends to the afterlife. If the female apostate did indeed kill herself in Ambrose Hall, then her restless spirit could still be waiting for the absolution that may never come.

THE PUTNAM MUSEUM

The Putnam Museum, founded in 1867, was one of the first museums west of the Mississippi River. In 1964, the museum changed its name to the Putman Museum of Science and History and moved to its present location at 1717 West Twelfth Street on Museum Hill. The museum houses 160,000 specimens and artifacts, such as Egyptian mummies and shrunken heads. Permanent exhibits include Ocean Voyages: People of the Pacific Islands; Images of the Floating World; Hall of Mammals; and Ocean Experience. A recent investigation by two groups of paranormal investigators has revealed a few "unofficial" exhibits inside the Putnam Museum.

On October 26, 2007, the Des Moines Iowa Extreme Paranormal Advanced Research Team (DIEPART) participated in a special event called "Haunted Hill." During the all-night investigation, the group recorded an EVP in the Egyptian Gallery of female laughter and another EVP of a woman's voice saying "Anna." However, the group did not gather enough evidence to label the museum as "haunted."

In 2008, another investigation was conducted by the Iowa Paranormal Advanced Research Team. The group had just begun their walk-through inside the museum when two Electron Magnetic Filed (EMF) detectors went off simultaneously. Matthew Sweet, who was stationed near the top of the IMAX Theater, registered a drop in temperature from 76 degrees to 68 degrees on his digital thermal thermometer. A few minutes later, members of the group heard soft bumping sounds and rustling sounds. The EVP of a woman's voice turned out to be the voice of the curator of the museum, Eunice Schlicting, who was observing the investigation.

Thousands of people visit the Putnam Museum annually. They come to see the exhibits and to watch movies in the IMAX Theater, which features a screen six stories high and seven stories wide. Attendance has most likely been boosted by the investigations of the area's paranormal groups as well. Following their investigation of the Putman Museum, the members of IPART were asked to assist the museum in gathering additional information for an exhibit called, "The Science of Ghost Hunting," which ran between September 5, 2008, and January 11, 2009. One cannot imagine a better venue for such a program.

DUBUQUE

Dubuque, Iowa, is one of the oldest settlements west of the Mississippi River. This region was claimed for France by La Salle in 1782. Julien Dubuque, the first permanent settler in the village that was to become Dubuque, arrived in 1875. Three years later, he was granted permission by the Spanish government to mine lead in the area. Control of Dubuque's rich lead mines shifted to France in 1880 and then to the United States in 1803. The city of Dubuque was chartered in 1833 on a large, flat plain adjoining the Mississippi River. Because of the region's large stands of timber, Dubuque soon became a center for the lumber industry. Between 1860 and 1880, Dubuque was one of the largest cities in the United States. In the late nineteenth and early twentieth centuries, the city's factories attracted a large wave of German and Irish Catholic immigrants. After the decline of industry in Dubuque in the 1980s, publishing and high technology became the city's fastest-growing businesses.

THE MATHIAS HAM HOUSE

In the mid-nineteenth century, Mathias Ham was one of Dubuque's most successful businessmen. After making a fortune in agriculture, lumber, shipping, and lead mining, Ham hired the architect John Francis Rague, the creator of Iowa City's capitol building, to design a palatial home for his family. Rague completed the Italian villa in 1856. The house's distinctive tower enabled Ham to keep watch on his ships as they floated down the Mississippi River. His wife, Margaret, died in 1874; Mathias followed her in death in 1889. Their daughters, May and Sarah, lived alone in the house until they passed away in the 1890s.

When Sarah Ham became the sole owner of the estate, she inherited more than just a rambling house. Shortly before he died, her father had alerted the authorities that he had spotted a gang of river pirates operating on the river not far from his house. Late one night in the 1890s, one of these pirates broke into the Ham House, seeking revenge. Sarah was lying in bed reading when she heard a strange noise on the first floor. By the time she crept down the stairs, the intruder had fled. The next day, she reported the break-in to her neighbors and advised them to be on the alert. She also told them that she would put a lighted lantern in her window if it happened again.

The next day, Sarah was awakened once again by the sound of someone moving around downstairs. She called out "Who's there?" but no one answered. She returned to her bedroom and placed the lantern in the window. Then she sat up in bed with her pistol at the ready. The minutes crawled by until, finally, she heard heavy footsteps climb the stairs to the second floor. When the footsteps stopped outside her bedroom, she fired two shots through the door. Aroused from their slumber by the gunfire, her neighbors hurried to Sarah's house. They followed the blood trail to the riverbank, where they found the body of the captain of the river pirates who had threatened her father so many years before.

The Mathias Ham House has been operated as a house museum since 1964. Visitors walking through the mansion get a view of the lifestyle of Iowa's wealthiest citizens before the Civil War. The dogtrot cabin, the one-room schoolhouse, and the replica mine shaft educate tourists about the lives of the state's less affluent citizens. An increasing number of visitors, however, visit places like the Mathias Ham House to learn about the paranormal.

Ever since the house was first opened as a museum, rumors have been circulating about the weird occurrences within the mansion. Staff members have talked about hearing phantom footsteps and the scooting of chairs on the wooden floors. Electricians have been called out to the old house on numerous occasions to investigate such electrical problems as lights that flicker or that cannot be turned on at all. The porch light can be turned on only by twisting the fuse. Rarely do electricians find anything wrong with the wiring or the lights when they examine the fixtures. Nonetheless, staff members are fairly certain about the cause of a strange light that moves from window to window and that sometimes flits around the outside of the house. The story goes that this mysterious light is actually the glow from a lantern carried by the ghostly pirate captain as he prowls around, seeking his revenge.

Something in the building also seems to enjoy manipulating objects. Ink pens or tools that are left in one place just before closing are moved to another location the next morning. The entity responsible for the disturbances in the house also seems to enjoy opening an upstairs window after the staff members have locked it.

The most common reported oddity in the Mathias Ham House is the feeling of cool breezes that waft through the house, even when the doors and windows are shut tight. Some staff members and visitors have walked into cold spots in certain parts of the house. The tower seems to have the most cold spots, but unusually frigid areas have also been detected on the stairs and in Sarah's bedroom.

THE GRAND OPERA HOUSE

The Grand Opera House was built at 135 Eighth Street in 1890. The lavish brick and sandstone building attracted acts that were rarely seen in the upper Midwest, such as ballets, minstrel shows, and stage plays. Stars like Lillian Russell, Sarah Bernhardt, and Ethel Barrymore appeared in stage productions at the Grand Opera House. Like many American opera houses, the Grand Opera House was converted into a movie theater in 1928 to attract more business. In 1986, the Barn Community Theatre Company took over the Grand Opera House. Following extensive renovations, the old opera house once again became a stage for live theater in Dubuque. Today, theater lovers enjoy productions produced by community theater members and by other outside groups. According to local lore, they are sometimes treated to unscheduled performances by the theater's ghosts.

Reports of ghostly activity inside the Grand Opera House first began circulating between 1928 and 1958 when movies were shown there. *In the 1930s, cleaning ladies were so unnerved by disembodied voices they heard coming from the stage area that they called the police. Reports of ghostly disturbances increased after the theater reopened in 1986. When the old building was being renovated, employees working alone continued to hear voices and even singing and laughter around the stage. Workmen said that they heard footsteps walking across the empty stage. The* first production performed at the theater after it reopened in 1986 was George Cohan's "Tintypes." According to the Web site Hauntedhouses. com, a few minutes after the play started, all of the lights went out in the theater except for the ones on stage. Electricians could find nothing wrong with the bulbs or the wiring. During subsequent productions, spotlights have risen up and down on their own. One night, an electrical box exploded. Moments later, an orb was seen floating across the stage. *In 1991, the ghosts began to manifest themselves visually. An employee was working alone in the theater when he saw two women sitting in the auditorium seats. They de-materialized within a few seconds. A few years later, a cameraman was filming a show when his lens suddenly began zooming in and out. When he examined the tape afterward, he was surprised to find a ghostly figure in one of the scenes.*

The ghost of a woman also seems to be active in the theater. Actors have seen a female figure walking past the windows of the booth where the spotlights are housed. A female spirit occupies the costume shop on the fifth floor. From all accounts, this spirit does not like women. One theater legend has it that years ago, a woman was pushed down the stairs by an invisible entity. A Ouija board session conducted on the fifth floor by a couple of women revealed that the name of the contentious spirit is "Sarah."

Unexplained occurrences are still reported in the Grand Opera House on a fairly regular basis. Doors in the lobby open and close at will. Light switches go off and on by themselves. Bumps, bangs, and knocks are heard in the balcony. People sitting in an empty row of seats sometimes feel the presence of someone sitting next to them. Once in a while, people feel cold blasts of air in parts of the theater where all of the doors and windows are closed. Objects left in one place are discovered somewhere else the next day. An actor who was on the stage when no one else was in the theater said he felt like someone was watching him from the balcony. None of these bizarre events seem to bother the director, who says that the theater's ghosts are not really menacing. In fact, they seem to enjoy the theater as much as the actors and the audience do.

Louisiana

NEW ORLEANS

Named after Philippe II, Duc d'Orleans, Regent of France, New Orleans was founded on May 7, 1718, by Jean-Baptiste Le Moyne de Bienville. In 1763, the Spanish took control of New Orleans. In 1801, the French regained control of the city. Following the Haitian Revolution of 1804, thousands of black and white Haitian refugees immigrated to New Orleans. On January 8, 1815, Andrew Jackson's militia defeated the British at the Battle of New Orleans. Between 1830 and 1840, New Orleans became the wealthiest city in the nation. Even though the largest slave market in the South was located in New Orleans, the city also had the largest and most affluent population of free persons of color in the United States. Still, the slave trade brought millions of dollars to the city before 1861. New Orleans surrendered to Union forces early in the Civil War and, as a result, was spared the destruction that many southern cities suffered. During Reconstruction, many blacks held political offices in New Orleans. However, in 1877, white southern Democrats stripped African Americans in New Orleans of their civil rights. In 1860, New Orleans was the largest city in the South, but after the Civil War, the city was surpassed by other southern cities that were growing at a much faster rate. An innovative drainage plan invented by A. Baldwin Wood enabled the city to expand into areas that had formerly been swampland. By the late 1980s, tourism became New Orleans's largest industry. New Orleans was devastated at the end of August 2005 by Hurricane Katrina, which flooded over 80 percent of the city and claimed 1,500 lives.

THE BOTTOM OF THE CUP TEA ROOM

The inconspicuous little shop at 732 Royal Street is the oldest operating tea room in the United States. Established in 1929, the Bottom of the Cup Tea Room has been a haven for lovers of fine teas and the paranormal for decades. Hundreds of tourists flock to the store to peruse the gift shop, sip tea, and have their fortunes read by professional psychics. According to employees and tour guides, some people have encountered the spirit world in a very personal way inside the Bottom of the Cup Tea Room.

In the early 1800s, hundreds of beautiful quadroons and octoroons—beautiful, educated young women descended from Spanish and African American stock—lived in the French Quarter. The minute trace of mixed blood that flowed through their veins lent them an exotic air that made them especially attractive to the sons of wealthy planters, who took them as their mistresses and set them up in lavish apartments. Although intermarriage between quadroons and octoroons and their lovers was forbidden at the time in New Orleans, the bonds that joined the couples together was so strong that many of these arrangements lasted for years, even if the woman's lover had another family. For many of these free women of color, living in the lap of luxury with fine clothes and expensive jewelry in expensively furnished apartments more than made up for the fact that they were the "other woman" in their lovers' life.

This was not true, however, for a lovely young woman named Julie, who lived with her wealthy white lover at the four-story walk-up at 732 Royal Street. She had everything she wanted except for a wedding ring. The handsome young French nobleman who had strong feelings for his gorgeous consort was reluctant to marry her because of the shame the union would bring upon his family. Consequently, he dodged the issue whenever his gorgeous consort was about to bring up the topic of marriage. After a while, his visits to 732 Royal became less and less frequent.

One cold, wet December night, Julie marched into the parlor and demanded that her lover marry her and move to France, where mixed marriages were legal. The Frenchman, who was expecting a visit from several of his male friends, told the girl that he would marry her if she proved her love to him by removing all of her clothing and spending the night on the roof of the building. Fighting back tears, Julie dashed up the stairs to the bedroom and slammed the door.

With his petulant girlfriend out of the way, the young man looked forward to spending a pleasant winter evening with his friends. Seated in front of the blazing fireplace, the men whiled away the hours playing cards, smoking cigars, and drinking cognac and absinthe. After the last of his guests went home, the young man realized that Julie was nowhere to be found. When he ran into their bedroom, he was shocked to find her clothes scattered on the floor. Suddenly, it dawned on him that Julie had taken his ridiculous request seriously and had spent the frigid night on the roof.

Practically flying up the attic stairs, he barged through the door and peered into the darkness, hoping to catch sight of his beloved. After a few seconds, panic gripped him as he spied the huddled figure of Julie lying by the fireplace. Nearly slipping on the ice that had collected during the night, he dashed over to the lifeless body and gathered her up in his arms, begging her to forgive him. In the weeks following Julie's senseless death, the young man secluded himself in his apartments at 732 Royal Street. His friends said that he spent all of his time seated in the parlor weeping and drinking cognac. A few months later, he, too, was dead, apparently of a broken heart.

The sad history of Julie and the handsome Frenchman lives on in tales told by tour guides, tourists, and clerks at the Bottom of the Cup Tea Room. It is said that on the coldest day in December, Julie's naked form can be seen walking back and forth across the roof, waiting for her lover to join her. She has also been seen through the dormer window, standing by the chimney. Supposedly, the New Orleans police department has a file of 911 telephone calls regarding sightings of a woman who spectators believe is going to jump off the roof of the old townhouse. When the police climb up the roof, no one is there.

In recent years, though, Julie's ghost has been making her presence known inside the tea room. For years, employees have identified her as the spirit that taps on the walls and moves objects inside the shop.

One day, a psychic named Otis Biggs was sitting in his booth when he heard the clicking of a woman's fingernails on the tabletop. Biggs has also smelled Julie's perfume and seen her image in the goldfish pond in the back courtyard. Another employee caught a glimpse of Julie's skirts whisking around the back corner of the shop. A few seconds later, the woman heard the faint sounds of female giggling. Another psychic named Philip Mullen was giving a customer a reading in a back room when he heard a rattling noise. He walked into the front of the shop and noticed that the small ornamental tree on a table in the middle of the room was shaking by itself. All of the crystals that had hung from the tree had been flung across the floor.

Customers have also met Julie's ghost. Women have felt invisible fingers running through their hair. One day, an attractive woman walked into the Bottom of the Cup Tea Room to do some shopping when, suddenly, her hair ribbon came untied, and her hair fell down around her shoulders. A few weeks later, a female tour guide wearing a full-length skirt led a group of tourists inside the tea room late in the afternoon. She was telling the story of Julie and her Frenchman when all at once, her skirts billowed up around her knees. It is widely believed in the French Quarter that the appearance of a beautiful woman inside her former home awakens her jealous rage.

Apparently, Julie bothers men as well inside the tea room. One day, a man who worked in a nearby Chinese restaurant walked into the Bottom of the Cup Tea Room holding a can of soda. While he was talking to the cashier, he set his soda can on the counter. Right in the middle of their conversation, the can began to rattle back and forth across the counter. A customer who witnessed the unusually "active" can was totally unaware that the shop was haunted when she walked in the door. By the time she left, she had become a believer in haunted houses. On another occasion, a carpenter was working in the attic late one evening all by himself. He stopped working just long enough to get a drink of water. When he returned to the attic, he could not find any of his tools. He looked all over the attic but could not find his tools anywhere. He then walked downstairs and asked if the store was haunted. He again walked back up to the attic and continued his search, eventually finding his tools hidden under the insulation.

The sad story of the octoroon mistress persists today as an indict-ment of slavery and of the prejudicial attitudes of many white south-erners at the time. In most versions of the tale, Julie's wealthy young French master loved her but did not marry her for fear of being ostra-cized and possibly even disinherited by his family. Many people say that he became a tragic figure, plagued with guilt and shame. His ghost, they say, can be seen through the windows seated at a chess board, all alone.

MAGNOLIA MANSION

Magnolia Mansion is one of the most magnificent of all the antebel-lum homes in New Orleans's Garden District. In 1857, a banker named Alexander Harris commissioned designer James H. Calrow to build the house for his bride, Elizabeth "Lizzie" Johnson Thompson, on a lot he had purchased on Prytania Street from McIlhenny for $12,000. Following Alexander's death from yellow fever on July 19, 2009, Lizzie Thompson Harris fell heir to the estate, which was worth $200,000. Lizzie eventually married Carneal Burke in 1871. In 1879, she sold the property to cotton mill owner John Henry Maginnis, who was one of the richest men in the entire South. On July 4, 1889, John Henry was struck and killed by lightning at his summer home in Ocean Springs, Mississippi. Some people viewed John's bizarre death as divine retri-bution for the deplorable working conditions in his cotton mills. The house was passed down to John's wife, Lizzie. Following her death in 1921, John and Lizzie's beautiful daughter, Josephine, inherited the house. Known as "Queen of Comus," Josephine was heavily involved in New Orleans's Mardi Gras parades for most of her life.

The Harris-Maginnis House, as it was known for many years, entered an entirely new phase in its history in 1939, when Josephine donated it to the New Orleans chapter of the Red Cross. Between 1939 and 1954, Red Cross volunteers tended to the needs of soldiers who had fought in World War II and the Korean War. During this period, the Red Cross, providing emergency relief for disaster victims, offered classes in home care for the sick and in first aid and water safety and also provided canteen service from its base in the Harris-Maginnis House. On December 5, 1954, the Red Cross sold the antebellum home to Dr. Clyde E. Cransons, who restored the old home to its former glory. Today, Magnolia Mansion is one of New Orleans's most beautiful and magnificent mansions. According to guests and staff, the ghosts of the former owners are not quite ready to give up ownership of their beautiful home.

Aside from being one of the most beautiful homes in the Garden District, Magnolia Mansion is also one of the most haunted. The ghost that has taken up residence in the old home is said to be the spirit of a mentally disturbed young woman who lived across the street from the mansion around the turn of the century back when the Maginnis family lived there. According to the legend, *the girl tried to kill herself by putting her head in the oven and by hanging herself from the balcony. Out of desperation, her parents finally placed their daughter in a mental institution. After a few months, the girl's condition improved so rapidly that her parents decided to treat her to a vacation. She was sitting in the train station in New Orleans with her mother while her father bought the train tickets. Suddenly, the silence in the station was shattered by the shrill whistle of an approaching train. The girl jumped out of her seat, ran outside, and placed her head on the railroad tracks just seconds before the train passed by. She was killed instantly.*

For years, the spirit of the disturbed girl was said to haunt her family home. People say that after the house was torn down, her ghost moved across the street to Magnolia Mansion. Her ghost first manifested itself while the old house was being converted into a bed and breakfast. *One day, a construction worker who was left alone in the house was talking on his cell phone when all at once, one of the 300-pound, ten-foot oak doors slammed shut with such force that one of the neighbors mistook the sound for a gunshot. The man was so shaken up that he ran out the front door and never returned, not even to pick up his paycheck.*

A few days later, the new owner of the house was inspecting the renovations when suddenly the chandelier in the main room began shaking. It seemed as if the shaking was being caused by the vibrations of footsteps upstairs. She walked up to the second floor, but no one was there. She returned to the first floor, but no one was there either. She had been alone in the house the entire time.

On another occasion, the owner of the bed and breakfast entered the house and found the construction workers sitting in the hallway, like kindergartners. Her first impression was that the crew was on break. Stifling her anger, she asked the foreman why they were lying down on the job when they were behind schedule. He simply pointed his finger and told her to go in the dining room and look at the wall. She walked into the room and was shocked to find that all the walls were wet. In fact, water was dripping off the walls onto the floor. She gazed around the room but could find no apparent leaks. When she accidentally brushed against one of the walls, she was surprised to find that the substance on the wall was oily in texture. Thinking that pranksters had broken into the house during the night, the workmen cleaned up the mess and returned to work.

The paranormal activity increased after the bed and breakfast opened for business. According to entries in the guest book, the most commonly reported disturbance in the old house is the sound of spectral footsteps, usually between two and three A.M. In recent years, guests have taken hundreds of photos of orbs in the various rooms. In February 2005, a guest caught the wispy image of a misty shape hovering over her husband, who was standing on the sidewalk in front of the building.

Some guests, however, have gotten "up close and personal" with the ghost of the mansion. A woman who was sitting in a chair on March 19, 2005, had just about fallen asleep when she felt a small hand grasp her wrist. It took a great deal of effort for her to pry the invisible fingers off her arm. On the eve of Daylight Savings Time in 2006, a young woman who spent the night in the room with the colorful title of "The Vampire's Lair" said that someone—or something—set her wristwatch back an hour. On January 20, 2007, a guest saw a little boy run through the dining room. No children were staying in the bed and breakfast at the time. That evening, a guest who had turned in for the night reported being touched by a ghostly hand. In July 2009, a couple who were staying in the Vamps Bordello Room heard something heavy, like furniture, being dragged across the room. When they turned on the lights, nothing appeared to have been moved around. On another night, the husband found one of his black shoes sitting at the end of his bed; the other was wedged between two pillows that had been placed on the floor.

One of the spirits haunting Magnolia Mansion is referred to as the "Caretaker" by the owners and staff. On July 28, 2004, a couple was spending their honeymoon in Magnolia Mansion. Sometime during the night, the woman took off the covers because she was not feeling well. A few minutes later, she felt someone pull up the covers, tuck her in, and brush her cheek with a cold hand. She looked over at her husband, but he was sound asleep.

Another woman made the acquaintance of the caretaker ghost on September 14, 2006. She had just returned from a wedding and decided to lie down in bed for a while. Suffering from an upset stomach, the woman was dizzy and nauseated. Suddenly, she felt a gentle hand stroking her face and hair. She became so relaxed that she fell asleep after only a couple of minutes. The next morning, she asked her husband if he had touched her face during the night, and he said no. As the woman and her husband were checking out of the hotel, she mentioned the incident to the owner, who told her that she had probably had an encounter with the mansion's ghostly caretaker.

Some of the strange incidents reported inside Magnolia Mansion take the form of poltergeist activity. On November 5, 2004, a woman was awakened early in the morning by the tinkling of a music box. Halloween night 2004, a woman who had been walking around the French Quarter returned to her room and found that her water glass had been turned upside down.

Magnolia Mansion tries to cater to as many different people as possible. Weddings and receptions are held here on a regular basis, as well as elopements and renewed vows. Not surprisingly, Magnolia Mansion was selected as one of 2007's top-10 Romantic Inns. However, the owners also try to attract people who visit New Orleans in the hopes of seeing a ghost. One of the mansion's most popular packages is its "Ghostly Get-Away Package for Two." Indeed, Magnolia Mansion was selected as one of 2006's Most Haunted Inns of America. There is a thin line, it seems, between romantic ambience and ghostly allure.

THE PONTCHARTRAIN HOTEL

The Pontchartrain Hotel, located on 2031 St. Louis Avenue in the Garden District, was founded in 1927 by Lyle Aschaffenburg. Named after the Count de Pontchartrain from the court of Louis XVI, the fourteen-story, 118-room luxury hotel featured polished marble floors and walls, splendid canvas murals depicting scenes of Louisiana bayous, and gleaming chandeliers suspended from an arching, sky-blue ceiling. The lobby, hallways, and guest rooms were furnished with priceless antiques. The Bayou Bar, added in 1947, became a favorite hangout for local professionals and visiting celebrities such as Frank Sinatra and Frankie Laine. Some of the city's most powerful business leaders and politicians started their day with a "power business breakfast" at Lafitte's Restaurant, which was added in 1948. For over eighty years, the Pontchartrain Hotel attracted the rich and famous from all over the United States, including Rita Hayworth, Jose Ferrer, Walt Disney, Charles Laughton, Richard Burton, Mary Martin, The Doors, George H. Bush, and Tennessee Williams, who worked on his play *A Streetcar Named Desire* during his stay at the hotel. Some of the Pontchartrain's best-known occupants, however, are not of this world.

The most commonly reported paranormal activity in the Pontchartrain Hotel is best described as a residual. Employees at the hotel claim that the spirit of the hotel's original owner and designer, Lyle Aschaffenburg, still continues his usual activities, which involve overseeing the hotel. He was most often seen darting around the corners of the hotel. Witnesses, most of whom describe him the same way, usually see him just out of the corner of the eye. When they took a second look, no one was there. He also creates disturbances in Room 910, the room where he lived for many years. Guests claim that the eyes of a portrait of Mr. Aschaffenburg in Room 910 seem to follow them around. In the late 1990s, a female guest woke up and made herself some tea. While she was waiting for the water to boil, she heard a gurgling sound coming from the bathroom. When she opened the door, she was surprised to find that someone—or something—had turned on the water faucet. She reported the incident to the hotel clerk, who informed her that other guests had had the same experience in Room 910. This revelation did not make her feel much better.

The ninth floor was also haunted by the ghosts of a pair of wid-
owed sisters. The women were known to ride around New Orleans
in their chauffeur-driven, black Lincoln. After they died, their spirits
refused to leave the hotel that had been their home for so many years.
For years, maids reported seeing the women walking down the hallway
and standing in their suite on the ninth floor. Guests staying on the
ninth floor have also reported hearing the ghostly voices of women on
the ninth floor.

In August 2005, the Pontchartrain Hotel survived the blasts of wind
and water from Hurricane Katrina but suffered considerable damage
from looting and vandalism. In July 2007, the hotel was closed for renovations. A year later, the owners of the Pontchartrain Hotel received
a $7.2 million building permit to convert the old building into a senior
living center. The various remodeling projects that have changed the
hotel over the years have uncovered a large, plaster-scrolled cartouche
above a window and hand-painted medallions with animals, birds, and
ships on the ceiling of the restaurant.

THE ANDREW JACKSON HOTEL

The Andrew Jackson Hotel has always been popular with tourists looking for a comfortable place to spend the night within walking distance
from antique shops and fine restaurants in the French Quarter. The
hotel is also a frequent stop for the ghost tours that highlight the Quarter's most haunted locations. The Andrew Jackson Hotel is located on
the site of an orphanage, which burned down in 1794. Supposedly, a fire
broke out in the orphanage after a hurricane raged through the city.
According to one account, five African American orphans were playing
in the attic when the building caught on fire. The boys were unable to
find a way out of the burning structure and perished in the fire. In other
stories, the number of casualties is given as eighteen orphans.

The orphanage was replaced by the first U.S. District Courthouse in
New Orleans. In 1815, United States attorney John Dick indicted General Andrew Jackson on charges of contempt of court. Dick added the
charge of obstruction of justice after Jackson imprisoned the judge who
had charged him with contempt. Because Jackson refused to answer
any questions, he was fined $1,000 and released.

In the 1840s the courthouse was razed, and the current building was erected on the site. For years, the Andrew Jackson Hotel was open to adults only. Ironically, guests staying in Rooms 208, 211, or 111 frequently complain about hearing the laughter of children in the courtyard, even though no living children were staying in the hotel. Spectral boys have been seen running through the lobby at full speed. Some of these spirits run into walls and disappear. Another guest was awakened by the bouncing of a ball against his door. The screams of children occasionally echo through the dark corridors as well. Experts in the paranormal refer to these sounds as a residual haunting, the psychic residue generated by the tragic fire of 1794. Most of the paranormal activity occurs during the off season when only a few guests are staying at the hotel.

Several adult spirits have been seen at the old hotel as well. The ghost of a woman who might have been a housekeeper has been known to rearrange objects in guest rooms. Another, more pensive spirit is the ghost of a man in a corner of the courtyard with his head down and his hands behind his back. He could possibly be the ghost of a convict who was tried in the courthouse and sentenced to be hanged. Desk clerks have also seen a ghost dressed in a military uniform who could be the spirit of Andrew Jackson.

The Andrew Jackson Hotel is a charming blend of the past and present. Guests can gaze out from their windows upon the cast-iron fountain in the traditional landscaped courtyard. Yet, free high-speed Internet access is available for those guests who want to keep in touch with the modern world while they are sampling the French Quarter's Old World charm. Occasionally, the past intrudes on the comfort of guests in the form of rambunctious children who are not ready to go to bed—permanently.

THE PLACE D'ARMES HOTEL

The Place d'Armes Hotel is one of the most picturesque buildings in the French Quarter. Located only a few yards from Jackson Square, two blocks from Bourbon Street, and one block from Café du Monde, the Place d'Armes Hotel attracts tourists from all over the world. Visitors are enchanted by the building's classic French Quarter atmosphere, enhanced by its exterior balconies and cast-iron railings. Actually, nine townhouses dating back to the eighteenth and nineteenth centuries have been incorporated into the Place d'Armes Hotel. According to local legends, several of the former occupants of one of the old structures that once stood where the hotel is located are still staying at the Place d'Armes.

Most of the paranormal activity at the Place d'Armes Hotel can be traced back to an eighteenth-century school that once stood on the site. On a fateful night in 1788, the school, which was the first in Louisiana, caught fire, and the headmaster and the children were burned alive while asleep in their beds. Some locals believe that because the children had no idea what was happening, they have retained their playful personalities. A couple staying in the hotel experienced the mischievous nature of the child ghosts in 2000. *Late one evening, the guests returned to their hotel room after spending the day taking photographs of the French Quarter's unique architecture. Exhausted, they placed their camera and their souvenirs on the dresser and went to bed. The next morning, the woman was shocked to find that over half of the film in her camera that she had loaded the night before was exposed. Her curiosity drove her to take the film to a local pharmacy to be developed. When she picked up her film a few hours later, she started flipping through the pictures. Shivers ran up her spine when she realized that all of the photographs on the exposed roll were of her husband and herself, sleeping in their bed. The different photographic angles suggested that the photographer moved around the room. She and her husband were certain that no one could have entered their room during the night because their door was securely locked.*

One ghostly child in particular seems to enjoy disrupting the routine of the hotel's staff. In her book *Haunted Inns of the Southeast,* Sheila Turnage tells the story of a ghost who appears anywhere on the fifth floor. Dubbed Melissa by the desk clerks, the little girl seems to favor Room 508. *One day when the hotel was being renovated, the switchboard operator received a telephone call from Room 508. She was puzzled because the telephone was supposed to be disconnected in that particular room. She walked upstairs and looked into the room, but no one was there. A week later, the same thing happened. An electrician was sent up to Room 508 to check on the wiring. He was walking down the hallway on the fifth floor when he saw a little girl in a white communion dress standing in the doorway. She appeared to be around twelve years old. Sensing that something was terribly wrong, he ran down the hallway and exited the hotel.*

One of the most frequently sighted ghosts in the hotel is known by the staff as "The Bearded Gentleman." This elderly, bearded gentleman dressed in the fashion of the early 1800s usually nods to guests and immediately disappears. In *Journey into Darkness*, author Kalia Katherina Smith recounts the story of a woman who was talking to a bearded man on the balcony. She assumed that the man was staying in the room next door. Later that day, she asked the desk clerk about the bearded man next door. She was told that that room was not occupied at the time.

LAFITTE'S BLACKSMITH SHOP

The little two-story, brick-and-stone building on the corner of Bourbon Street and St. Phillip Street is the second-oldest building in New Orleans. Erected some time before 1772, it miraculously survived the fires of 1788 and 1794, which destroyed many of the city's wooden structures. The little cottage was designed using the "briquete entre poteaux" (i.e., "bricked between posts") technique. Tradition maintains that Jean Lafitte and his brother Pierre used the blacksmith shop as a front for several of their illegal enterprises, such as the trafficking of slaves. The business was located on the first floor; the owners lived on the second floor. Locals claim that the Lafittes buried treasure in backyards surrounding the blacksmith shop. Although no records exist documenting the Lafittes' ownership of the business, history shows that Jean Lafitte did base his headquarters from Barataria Island in Barataria Bay, just south of New Orleans. Chances are good that the pirate-turned-patriot who supplemented General Andrew Jackson's forces during the Battle of New Orleans in 1814 really did make clandestine visits to the blacksmith shop on Bourbon Street. People who truly believe Lafitte's legendary connection to the old pub usually have no trouble believing that his spirit has never really left.

Patrons of one of the most popular bars in the French Quarter have been reporting sightings of the old pirate for many years. They claim that they have seen his apparition strutting through courtyards, hanging from the rafters, and leaning on a barstool. Customers have also seen his ghost standing in dark corners on the first floor, twirling his mustache. His spirit also enjoys sitting at a table, drinking and smoking cigars. The privateer's frequent appearance in the women's restroom suggests that Lafitte's interest in the ladies has not diminished over the years.

A spirit of a woman shows up in the bar on occasion. The spectral reflection of a woman dressed in black with long, black hair has been seen in a mirror in a room on the second floor. The apparitions also make nocturnal visits to the bar and an upstairs office. People have speculated that she could be the spirit of one of the former owners of the old shop or of one of the women who enjoyed the company of pirates. Another theory identifies the ghost as the spirit of voodoo queen Marie Laveau or the sinister Madame Delphine LaLaurie.

The Creole cottage known today as Lafitte's Blacksmith Shop has had a number of different owners in the past three hundred years. Yet, there is no historical evidence of its ever having housed a blacksmith shop. It stands to reason, though, that the same people who believe in spirits will not let the absence of historical documentation convince them that Lafitte's Blacksmith Shop is not haunted.

LE PETIT THEATRE

The building that now houses Le Petit Theatre is located on the site of the bishop's house, which burned in 1788. It was rebuilt in 1789 as the home of Don Josef de Orue y Garbea, the head accountant of the Spanish royal finance office. In 1794, 50 percent of the building was destroyed in a fire that claimed the lives of a number of slaves. The second building, where the auditorium and the main stage are located, was built in 1922. It was razed in 1962 and rebuilt a year later. The flooring in the Helen Hayes foyer is made from ballast removed from ships.

According to actors, stagehands, and patrons, the floor is not the only unusual aspect of Le Petit Theatre.

The ghosts of two women are said to haunt Le Petit Theatre. One of these apparitions is the spirit of a twenty-two-year-old actress named Caroline. In 1924, Caroline fell in love with a young actor who was working with her in a play at Le Petit Theater. Despite the fact that she was married and the actor was too, Caroline and the young man fell in love and embarked on a clandestine affair. Most of their trysts took place in a little storage room on the upper floor. One night, they were locked in a passionate embrace on the attic balcony overlooking the courtyard when Caroline lost her footing and tumbled over the railing to her death below. Caroline is a gregarious ghost who is often seen in the company of the spirits of children who dance and sing around her. Her ghost is often dressed in a wedding gown, which is the costume she was wearing at the time of her death. However, her ghost has been sighted wearing other dresses and costumes as well. Sometimes, her long blonde hair hangs loose on her shoulders; at other times, it is piled on top of her head. Caroline is very popular with the thespians and crew members for whom Le Petit Theatre is a second home. Whenever someone loses an object in one of the most cluttered areas of the theater, like the attic, he or she asks Caroline to locate the missing item. Usually, the object shows up within a very short period of time.

The other female spirit is a very morose, tragic entity. In 1926, an unknown actress working in New Orleans had achieved recognition for a few bit parts, but she had not had a starring role in a play. One day, she caught the eye of a director who promised her a big role in an upcoming production at Le Petit Theatre. She was so desperate for fame that she succumbed to his advances and became his mistress. A few days before the play opened, the director replaced her with another actress who had become his new paramour. Grief stricken, the actress hurried back to her apartment and plotted her revenge. On opening night, she climbed up the catwalk and waited above the stage. Just before curtain call, she tied a weighted rope around her neck and jumped. The audience gasped in horror as they gazed upon the corpse of the young woman dangling from the end of the rope. Since then, cast members and stagehands have reported being overcome with a feeling of intense sorrow at the foot of the stage. She is also said to be responsible for a cold spot that people occasionally experience within the theater. She has been identified as a female apparition with long, black hair who wears a yellow dress.

Unlike Caroline, one of the theater's adult male ghosts is not a helpful spirit. Sigmund, a German stage carpenter who began working at Le Petit Theatre in 1922, is a mischievous ghost who enjoys playing pranks. Whenever a tool turns up missing, Sigmund is usually blamed for hiding it. He has also been known to disconnect the spotlight, interfere with the stereo system, and close the stage curtains prematurely.

Another male ghost in Le Petit Theatre is the spirit of an old Spanish gentleman dressed in formal attire named Alejandro Venegas. Alejandro has been described by eyewitnesses as being a tall man with thick black hair and a mustache. His ghost has usually been sighted in the front row of the balcony section of the main auditorium. Alejandro is so attached to his favorite seat, the second seat in from the left aisle, that when a patron who has paid for that seat asks him to leave, he flatly refuses to move. When the irate patron complains at the box office, he is usually told that when he returns to his seat, the well-dressed man will be gone.

The third male spirit that haunts the theater is known only to the staff as "The Captain." According to the legend, he was a gentleman who fell in love with a beautiful actress in the late nineteenth century. He attended every one of her performances, possibly in the hope that he would actually have an opportunity to talk to her. The actress's anonymous lothario passed away before he confessed his love for her. Since the poor man's death, his ghost has been sighted at every performance in the theater, usually in a balcony seat three rows back on the right-hand side.

The ghosts of children occasionally make their presence known at Le Petit Theatre. For years, a group of singing, laughing youngsters has been seen running through the theater. Like most "real" children, these ghost kids seem to have a playful side. For example, one day, every piece of equipment in the front office turned on by itself. Assuming that the little ghosts were responsible, the office manager yelled, "Children, cut it out." Almost instantly, the copier, fax machine, and telephones turned themselves off.

In a sense, Le Petit Theatre is very similar to most of the other haunted theaters in the United States. Troy Taylor, author of *Haunted New Orleans*, says that theaters are likely candidates for paranormal activity because "the energy, emotions, and constant stream of personalities are the vital ingredients for ghostly activity." The drama that has occurred off-stage seems to be responsible for the residual ghostly activity inside the old theater.

O'FLAHERTY'S IRISH CHANNEL PUB

O'Flaherty's Irish Channel Pub actually consists of two buildings constructed in the late eighteenth century and the early nineteenth century. In the 1800s, the first floor of the buildings housed businesses; the owners of the businesses lived on the upper floors. During the yellow fever epidemic, the second floor was utilized as a clinic for people in the last stages of the disease. Since the late 1980s, the old buildings have been transformed into a popular eatery called O'Flaherty's Irish Channel Pub. With the help of authentic Irish cuisine and Irish music, patrons tap into the spirit of the Emerald Isles. Legend has it that patrons of the restaurant occasionally connect with spirits of a far different sort.

O'Flaherty's Irish Channel Pub is reputed to be haunted by the spirits of one man and two women. *In 1803, the owner of one of the buildings, Don Guillame, married twenty-one-year-old Mary Wheaton from Cumberland, New Jersey. Following her husband's death, she married Joseph Bapentier and moved into the second floor of the building she had inherited from Don Guillame. Bapentier operated a feed store on the first floor. A few months after his marriage, Bapentier took an attractive young French woman named Angelique as his mistress. Before long, Angelique became dissatisfied with the arrangement. Angelique began nagging Bapentier to divorce Mary and take her as his wife. One fateful day in 1810, Bapentier and Angelique began arguing on the patio of the courtyard. She told her lover that she was tired of being the "other woman," and she threatened to reveal the whole affair to Mary. Within a matter of minutes, the argument turned physical. Bapentier chased Angelique through the courtyard. When he caught up with her, he grabbed her by the neck and pulled her into the building. Bapentier half-dragged, half-carried the terrified young woman up the stairs to the third floor. In a fit of rage, he threw her from the balcony. Angelique landed head-first on the hard pavement and broke her neck. Fearing discovery, Bapentier ran down the stairs to the courtyard and carried Angelique's corpse to a sewage well. As he was lowering her into the dark mouth of the well, he looked over his shoulder. Standing in a window was the small son of one of his slaves. As soon as their eyes made contact, the little boy ran off, probably to get help. Realizing that he would soon be tried and convicted of murder, Bapentier slowly walked up to the third floor and hanged himself in one of the rooms.*

The tragic history of O'Flaherty's Irish Channel Pub is very much a part of the present. People standing in the courtyard have seen Mary's ghost staring out of a second-floor window. Her ghost has also appeared in the bar, the restaurant, and the balcony overlooking the Ballad Room. Cold spots have been detected in specific areas in the courtyard. Some customers and waiters claim that cold spots travel between the tables and chairs. The ghost of an unidentified man wearing turn-of-the-century clothing has been seen sitting at the end of the bar watching television. After a few seconds, he disappears. The ghosts of the pub have also been known to "get physical" with the patrons. Angelique's ghost is said to touch the hands of children and young man. Joseph's ghost is much more aggressive. His ghost has left marks on the arms of customers. A ghost matching his description—a tall, fat man—has pushed several customers down over the years. Without a doubt, the interactive spirits of the Irish Channel Pub help make drinking and dining there an unforgettable experience.

THE CABILDO

The Cabildo on Chartres Street in New Orleans is one of the most important buildings in the state of Louisiana. It was rebuilt between 1795 and 1799 on the site of the original Cabildo, which burned in 1788. It served as the seat of the colonial Spanish government until 1803, when the Louisiana Purchase was signed there. From 1803 to 1812, it housed the Louisiana Territorial Supreme Court. The New Orleans city council convened in the Cabildo until the 1850s. In the 1840s, the Baroness Micaela Almonester de Pontalba supervised the addition of a third story to the building, as well as the installation of massive cast-iron gates at the main entrance. During the Civil War, the Union army used the Cabildo as barracks, offices, and a warehouse. Between 1868 and 1910, the Cabildo became the home of the Louisiana Supreme Court. In 1911, the Cabildo was converted into the Louisiana State Museum. The Cabildo has survived a number of natural and man-made catastrophes in the past two centuries, including the Civil War, a devastating fire that destroyed the entire third floor in 1988, and Hurricane Katrina in 2005. Six years later, the Cabildo was reopened to the public. Today, the Cabildo displays artifacts from three centuries of Louisiana's history. Some employees of the museum swear that the Cabildo also contains spiritual vestiges of the city's turbulent past.

The renovations of the Cabildo following the 1988 fire seem to have activated the spirits trapped inside the old building. One of these apparitions could be the spirit of a British sympathizer who was imprisoned in the Cabildo during the War of 1812. After being tried and found guilty of spying on the American army, he was hanged in the courtyard. In his book *Ghost Hunter's Guide to New Orleans*, Jeff Dwyer reports that tourists walking through the courtyard occasionally find themselves in the throes of depression. A few people have actually seen the apparition of a soldier swinging from a rope in the courtyard. The spirit of a running man, dressed in early nineteenth-century attire, has been seen on the second floor.

The other ghosts inside the Cabildo might have a connection to a display of Civil War artifacts. Security guards have seen men wearing gray or blue uniforms walking around the exhibits at night. The ghost of a soldier in a tattered uniform has been sighted strolling around the courtyard early in the morning. History certainly comes alive at the Cabildo, in more ways than one.

THE LALAURIE HOUSE

No other house in the French Quarter has excited the imagination like the LaLaurie House at 1140 Royal Street. Madame Marie Delphine

LaLaurie and her husband, Dr. Leonard Louis LaLaurie, built the house in 1832. Marie had been married twice before. On June 11, 1800, she married Don Ramon De Lopez y Angulo. Following his death in 1808, Marie married Jean Blanque later that same year. Jean died in 1816. The causes of the deaths of her first two husbands are unknown. Marie married her third husband, Leonard Louis LaLaurie, in 1825. Once the LaLauries took up residence in the French Quarter, their beautiful new home became the showplace of New Orleans. Madame LaLaurie regaled her guests with lavish soirees. For the next two years, she and her husband were the toast of New Orleans. None of the friends knew that this glamorous couple harbored a deep, dark secret in the very house where they were sipping champagne and sampling French cuisine.

It was during one of the LaLauries' famous parties that the couple's dark side came to light. On April 19, 1834, the local fire brigade responded to a report of a kitchen fire at 1140 Royal Street. The officers followed the plume of smoke to the kitchen entrance of the house. After forcing open the door, they were shocked by the sight of an elderly slave woman who had been chained to a wrought-iron stove. While they were extinguishing the flames, the old woman admitted setting the blaze herself in order to attract public attention to her plight. Their curiosity aroused, the policemen followed the old woman to the attic, where they beheld a scene that fueled their nightmares for the rest of their lives. According to an account published in a local newspaper, the *New Orleans Bee*, the policemen found more than a dozen slaves chained to the wall. Most of them were severely malnourished.

Almost immediately, the citizens of New Orleans began to embellish the official report of the LaLauries' abuse of their slaves. Some people said that several of the slaves had been strapped to operating tables. The attic floor was littered with human body parts and naked corpses in various states of decay. A woman who had been disemboweled was tied up with her own intestines. The fingers and toes of a number of slaves had been amputated and discarded. Someone had filled a woman's mouth with feces and sewed her mouth shut. Inside a cage big enough for a large dog was a woman whose limbs had been broken and reset at odd angles so that she resembled a human crab. The lurid allegations of the LaLauries' crimes persisted well into the twentieth century. According to Jeanne de Lavigne's 1946 book *The Haunted House of the Rue Royale*, the doctor and his wife performed horrendous experiments on their slaves: "[The slaves] had their joints skinned and festering, great holes in their buttocks where the flesh had been sliced away, their ears hanging by shreds, their lips sewed together, their tongues drawn out and sewed to their chins, severed hands stitched to bellies, legs pulled joint from joint" (258). Supposedly, a number of the firemen were so sickened by the horrors in the attic that they vomited on the spot. A few others fainted.

Word of the LaLauries' nefarious activities quickly spread throughout the Quarter. Hundreds of people gathered around the house at 1140 Royal Street and demanded that the doctor and his wife be brought to justice. Sensing that their lives were in jeopardy, Dr. LaLaurie and his wife somehow managed to climb into the same carriage that had taken them on their daily rides through New Orleans. Whipping the horses into a frenzy, Dr. LaLaurie managed to drive the carriage through the mob and out of the city. The LaLauries made their way to St. John's Bay, where they paid the captain of a schooner to transport them to Covington Mandeville. Some people said that the LaLauries lived for a while in Mobile or New York and ended up in Paris, where Madame LaLaurie was gored and killed by a bull. Others swore that the infamous Madame LaLaurie lived on the north shore of Lake Ponchartrain under the name "Widow Blanque."

Once the truth of the LaLauries' sadistic experiments was finally revealed, many of their friends and neighbors were reminded of an incident that had occurred just a year before. In 1833, several people saw Madame LaLaurie chasing a twelve-year-old slave girl named Lia through the courtyard of the house. Apparently, Marie had become enraged when the comb the girl was using to brush her mistress's hair became snagged on a few strands. Brandishing a strip of cowhide in her hand, Madame LaLaurie chased the terrified girl across the yard, up the winding stairway, and through the galleries. The crazed woman's pursuit of Lia ended on top of the roof. No one knows why—or how— Lia plummeted from the roof to her death on the bricks below. The police, who were troubled by the rumored disappearance of a number of the LaLauries' slaves in the past, confiscated all of their servants.

Later on, the slaves were sold at auction, and the LaLauries were fined $500. Not long thereafter, the LaLauries' friends—the same people who later found themselves sickened by the detailed descriptions of the torture chamber—secretly bought the slaves and returned them to the doctor and his beautiful wife. One can only imagine the guilt that these people must have experienced upon learning of the true nature of their former friends.

For several years, the still-imposing mansion at 1140 Royal Street became a shunned house. Some people even walked across the street when passing by the house. Following extensive renovations, the house was purchased by a man who lived there only three months because he was constantly awakened by cries and groans during the night. The house was abandoned until 1865, when it became an integrated high school for girls of the lower district. The school closed in 1879 after the school board restricted enrollment only to black girls. In 1882, the house became a conservatory of music and dance, but it closed when the director was accused of taking improprieties with students.

The old residence once again acquired a reputation as a "haunted house" in the late 1890s when it was sectioned off into apartments. Most of the occupants of the tenement house were Italian immigrants. Children claimed that a madwoman chased them around the house with a whip. Several people claimed to have been attacked by a black man wrapped in chains. A young mother saw the apparition of a beautiful woman in a fine gown bending over her sleeping baby. Many people complained of being unable to sleep because of all of the screams and moans that permeated the night air inside the house.

The house went through a variety of changes in the twentieth century. In 1923, William Warrington purchased the tenement building and converted it into a home for delinquents. Between 1923 and 1942, the house was owned by the Grand Consistory of Louisiana. It was eventually turned into a department store. The story goes that a few days after the store opened, the owner opened the door one morning and was shocked to find his merchandise covered in feces, urine, and blood. After spending hours cleaning and disinfecting the furniture, the man spent the night inside the door with a shotgun cradled in his arms. When he awoke the next morning and walked into the showroom, he was amazed to find that once again, someone—or something—had soiled his entire stock. He closed his business for good that same day. An enterprising bartender tried to capitalize on the ghost stories circulating around the building by opening what he called "a haunted saloon" on the premises, but locals, most of whom took these tales very seriously, refused to patronize the bar. It closed as well.

In 1969, a physician purchased the LaLaurie House. He remodeled it in 1976 and 1980, restoring the house to its 1830s luster. In December 2008, actor Nicholas Cage, who has always been fascinated by the paranormal, purchased the LaLaurie house for $3.45 million. He sold it in 2009 for $3.55 million.

Paranormal investigators have not been allowed inside the LaLaurie House for many years. Nevertheless, the LaLaurie House's ranking as one of the most haunted houses in the United States does not seem to be in jeopardy. It is also a popular stop on New Orleans's ghost tours. Once in a while, passersby who are totally unaware of Madame LaLaurie hear shrieks and moans coming from the infamous mansion, even when no living people are inside.

WHITE CASTLE

White Castle, Louisiana, was founded in 1883 on the White Castle Plantation, formerly owned by George Wales. At the turn of the century, the fledgling town depended heavily on logging operations in the Cyprus swamps in the area. Sugar cane became the area's primary industry after the Cypress swamps were depleted. By the 1970s, three major sugar mills were located in White Castle. The chemical industry, which came to White Castle in the 1950s, also brought considerable economic growth to the city.

NOTTOWAY HISTORIC INN

The most imposing structure in White Castle, Louisiana, was the home of a wealthy planter named John Hampton Randolph. Born on March 24, 1813, John grew up in Virginia but moved to Elmwood

Plantation in Woodville, Mississippi, where his father was appointed a federal judge by President Andrew Jackson. In Mississippi, John met the love of his life, Emily Jane Liddell, who lived on a plantation not far from Elmwood. John and Emily were married on December 14, 1837. By the time John and Emily moved to a cotton plantation in Louisiana named Forest Home, they already had two children. Even though the Randolphs loved Forest Home, where they eventually raised ten children, John dreamed of building an even more magnificent plantation home for himself and his family. His fortunes increased considerably after he converted his cotton plantation to sugar cane, enabling him to begin planning his new house in earnest. In 1855, John's servants cut cypress trees growing at Forest Home and soaked the logs in water for four years to make the lumber resistant to termites. Meanwhile, his other servants made bricks in kilns on the plantation. To ensure that his new home would be the finest private residence in the region, John hired a renowned architect named Henry Howard, who had built many of the finest buildings in New Orleans in the Italianate and Greek Revival styles.

In 1859, John's lavish new mansion, Nottoway, was completed five miles from Forest Home at a cost of $80,000. The sixty-four-room plantation house had six inside staircases, three bathrooms, twenty-two huge columns, and fifteen-and-a-half-foot ceilings. His favorite room, the semicircular White Ballroom, was painted white to highlight the natural beauty of his seven daughters. The Greek Revival-Italianate mansion is furnished with lace curtains, brass and crystal chandeliers, hand-painted Dresden porcelain doorknobs, twelve hand-carved Italian marble fireplaces, and even a bowling alley. After John Randolph died in 1889, Mary sold the plantation for $50,000. Several decades later, Nottoway was sold for $10,000 because the owners could not pay the taxes. Today, Nottoway Plantation is an inn and meeting place for special events. It is also, according to the staff, a hotbed of paranormal activity.

Most of the ghostly activity at the Nottoway Historic Inn has been reported on the third floor. A woman wearing a black dress with a white ruffle around her neck has been seen on the third-floor staircase. Sometimes, she is seen as a solid, shadowy shape that walks up to the top of the stairs and then runs away. The woman in black has also been seen staring out of a window in a third-floor bedroom. Witnesses say that she seems to be waiting for someone to arrive. One day, the housekeeper walked into a third-floor bedroom and saw a young woman in nightclothes sitting on the edge of the bed. One young man who was taking a tour of the house spotted the lady in black at the top of the stairs. He told the tour guide that she bore a strong resemblance to Emily Randolph, whose portrait hangs in the master bedroom, next to a portrait of John Randolph.

Occasionally, guests staying at Nottoway have encountered the ghost. In the early twenty-first century, a couple was honeymooning in a room on the third floor of the historic inn. The bride was walking down the hallway on the third floor when she felt someone take her hand. Thinking that her husband had just walked up beside her, she turned to look at him. To her amazement, no one was there. A few months later, a woman was sitting in a room on the third floor when she heard noises in the hallway just outside her door. Suddenly, a picture hanging on the wall flew across the room, barely missing her. Guests have also experienced cold spots on the third floor.

Today, Nottoway Historic Inn truly lives up to its reputation as an American castle. Its antebellum grandeur has made it a popular setting for weddings and wedding receptions. The Randolph Ballroom, which has over 350 seats, is often used for corporate meetings. Nottoway Historic Inn also offers fine dining at the Mansion Restaurant. Blue crab cakes, crawfish bisque, ricotta gnudu, tandori, and spiced lamb chops are just a few of the dishes that have delighted the palates of guests at the inn for years. The Nottoway Historic Inn has another feature that distinguishes it from the run-of-the-mill southern inns: the woman in black.

Minnesota

ST. PAUL

The Sioux Indians were the first inhabitants in what is now St. Paul, Minnesota. In 1819, the U.S. Army established Fort Anthony in the area as a temporary fort. It became a permanent fort between 1820 and 1822. It covered a large area on the west side of the Mississippi River. The fort was renamed Fort Snelling in 1825. Because of the protection the fort afforded, hundreds of settlers began moving into the area. In 1840, a French-Canadian trader, along with several families, left the military outpost and moved east, where they founded the settlement that eventually developed into St. Paul. Over the next decade, St. Paul became an important trading post and steamboat port. It was incorporated as a city in 1854. Thousands of European immigrants moved to St. Paul because of the economic opportunities offered by its farmland, iron mines, and large stands of timber. Around the turn of the century, railroad financier James J. Hill improved the city's cultural and industrial development. By 1893, he had extended the Great Northern Railway from St. Paul to Puget Sound. Large flour mills also aided in the growth of the city. St. Paul's economy declined in the 1920s and 1930s, but the city underwent a period of revitalization with the construction of the Capitol Centre in 1970 and the St. Paul Civic Center in 1973 and the completion of the Town Square Project in 1980.

FOREPAUGH'S RESTAURANT

Joseph Lybrandt Forepaugh was one of those enterprising businessmen who seemed to have achieved the American Dream. He made a fortune in the dry-goods business in St. Paul in the 1860s. By the end of the decade, he was the senior partner in J. L. Forepaugh and Company, which manufactured and sold boots and shoes, among other things. In 1870, Forepaugh purchased five lots in the fashionable Irving Park neighborhood. In the center of the property, Forepaugh constructed a three-story Victorian mansion at a cost of the then exorbitant sum of $10,000. His dream home was highlighted by beautifully landscaped lawns and gardens. The interior of his house was richly furnished with hand-crafted furniture. Forepaugh's neighbors included Civil War generals and territorial governors. From all appearances, Joseph Lybrandt Forepaugh had it made. In reality, he was a tormented man whose miserable spirit still haunts the mansion that bears his name to this day.

Forepaugh and his wife, Mary, appeared to have had a happy marriage, and they did, for a while. However, Forepaugh eventually found himself seeking love and comfort in the arms of a maid he had hired named Molly. One afternoon, Mary caught the pair in bed together. Instead of divorcing Joseph and giving up her life of wealth and privilege, Mary ordered her husband to end the affair. After Joseph broke it off with Molly, she became extremely despondent. When she learned that she was pregnant, Molly walked up the stairs to the third floor and tied a rope to a chandelier. After slipping the noose around her neck, Molly threw herself out the window and hanged herself.

The next year, Joseph sold the mansion to General John Henry Hammond, a Civil War veteran. He and Mary traveled to Europe in an effort to rebuild their marriage. After the couple returned to the United States in 1889, Henry built a second showplace at 302 Summit Avenue. Even though Joseph seemed to have everything he had ever wanted, he became increasingly depressed over the next three years. He told his friends and relatives that he was concerned about his business, which was doing very well at the time. Those who were closest to him speculated that he had never really recovered from Molly's death. In 1892, Joseph Lybrandt Forepaugh's corpse was found in a nearby park with a bullet in his head. A pistol was still clenched in his hand. He was fifty-eight years old.

The mansion at Irvine Park has changed hands many times over the years. In 1983, James Crankovich purchased the old house and began restoring it to its former glory. Beautifully decorated dining rooms were placed on all three floors. From the second-story patio, diners have a striking view of St. Paul's downtown area. Today, Forepaugh's Restaurant is famous for its French cuisine, which includes fragrant striped bass pistou, rare shears of thyme-infused lamb loin, slow-roasted salmon with a potato leek fondue, colorful soups, and elegant desserts. For people interested in the supernatural, the restaurant's ghost stories are definitely a bonus.

Two different ghosts have been sighted at Forepaugh's Restaurant. One of these spirits is the ghost of Joseph Forepaugh. His full-bodied apparition, dressed in nineteenth-century attire, has been seen strolling through the dining room with a pleased look on his face. Apparently, he approves of the way the old house has been restored to the way it looked when he lived there.

Molly's ghost seems to be the most active spirit in Forepaugh's Restaurant. Her ghost has been sighted standing in the third-floor room where she hanged herself. She is described as wearing a brown hood or cape. One night, a server saw Molly's ghost open the door, walk in the room, and shut the door. A few weeks later, a waiter and a bus boy were setting up tables in a room on the third floor. These tables had heavy sides, which folded down. When one of the heavy tables was moved to a corner of the room, the sides flipped up by themselves. In an interview with Jim Longo, a longtime employee said that a waitress carrying a tray of drinks was walking through the room when something knocked the tray out of her hand. On another occasion, two antique tables lifted off the floor a few inches and lowered to the floor.

Spectral footsteps are occasionally heard coming from the third floor. In the late 1990s, management called the police to investigate loud stomping sounds that were coming from the third floor. One of the policemen had great difficulty persuading his German shepherd to climb the stairs. As soon as the policemen reached the top of the stairs, the stomping sounds stopped.

For the most part, though, Molly is a very out-going spirit who enjoys crashing weddings and receptions. Hanging from one of the walls in the restaurant is a wedding picture that clearly depicts the spectral form of a woman. During one of these receptions, all of the waitresses were wearing nineteenth-century period dresses. Midway through the reception, a woman wearing one of these old dresses floated down a hallway and disappeared into a wall.

Poltergeist activity has been reported in the restaurant as well. When the house was being restored, workmen became annoyed when buckets of nails or hammers seemed to move from the spot where they were left to a different location altogether. After the restaurant opened, the kitchen staff had the same problem with pots and pans, which seemed to be relocated by some invisible force. Sometimes, the telephones ring incessantly, and the air conditioner comes on by itself. In the basement, people have been overcome by a chilly feeling. The sweet scent of lilac perfume often wafts through the air. The lights turn themselves off and on as well.

To date, only one person became too frightened to finish her meal in Forepaugh's Restaurant. As a rule, when a customer experiences the uncanny in the restaurant, the servers tell him or her that Molly's ghost creates these disturbances as a way of drawing attention to herself. Perhaps her spirit is still craving the attention that Joseph Forepaugh was not able to give her.

THE GRIGGS MANSION

The Griggs Mansion was built by a wealthy businessman named Chauncey Griggs in 1883. He made his fortune in the wholesale grocery business. He lived in his beautiful sandstone mansion for only four years before moving to the west coast, where he expanded his business interests to include transportation and lumber. For the next few decades, each family that moved in and made costly renovations to the house ended up moving out after a year or two without giving any explanation to their neighbors. The Griggs Mansion is not only the most haunted house in St. Paul, but it might be the most haunted house in Minnesota as well.

The identity of two of the ghosts that haunt the Griggs Mansion is known. One source of the hauntings can be traced to the death of a maid. In 1915, the young woman became so despondent after breaking up with her boyfriend that she hanged herself near the fourth-floor landing. In

1920, a maid was asleep in her room when she was awakened by the figure of a young girl in a white gown who stretched out her hand to the horrified servant and vanished. Another ghost is the spirit of Charles Wade, who was the caretaker and gardener. His ghost seems to favor the mansion's library, where he spent hours reading his master's books.

In 1939, the Roger B. Shepherd family donated the old house to the St. Paul Gallery and Art Museum. For over twenty years, faculty and students reported feeling as if someone—or something—was constantly watching them. Many people also heard disembodied footsteps on the stairs when no one was present. In the early 1950s, an instructor at the school, Dr. Delmar Kolb, said he was trying to sleep in his front basement apartment when he saw the ghost of a tall, thin man in a black suit and top hat. Kolb guessed that the man was in his sixties. In 1959, two college students who were sleeping in Kolb's apartment had a bone-chilling encounter with the ghost of a little girl. One student saw that spectral form of a little girl floating above his bed. The other student felt icy fingers pressed against his forehead.

In 1964, Karl Weschke, the publisher of *Fate Magazine*, purchased the Griggs Mansion after the new Arts and Sciences center opened. In *Ghost Stories of Minnesota*, author Gina Teel says that Weschke suspected that something was amiss when a window that he shut was open again the next day. For three days, Weschke tried in vain to keep the window shut. In desperation, he nailed the window shut. The next day, he was amazed to find that it was open again. A few months later, he too saw a thin, old man in a dark suit in the same room where Delmar Kolb stayed. Weschke's most nerve-wracking experience occurred when an invisible entity picked him up and threw him in the air.

In 1969, two reporters and a photographer from the *St. Paul Pioneer* set out to spend the night in the Griggs Mansion. Their original intention was to debunk the stories that had been floating around St. Paul for decades. While staying in a room on the third floor, the trio heard the unmistakable sound of footsteps marching up and down the staircase. By four A.M., the journalists had had enough. They bolted out of the front door, their skepticism gone forever.

From all appearances, this grand four-story sandstone mansion is just one of a number of lavish Victorian mansions on Summit Avenue.

The people who have lived in this old house over the years hoped that the Griggs Mansion's sinister reputation would just disappear, just as the spirits in the ghost stories have done. Today, the Griggs Mansion is a private residence. The owners do not welcome visitors eager to catch sight of its ghostly inhabitants.

GIBBS FARMHOUSE MUSEUM

In 1833, a young girl named Jane De Bow was kidnapped by the Stevens family and taken from her home in New York to a mission near Fort Snelling on the shores of Lake Calhoun. While growing up in what is now present-day Minneapolis, Jane learned the culture of the Dakota Indians, many of whom lived in the mission. The Stevens spent more than a decade living among the Indians in Minnesota, before moving to Illinois. After living in Illinois for a few months, Jane met Herman Gibbs, an Indiana schoolteacher who was fourteen years older than she was. Gibbs had left Indiana to seek his fortune in the mine fields. The couple fell in love and were married in 1847. Two years later, Jane convinced her husband to return to the Minnesota territory, where they purchased 160 acres at $1.25 an acre. For the first five years of their marriage, Herman and Jane lived in a dug-out 10' x 12' sod house, the foundation of which has been recently excavated. Coincidentally, the trail that the Dakota took on their northern migration crossed through the Gibbs's farm. To her delight, Jane was reunited with her Dakota friends. In 1854, Herman built a much larger house. To accommodate his growing family, Herman added a second floor, a parlor, and a guest room. In 1873, Herman added a hired hand's room and a summer kitchen. He died in 1891. After Jane's death in 1910, her daughter, Abbie, inherited the farm. The white barn that now stands on the property was built that same year. The Gibbs's farm was sold to the University of Minnesota in 1943. Six years later, the farm came under the control of the Ramsey County Historical Society, which opened it to the public as a museum. The Stoen School, built in the 1880s, was moved to the Gibbs farm in 1966. Today, visitors can catch a glimpse of pioneer life through the museum's pioneer crop garden, its Dakotah medicine garden, and its ghost stories.

The hauntings in the Gibbs farmhouse started soon after it was opened as a museum. The presence in the house could be the spirit of Jane and Herman's third child. In 1867, just after Herman had completed the addition to his house, a prairie fire started not far from his farm. His nine-year-old son, William, was helping beat back the flames when he was overcome by smoke and fainted. The grass fire spared the farmhouse, but the brave little boy died of smoke inhalation.

Many of the disturbances in the old house seem to be a form of poltergeist activity. For example, staff and tourists have heard footsteps in the hallway behind the kitchen. The source of the footsteps has never been found. People have also seen a rocking chair rock by itself. Doors and cupboards have opened on their own. Toys that were locked away in the closet just before closing have been found scattered around the boys' room the next day.

As if one needed any more proof that the Gibbs farmhouse was haunted, the apparition of William Gibbs has been sighted on at least two occasions. A tour guide who was sitting on the porch, waiting for her next tour to begin, caught sight of a boy staring at her from a window. Within just a few seconds, the child vanished. On another occasion, a policeman passing by the house several hours after it had closed saw the face of a child gazing out of a second-story bedroom window.

In recent years, the Gibbs Farmhouse Museum has offered visitors the opportunity to sample Halloween as it was celebrated in the nineteenth century by carving jack-o-lanterns and listening to ghostly folk tales. At the Stoen School, children can watch re-creations of classic ghost tales like "The Legend of Sleepy Hollow." Actually, the ghost stories that have been told about the Gibbs farmhouse are scarier than their literary counterparts because of their basis in fact.

THE LANDMARK CENTER

In the late 1890s, the architect Willoughby J. Edbrooke began drawing up the plans for what he hoped would be one of Minnesota's most impressive governmental buildings in St. Paul's fashionable Rice Park. In 1902, contractor Cass Gilbert completed construction on the castle-like structure with its hipped red-tile roof, gables and dormers with

steeply peaked roofs, and cylindrical corner towers with conical tur-
rets. The costs totaled $2.5 million. Initially, the customhouse, the post
office, and the federal courts were housed in the new building. Within
a few years, all of the federal offices in the upper midwest were moved
to the building. By the 1960s, the old building was in dire need of repair.
In 1967, the federal offices were moved to the newly constructed federal building. The cost of renovating the old building was too high, and
it was scheduled to be razed. Just one week before the building was
demolished, the community raised enough money to save it from the
wrecking ball. The building was extensively renovated between 1972
and 1978 and renamed the Landmark Center. Today, St. Paul's arts
and cultural center houses a number of community organizations,
such as the American Association of Woodturners, the Schubert Club
Museum of Musical Instruments, and the Ramsey County Historical
Society Center. According to the legends, the ghost of a gangster also
calls the Landmark Center home.

From a criminologist's perspective, the most-intriguing chapter
in the old building's long history unfolded during the 1930s. A number of America's most infamous gangsters, including Babyface Nelson, Alvin Karpis, and Machine-gun Kelly, were tried in the Ramsey
County Courtroom, Room 317, the building's largest courtroom. A former bellhop and speakeasy owner named Jack Peifer was one of the
lesser-known criminals who was meted out justice in Room 317. Some
of the gangsters who frequented Peifer's bar convinced him that he
could make much more money working for them. Peifer started out
laundering money for the likes of Alvin Karpis and "Doc" Barker, Ma
Barker's son. In 1933, he played a pivotal role in the kidnapping of brewery heir William Hamm. In 1934, Peifer tried to dissuade Alvin Karpis
from abducting a banker named Woodward Bremer because Edward
Bremer Sr. was a good friend of President Franklin Delano Roosevelt.
Eventually, Peifer and other members of the Karpis/Barker gang were
apprehended and tried in the Ramsey County Courtroom. Peifer was
convicted and sentenced to thirty years in Leavenworth prison. The
prospect of spending three decades in a virtual hell proved to be too
daunting for the former bellhop. Shortly after he was sentenced, Peifer
committed suicide by ingesting potassium cyanide in his jail cell.

An entity usually identified as the ghost of Jack Peifer has been active in the Landmark Center ever since it first opened its doors. His ghost seems to enjoy tormenting women in restrooms throughout the building, but he seems to be partial to the restroom on the second floor. An invisible hand is said to open and close the stall doors. One July evening in 2001, two women saw a sinister-looking man standing in a second-floor restroom. Before they could focus on the strange figure, he vanished. The women ran out of the bathroom and told their weird story to a puzzled security guard. On another occasion, a woman standing at a sink in a restroom heard a man's spectral laughter behind her. She spun around, and no one was there.

Peifer's spirit also roams around the third floor of the Landmark Center. Elevator doors open and close mysteriously on the third floor, leading some to theorize that Peifer the bellboy is still on the job. In *Ghost Stories of Minnesota*, Gina Teel tells the story of a tour guide and a history buff who were standing on the landing on the third floor in 1985 or 1986. They were looking down at an elevator that was on its way up. As they peered trough the glass top, they noticed a transparent man dressed in a bellhop's uniform. When the elevator reached the third floor, no one was inside. A few weeks later, a young woman was riding up the elevator to the third floor when she felt the pressure of an invisible arm around her shoulder and somebody's hot breath on her neck. The girl was visibly shaken by the strange incident for at least an hour.

Peifer also enjoys joining in on celebrations where alcohol is present, just as he did when he operated his speakeasy. Sometimes during wedding receptions in the bar area, gin bottles topple over on their own and shot glasses shatter mysteriously. Gina Teel tells the story of the day Peifer's wedding crashing was caught on film. One cold March day in the early 2000s, Kimberly and Joseph Arrigoni were having their wedding pictures taken on the sweeping staircase. When the couple examined one of the photographs a few days later, they were shocked to see the transparent figure of a man standing behind the five-year-old ring bearer. On the man's right side, the stained glass of a cathedral window was clearly visible.

The ghost of Jack Peifer is clearly a restless spirit. People who are familiar with the story of Jack Peifer have surmised that he might be unable to rest because he hates himself for participating in the gangsters' schemes. According to Rosemary Ellen Guiley, author of *The Encyclopedia of Ghosts and Spirits*, one of the reasons why ghosts return is to complete unfinished business. Could it be that maybe Jack Peifer is also looking for redemption?

THE FITZGERALD THEATER

The Schubert Theater is the oldest operating theater in St. Paul. Built of concrete and steel in 1910, the local newspapers proclaimed it as one of the safest theaters in the state when it opened on August 29, 1910. The state-of-the-art theater boasted 2,000 electric lights, a built-in vacuum-cleaning system, a stage that could be raised and lowered, and sixteen dressing rooms. Originally designed as a vaudeville theater, the Schubert thrilled and delighted audience for over twenty years with a wide variety of acts, including singers, dancers, ventriloquists, and acrobats. In 1933, the Schubert Theater was converted into a movie palace and renamed as the World Theater. In 1980, the old theater was purchased by Minnesota Public Radio, which made much-needed repairs on the inside and outside. One year later, Garrison Keeler's "A Prairie Home Companion" radio program began broadcasting from the World Theater. Keeler headed the drive to change the name of the old theater to the Fitzgerald Theater in honor of St. Paul native F. Scott Fitzgerald, author of *The Great Gatsby*. In 2006, the Fitzgerald Theater was featured in director Robert Altman's film *A Prairie Home Companion*. Not surprisingly, the renovations that took place in the 1980s might have stirred up part of the theater's past.

People started talking about the haunted activity in the theater in 1985 when it was remodeled extensively. When workers removed one of the false ceilings, they not only discovered a balcony that had been hidden for years, but they also found an old note written to a stagehand named Ben. Soon afterward, bizarre incidents began occurring on a regular basis. People walking through specific areas in the theater detected cold spots. Old, dusty bottles of muscatel began turning up in odd places. Tools that workers had left in specific spots were found in different locations the next day. According to Gina Teel, author of *Ghost Stories of Minnesota*, the possibility that a ghost was responsible was confirmed when the theater manager watched a man in a workman's uniform walk up to a brick wall and pass through it in the exact spot where a door leading to Wabasha Street once existed. The theater's usually playful ghost exhibited more malicious behavior one day when a couple of employees holding flashlights were making their way through the backstage area. Suddenly, a large chunk of plaster fell from the ceiling and crashed to the floor, almost hitting the two men. When the startled men aimed their flashlights up toward the ceiling they saw a man on the catwalk. He took a few quick steps and disappeared.

In *The Nearly Departed*, author Michael Norman tells the story of a young woman who worked in the theater's box office. Late one afternoon, as she was cleaning up for the night, she noticed a strange man looking into a seldom-used box office window. Before the stranger faded into the shadows, she observed that he had black hair and was wearing a plaid shirt. She returned to her paperwork when something told her to look back at the side window. She turned her head and caught a glimpse of the man as he retreated into the darkness. In a quivering voice, she announced that she was closing up. Sensing movement to her right, she turned around and found herself standing face to face with a thin man in a plaid shirt. He faded away after she stared at him for a few seconds.

Employees at the Fitzgerald Theater have also made the acquaintance of a female entity, whom they have nicknamed Veronica. Supposedly, she was an actress who performed at the Fitzgerald Theater early in its history. The lilting tones of a woman's distinctive singing have often been heard after the lights have been turned off. She also makes her presence known by "kissing" the mirror in the lobby and dressing rooms, leaving the unmistakable imprint of lipstick-smeared lips on the glass.

Many haunted theaters can be found in the United States. The most common ghosts found in these theaters are the spirits of stagehands or of actresses. The Fitzgerald Theater is unique in that it has both types of ghosts.

MINNEAPOLIS

The first inhabitants in the area now occupied by the city of Minneapolis were the Dakota Sioux, who met the French explorers when they arrived in 1680. The founding of Fort Snelling in 1680 spurred growth in the region. In 1856, the Minnesota Territorial Legislature established Minneapolis as a town on the Mississippi River's west bank. It was incorporated as a city in 1867. That same year, the railroad was extended between Minneapolis and Chicago. Most of the city's growth centered around St. Anthony's Falls. Between 1880 and 1930, the city harnessed the waterfall's power. By 1871, twenty-free businesses were located on the west bank of the river, including ironworks, woolen, and cotton, paper, and planing wood mills. Grain produced by local farmers was sent to the city's thirty-four flour mills. By 1905, 10 percent of the nation's flour was milled in Minneapolis. In the 1950s and 1960s, two hundred buildings were razed as part of the city's urban renewal project. In the 1960s, Minneapolis became the birthplace of the American Indian Movement.

THE MINNEAPOLIS CITY HALL

The Minneapolis City Hall at 350 South Fifth Street was built between 1888 and 1909 at a cost of $3,554,000 on the site of an older building. The architectural firm of Long and Keys modeled the Richardsonian Romanesque building after the Allegheny County Courthouse in Pittsburgh, Pennsylvania. The castle-like structure includes two towers: a clock tower and a prison tower where prisoners awaiting execution were housed. In the 1940s, the terra cotta roof was covered over with copper sheathing to prevent leaking. Inside the rotunda is artist Larkin Goldsmith Mead's 1906 sculpture "Father of the Waters." Over the years, the building has been used as the Hennepin County Courthouse and as the seat of city government. It has also housed city offices and the police, jail, and court system. Today, the most famous person associated with city hall is not a former mayor; it is the ghost of John Moshik.

In 1898, John Moshik, the leader of St. Paul's infamous Rice Street Gang, killed a man and robbed him of $14.00. He was incarcerated in a jail on the fifth floor. During the trial, Moshik pleaded "inherited insanity" for his crimes, but the jury found him guilty anyway. After Moshik was convicted of the crime, he was scheduled to hang on March 18, 1898. On the day of his execution, the hangman placed the noose around Moshik's neck and told him to stand on a chair. First, the hangman taped Moshik's mouth shut. Then he bound Moshik's feet and kicked the chair away. In one account of Moshik's execution, the rope slipped up under Moshik's chin, slowly strangling him for three minutes. John Moshik bears the dubious distinction of being the only man ever hanged in city hall and the last man hanged in Hennepin County.

John Moshik's ghost still prowls around the last place he called home: the abandoned death row on the fifth floor in the South Tower. Today, the jail cells have been ripped out, but the iron bars are still in place. According to deputies who worked on death row years ago, many prisoners swore that when they were in the common room, they saw a man looking in the window. Strangely enough, the man's image was never captured on the video monitors. Some prisoners complained about seeing a weird man wearing only boxer shorts ogling them through the bars of their cells. Guards also reported seeing an oddly dressed man walking down the hallways. Moshik's apparition is also said to take the form of a shadowy figure that lurks around dark corners. Strange noises, such as disembodied footsteps, have echoed throughout the fifth floor for years.

Gina Teel's *Ghost Stories of Minnesota* recounts a bizarre incident that occurred in city hall several years ago. One day, a city employee was walking down a hallway when he discovered that a framed photograph had fallen off the wall. The glass was shattered, and the photograph was covered in blood. The man hurried over to the janitor's closet. When he returned with a broom and a dustpan, he was surprised to find that the photograph was back on the wall. The glass was intact. Coincidentally, the photograph was a picture of the judge who condemned John Moshik.

John Moshik's ghost is still very active in the Minneapolis City Hall. Staff members claim that toilets flush themselves late at night. Visitors have reported feeling cold breezes on the fifth floor. Less frequently, visitors claim to have seen the apparition of a man walking around the fifth floor. Legend has it, though, that all anyone who feels uncomfortable in city hall has to do is rub the big toe of Father Walters's statue. Not surprisingly, Father Walters's big toe has become very shiny over the years.

THE MINNEAPOLIS INSTITUTE OF ARTS

The idea for creating an arts center in Minneapolis was born in a meeting of a group of twenty-five business and professional leaders in 1883. The group, which eventually became known as the Minneapolis Society of Fine Arts, began organizing art exhibits throughout the city. The first home of the society, which changed its name to the Minneapolis Institute of Arts, was the Minneapolis Public Library. In 1915, the Minneapolis Institute of Arts was moved from the library, where it had been housed for twenty-six years, to a new museum, designed by the firm of McKim, Mead and White. Built in the Beaux-Arts architectural style, the museum was located on land donated by the Morrison family in the Washburn–Fair Oaks Mansion District. Additions to the museum were built in 1974 and 2006. Today, over 80,000 objects are housed in the Minneapolis Institute, including paintings, prints and drawings, and textiles. The museum is divided into seven "curatorial areas": Africa, Oceania, the Americas; Architecture, Design, Decorative Arts, Craft, and Scupture; Asian Art; Paintings and Modern Sculpture; Photographs; Prints and Drawings; and Textiles. The museum's collection of Asian art is one of the finest in the entire United States. One of the museum's most popular attractions is its collection of forty-two works by Georgia O'Keefe. According to employees, the museum's ghosts are sometimes on display as well.

In his book *The Nearly Departed*, Michael Norman tells the story of museum security guard Sam Rowan's ghostly encounter in the Queen Anne Room late one September night in 1996. He had just walked out of the Queen Anne Room when he saw a shadowy female figure slip out of a doorway across the hall and walk quickly into the Queen Anne Room. Rowan rushed back into the room, but no one was there but him. The uneasy feeling that Rowan experienced at that moment stayed with him for several months.

Rowan's next ghostly encounter occurred in 2005. He was walking into the Northumberland Room when he noticed a human leg walking next to him. The leg was clothed, and it wore a shoe. Only Rowan's footsteps made a sound. The possibility that he might be walking with part of a ghost did not occur to him at the time because he thought it was just his shadow. After he left the room, he realized that the light in the room was in the wrong position for his leg to have cast a shadow.

The museum's best-known paranormal incident occurred in 2007. Late one night, a security guard who was supposed to be watching a monitor in the communications room fell asleep. He had only been sleeping for a few minutes when he heard a sharp tapping on the glass of the room. When he opened his eyes, he saw an elderly lady wearing a cream-colored gown shaking her finger at him. She then passed through the closed door, floated into the room, and vanished. Almost instantly, he recognized the ghostly woman as the figure in a 1920 painting by George Wesley Bellows hanging in the corridor. The title of the painting was "Mrs. T. in Cream Silk, No. 2."

Most of the people who have seen the ghosts in the Minneapolis Institute of Arts have been employees. However, a number of visitors have experienced cold spots in the museum, especially in the Connecticut Room, which contains nineteenth-century exhibits.

THE FIRST AVENUE CLUB

The First Avenue Club was originally called The Depot because it was built in 1937 as a Greyhound bus station. At the time of its construction, the bus station was considered a very special place because of its air conditioning, its classic terrazzo floors, its shower rooms, its huge chromium trimmed chandeliers, its public telephones, and its sidewalk made of shiny blue bricks with white trim. In the 1930s, it was hailed as one of the most modernistic travel centers in America. In 1968, the bus station closed. In 1970, Allen Fingerhut, heir to the Fingerhut catalog fortune, rented the old depot with the intention of converting it into a nightclub called Sam's. On April 3, 1970, Fingerhut opened his club as the only venue in downtown Minnesota featuring both rock bands and alcohol. Some of the nation's most famous musical acts of the 1970s performed there, including the Allman Brothers, Ike and Tina Turner, the Kinks, The Stooges, Canned Heat, Pat Benatar, the Ramones, U2, and Frank Zappa and the Mothers of Invention. In 1980, Steve McClellan and Jack Meyers took over the nightclub. In 1981, they changed its name to the First Avenue Club. From the outset, McClellan and Meyers began booking heavy metal and alternative rock acts as well as up-and-coming local artists. In the early 1980s, local artist Prince began performing regularly at the First Avenue Nightclub. In the 1990s, the First Avenue Nightclub received rave reviews in *Rolling Stone* and *Time* magazine. In 2000, the nightclub purchased the building that had been its home for thirty years. Today, the First Avenue Nightclub and the Seventh Street Eatery, located inside the nightclub, are considered to be a cornerstone of the Midwest music scene and one of the most haunted places in Minnesota.

The paranormal activity inside the First Avenue Club could be generated by the deaths of several homeless people inside the old depot. The most frequently sighted ghost is the spirit of a teenage girl who hanged herself in stall five in the women's restroom. Eyewitnesses describe the ghost as having long blonde hair and red eyes. She wears a green army jacket and bell-bottom pants. Several people said they saw the girl for only a few seconds before she vanished into the darkness. In the early 2000s, a young director was making a documentary at the old bus depot. He walked into the women's restroom and immediately saw the image of a young girl with blood on her dress. Around the same time, two girls inside the women's restroom heard the sound of a woman crying. They opened up all of the stall doors, but no one was in the room besides them. The most bizarre encounter in the women's restroom occurred in the early twenty-first century. A woman was standing in the room when the figure of a teenage girl suddenly appeared in front of her. She took the woman over to stall five and was explaining how she hanged herself when, all at once, she disappeared.

The stage and dance floor are also centers of ghostly occurrences to the First Avenue Club. A number of musicians have reported seeing their equipment being moved and even thrown around by an invisible force. Disc jockeys have heard strange noises coming from the head-sets. Patrons dancing on the dance floor claim to have seen a dancing ghost with no legs.

The First Avenue Club has been a popular nightspot of the city for decades. The musicians who have performed there represent some of the most popular musical trends of the twentieth and twenty-first centuries, ranging from punk, heavy metal, grunge, and reggae to goth, rap, and techno. In recent years, the First Avenue Club has become just as famous for its ghost stories as it has for the cutting-edge performers who have graced its stage.

HENNEPIN HISTORY MUSEUM

Shortly after arriving in Minneapolis in 1866, George H. Christian became manager of the Washburn-Crosby Company. Before long, he perfected a revolutionary process for milling spring wheat. As a result of this process, Minneapolis became the flour-milling capitol of the world from 1880 to 1930. Christian became so wealthy that he retired in 1875 and devoted his time to the pursuit of art, philosophy, music, and philanthropy. In 1917, Christian hired the firm of Hewitt and Brown to design a mansion for him and his family. Edwin Hewitt's design draws from Renaissance and late English Gothic styles. Christian's lavish mansion was completed two years later. The brick façade of the house has a two-story window bay. The interior of the house has African-cypress floors and ironwork created by the artist Samuel Yelin. Unfortunately, Christian's wife and grown son died before the mansion was finished. Years later, Christian's daughter-in-law, Carolyn McKnight Christian, inherited the property. In 1957, she donated the house to the Minnesota Society of Fine Arts, which, in turn, sold the house to the Hennepin Historical Society that same year. Despite the fact that no one is known to have died here, the Hennepin History Museum is very haunted.

Even though no apparitions have been sighted in the museum, enough bizarre occurrences have taken place to convince many visitors, staff members, and volunteers that the Hennepin History Museum is haunted. A number of female visitors have reported feeling as if someone was hovering near them. When they turn around, no one is there. A variety of strange smells have been detected in the museum, such as the odor of pipe smoke and perfume. Occasionally, people walk into what they describe as "cold spots" or "hot spots" inside the building. In *Ghost Stories of Minnesota*, author Gina Teel says that in 2000, the museum curator Jack Kabrud walked into his office and was shocked to see the water in the drinking water dispenser spinning around. The spinning lasted for about thirty seconds.

The reasons for the haunting of the Hennepin History Museum can probably be traced to the exhibits and artifacts contained within. Many paranormal investigators believe that psychic energy sometimes attaches itself to objects. If this theory is true, then it is possible that the exhibit "Icons for the Bereaved: Traditions and Artifacts for Mourning" includes artifacts like mourning clothing and jewelry that reflect the personalities of the people who once owned them.

WINONA

Winona, Minnesota, is located in the bluff country on the Mississippi River. Winona's most prominent landmark is Sugar Loaf, a rock pinnacle rising from one of the bluffs along Highway 61. The town was founded by Orrin Smith on October 15, 1851. Henry D. Huff, who bought an interest in the town site, in 1853, gave the town its name—"Winona"—which is a Dakota Indian word meaning "first-born daughter." Winona owed its growth in the 1850s to its railway and steamboat transportation systems. In the 1870s, Winona was the fourth-largest wheat shipping port in the United States. By 1892, sawmills in Winona were producing over 160 million board feet annually. The city's population declined as a result of the decline of the lumber industry in the early 1900s. In 1868, J. R. Watkins started the company that eventually came to be known as the J. R. Watkins Medical Company, one of the oldest companies in the United States. Winona was the home of actor William Windom and Carol Bartz, CEO of Yahoo!

ST. MARY'S UNIVERSITY

St. Mary's College was founded was founded in 1912 by Bishop Patrick Richard Heffron. In 1925, the school became a four-year liberal arts college. The De La Salle Christian brothers took over the school in 1933. St. Mary's College became coeducational in 1969. During the building boom of the 1980s, the Ice Arena (1986) and the Performance Center (1987) were constructed. A series of nontraditional graduate and professional programs was launched in 1985. St. Mary's College was renamed St. Mary's University in 1995 to reflect the expanded role of graduate programs. Today, the private institution has an annual enrollment of over 5,000 students and is run by the Brothers of the Christian Schools. The school is known not only for the high quality of its instructors and courses, but also for a sensational crime that was committed there in the early years of St. Mary's history.

Heffron Hall is the second major building to be erected on the campus of St. Mary's University. It is named after Bishop Patrick R. Heffron of the Diocese of Winona, who founded the school in 1912. Built in 1921, the dormitory is home to ninety-three coed sophomores, juniors, and seniors. Each of the 8.6' x 13.5' rooms has a sink. The dormitory has one kitchen, a laundry, and two TV lounges. If the stories can be believed, it also has a ghost.

St. Mary's University's most famous ghost story begins on the morning of August 27, 1915. Bishop Heffron was kneeling at the altar in the chapel when fifty-five-year-old Father Laurence M. Lesches, a tutor at the university, threw open the door and started running toward the praying bishop. The bishop turned around in time to see Father Lesches pull a handgun and begin firing. The bishop was struck in the leg and the chest. His third shot hit the altar. While Bishop Heffron lay bleeding on the floor of the chapel, Father Lesches hurried back to his room, where the police later caught up with him still in possession of the pistol.

After Bishop Heffron recovered sufficiently in the hospital to talk to the police, he said that Father Lesches was an arrogant man with a volatile personality who had difficulty making friends. The truth was that Bishop Heffron dealt harshly with faculty members who could not meet his high standards. Just a few days before the attack, Bishop Heffron had denied Father Lesches's request for a parish of his own on the grounds that he was emotionally unstable. This fact came out during the trial that followed in December 1915. It was revealed during the trial that the two men had never really liked each other in the seventeen years that they had known each other. After the two-day trial had ended, the jury deliberated for only two hours and found Father Lesches innocent on the grounds of insanity.

Father Lesches was committed to the State Hospital for the Dangerously Insane. In 1931, four years later after the death of Bishop Heffron, the doctors at the State Hospital found Father Lesches to be of sound mental health. The disgraced priest applied for release from the State Hospital, but Heffron's successor refused to sign his release papers. In 1943, Father Lesches passed away in the State Hospital at the age of eighty-four. He had spent twenty-nine years there.

In 1931, the same year that Father Lesches's petition for release from the State Hospital was turned down, he was blamed for the harm to another priest on St. Mary's campus. Not long after Father Lesches's release was denied, a maid found the charred body of Father Edward Lynch in bed. Only Father Lynch's corpse and his Bible were touched by the flames. Even the sheets on which his body lay were not burned. Coincidentally, Bishop Heffron and Father Lynch were friends, and neither one of them liked Father Lesches. The Winona County coroner P. A. Mattison concluded that Father Lynch had been electrocuted when he reached over to shut off a reading lamp attached to his metal headboard and simultaneously touched a steam radiator. Nevertheless, rumors quickly spread throughout the campus that Father Lesches had put a curse on Father Lynch. Interestingly enough, four other priests at St. Mary's University perished that same year, one by fire and three in a plane crash.

Heffron Hall gained a reputation for been haunted soon after the death of Father Lesches in 1943. Several times, Father Lesches's apparition has appeared to students on the third floor. Students living on the third floor also reported feeling cold drafts and hearing spectral footsteps and the tapping of a cane. Announcements attached to bulletin boards have fluttered, just as if a breeze was blowing through the hall. Late one night, a seminary student heard footsteps and a knocking on his door. When he opened the door, a cloaked figure was standing on the stoop. Thinking that the man was a priest, the student asked him what he wanted, and the man replied, "I want you!" Terrified, the student punched the strange man in the jaw and broke almost every bone in his hand.

In 1969, the staff and the advisor of the college newspaper, the *Nexus*, decided to investigate the stories that had been circulating around the university for almost thirty years. The group spent two nights in the hall collecting evidence. On both nights, the temperature dropped fifteen degrees at 1:45 A.M. This is the exact time at which Father Lesches is said to have died. Photographs that the staff took of cold spots captured blurred, amorphous shapes. The staff also detected cold spots, which moved one hundred feet in thirty seconds.

Sightings in Heffron Hall continued well into the twenty-first century. A student who lived in Heffron Hall in the early 2000s said that televisions in several of the rooms on the third floor turned off and on by themselves. He also said that doors slammed shut on their own. In 2006, another student who lived in town was visiting a friend in the dormitory. When she went to the bathroom, she felt a hand touch the back of her neck. She was so scared that she never returned to Heffron Hall. Between 2000 and 2010, a number of students living on the third floor reported dreaming about a cowled figure sitting on their bed. Most of these students had the dream at 1:45 A.M. If Father Lesches is indeed the restless spirit that is responsible for the disturbances in Heffron Hall, he could possibly be "acting out" because he still does not believe that he received just treatment.

WINONA STATE UNIVERSITY

The first Minnesota State Legislature established Winona State University in 1858 to prepare teachers. Classes began in 1860, but the school closed in 1861 after the outbreak of the Civil War. It reopened in 1866. The first new building after the Civil War, Main Hall, was constructed in 1866. Phelps Hall, which housed the gymnasium, the library, and the teaching lab, was constructed in 1890. In 1921, the school became Winona Teachers' College and was granted the authority to award bachelor's degrees. A number of new courses and departments were created between 1920 and 1941. The school's name was changed to Winona State College in 1957. In 1977, it became Winona State University. Today, Winona State University is composed of five colleges: Business, Liberal Arts, Nursing and Health Sciences, Science, and Engineering. Winona State University is not only the oldest member of the Minnesota State College and Universities System. It is also one of the most haunted.

Lourdes Hall, a women's dormitory, is said to be haunted by the ghost of a former student named Ruth. During the early 1800s, Lourdes Hall was a part of St. Teresa's College. Ruth, a nursing student, lived on the fourth floor in Room 4450. The story goes that the girl had an affair with a married priest named Father William. When Ruth discovered that she was pregnant, she hid herself in the infirmary on what is now the fourth floor of Lourdes Hall. She remained there until her baby was delivered. After Father William learned that Ruth had had her baby, he ran over to the infirmary, grabbed the baby from Ruth's arms, and threw it down an elevator shaft at the south end of the floor. Ruth was so devastated by the death of her baby that she threw herself down the third-north stairwell. Racked with guilt, Father William hanged himself one week later in an area that is now the Lourdes pool. Students swimming in the pool claim to have seen the body of Father William drifting over the pool. A few swimmers have felt a strange pull on their legs in the pool. A group of students using a Ouija board in Room 4450 claim to have made contact with Ruth's spirit.

Phelps Hall is also rumored to be haunted. In the 1970s, a day-care center was housed on the third floor. One tragic afternoon, a fire broke out on the third floor, killing three children. Late one evening in 2003, a custodian at the end of her shift was locking up when she heard the screams of three young children. She checked all of the rooms on the third floor but was unable to find any children. Since that time, she has refused to work on the third floor alone in the evening.

The most haunted building on campus is the Performing Arts Center. On October 5, 1973, a student named Christopher Robb

Neidringhous was discovered lying on the floor of the stage, unconscious. He had apparently fallen from the fly gallery sometime during the evening. The next day, Christopher died from internal bleeding. Students who knew Christopher said that just before he died, he appeared despondent and, possibly, under the influence of drugs. A few of his friends theorized that he might have committed suicide by jumping off the fly gallery. *The paranormal activity inside the Performing Arts Center began in June 1974, eight months after Christopher's death. His ghost was blamed for the flickering of lights on the stage. During a production of* The Crucible, *a blue light floated down from the sound booth and hovered around one of the actors. A light placed along the catwalk began to blink at odd times. Phantom footsteps have also been heard from this catwalk, the same catwalk from which Christopher plunged to his death.*

Unlike some colleges, which tend to downplay their ghost stories, Winona State University takes pride in its oral ghost narratives. In fact, versions of the university's signature ghost stories appear in a yearly program entitled "Ghost Stories from the Lourdes Attic." Ghosts, it seems, are just as integral to Winona State University's identity as its football team and homecoming celebrations.

WABASHA

Wabasha is the oldest city in Wisconsin. The area has been continuously occupied since 1826, but it was officially established as a town in 1830. The city is named after a Sioux Indian chief, Chief Wa-pa-shaw. During Wabasha's Historic Walking Tour, tour guides regale visitors with stories of the town's historic buildings, over fifty of which are listed on the National Register of Historic Places. Tourists also come to Wabasha to catch a glimpse of its eagles, which flock to the town in the winter months. Other attractions include the historic Anderson House, the Wabasha County History Museum, and the Arrowhead Bluffs Museum. The movies *Grumpy Old Men* (1993) and *Grumpier Old Men* (1995) were filmed in Wabasha.

THE RACING SCALAWAG

The phantom racer is a motif commonly found in twentieth-century folklore. One of the best-known examples is the story of Hotrod Haven, a treacherous stretch of road in Louisville, Kentucky, called Mitchell Road. In one version of the tale, a young woman and her boyfriend were driving at a high rate of speed on Mitchell Road late one night in 1950 when they missed a sharp turn and tumbled down the hill. To this day, people driving down Mitchell Road late at night report being pursued by a ghost car that attempts to force them off the road. Interestingly enough, a similar story was generated in the late nineteenth century in Wabasha, Minnesota.

Between 1875 and 1900, the residents of Wabasha were tormented by a very annoying ghost. People driving their buggies down Wabasha's lonely back roads at night have claimed that sometimes a strange-looking carriage would pull up behind them. Then, without warning, the carriage would speed up and disappear into the darkness just before pulling ahead. Invariably, the horse that was being passed would become agitated and bolt. No one ever saw the face of the phantom driver because he never really passed anyone.

Even though the speeding driver, dubbed the "Racing Scalawag," never caused any fatalities, local authorities were under a great deal of pressure to apprehend him because over the course of a decade, several carriages and wagons were overturned, and a few people were seriously injured. Finally, in 1900, the local sheriff concocted a plan to catch the "Racing Scalawag." With the assistance of several policemen from Red Wing, the sheriff began patrolling Wabasha's lonely country roads. One night, the policemen spotted a carriage matching the description given by eyewitnesses. The police followed him down a road near Zubrota where escape would have been impossible. Incredibly, the "Racing Scalawag" found a way to elude his pursuers.

A few weeks later, the police once again took off after the Racing Scalawag down a rural road. When the carriage pulled into a barn near Lake City, the sheriff and his men were certain that they had him trapped. While his men surrounded the barn, the sheriff walked into the barn with guns drawn. To his amazement, no one was there.

The Racing Scalawag's uncanny ability to evade capture led many people in Wabasha to conclude that the driver and his horse and buggy must have been ghosts. However, folklore provides evidence suggesting that the driver might have been the devil himself. Racing with the devil is a fairly common motif in American and European folklore. For example, people living in Bucks County, Pennsylvania, say that the devil races people from Mount Gilead Church to an abandoned graveyard. The fact that some people racing in Wabasha were injured suggests that this could have been the Racing Scalawag's intention all along.

THE ANDERSON HOUSE

The Anderson House was a fifty-two-room hotel built in 1856 on the corner of Main and Bridge Streets by Mr. Hurd, just two years before the village of Wabasha was incorporated. In 1901, "Grandma" Ida Anderson, who was from the Amish colonies in Lancaster, Pennsylvania, purchased the hotel, which bears her name to this day. A big attraction was Grandma Anderson's Dutch cooking. For years, her great-grandson, John Hall, continued the tradition of serving up her dishes in the hotel's restaurant. At the end of the twentieth century, the Anderson Hotel had become just as famous for its cats as it was for being the oldest continuously operating hotel in Minnesota. One of these cats was featured in the children's book *Blumpoe the Grumpoe Meets Arnold the Cat.* Visitors were allowed to "borrow" the cats for the night. The spirits who haunted the old hotel were not nearly as cuddly.

Teresa and Mike Smith, who owned the hotel between 2004 and 2010, heard many stories of three ghosts who appeared to the guests. People claimed to have seen the apparitions of a man and woman dressed in Victorian attire climbing the staircase and then vanishing. An even more terrifying entity was the ghost of a train conductor who approached guests on the third floor and asked for their tickets before disappearing. The cats seemed to sense that they were sharing the house with otherworldly presences. Sometimes, they stared and hissed at the corner of some of the rooms and leaped at the walls.

In the March 23, 2009, edition of the *Star Tribune*, Teresa and Mike Smith announced that the historic Anderson House was closing its doors. At least a dozen of the hotel's cats had found new homes by that time. There is no word on what has happened to the ghosts that haunted the Anderson House.

RED WING

Steamboats brought settlers from New England to Red Wing, Minnesota, in the 1850s to raise wheat on the area's fertile farmland. By 1873, Red Wing led the country in wheat production. By the end of the nineteenth century, hundreds of immigrants from Germany, Ireland, and Sweden had flocked to Red Wing. Early industries included the production of bricks, barrels, buttons, and pottery. Red Wing is the home of the Red Wing Shoe Company.

ST. JAMES HOTEL

In 1874, a group of eleven businessmen formed a stock company to build a luxury hotel. When the St. James Hotel was completed in 1875, the Italianate building was the most elegant hotel west of Chicago. Its primary clientele were passengers from the trains that passed through Red Wing. In 1975, the St. James Hotel was in dire need of repair. That same year, the Red Wing Shoe Company bought the old hotel and immediately set about to renovate and expand the structure. Today, the St. James Hotel has sixty-one Victorian-style guest rooms, no two of which are like. It is also said to have a number of ghosts.

Many reasons have been given for the large number of sightings in the St. James Hotel. Legend has it that the hotel was built over an Indian burial ground. Desecrating sacred ground, especially Indian burial grounds, always has dire consequences in American folklore. It is also said that a little girl drowned in a well on the property around the turn of the century. Most of the employees of the old hotel say that a former owner of the hotel who committed suicide is now haunting the St. James, along with the ghost of his wife.

Employees and guests of the St. James Hotel have reported some very strange experiences. Housekeepers have seen shadowy figures moving around in the rooms. However, when they investigate, the rooms are always entirely empty. Chefs working in the basement of the hotel have seen disembodied heads floating in the air, staring at them. A new employee said that one morning, she walked into the office and found a note that read: "Who are you?" The crude handwriting suggested that a child wrote the note. At first, she thought that a co-worker had played a prank on her. Then she realized that the office is always locked because of the sensitive information that is stored there. Several times, guests have checked out in the middle of the night, usually because the blinds on their windows began flapping on their own. The windows were closed at the time.

The Red Wing Shoe Company managed to restore the Victorian elegance of the St. James Hotel and expand it at the same time. The old hotel has thirteen meeting or banquet rooms that can serve groups of three hundred people. In the St. James courtyard, guests can explore twelve distinctive shops. The old hotel is so luxurious, in fact, that no one seems eager to leave, not even the St. James's dead guests and employees.

Mississippi

NATCHEZ

The first inhabitants of Natchez, Mississippi, were the Natchez Indians. Hernando De Soto, La Salle, and Bienville all made contact with the Natchez Indians. The French founded Fort Rosalie in 1716 to protect the newly established trading post. In 1729, the Natchez Indians massacred 229 French colonists. Over the next two years, most of the Natchez Indians were killed. In 1731, hundreds of Natchez Indians were transported to New Orleans, where they were sold as slaves. The burgeoning town, which was named Natchez, passed into British and Spanish control until the British ceded the town to the United States in 1783. In the late eighteenth and early nineteenth centuries, Natchez served as the jumping-off point for the Natchez Trace. At this time, Natchez became a bustling port city. Planters loaded their cotton bales onto steamboats at a notorious landing called Natchez-Under-the-Hill. Thousands of slaves were sold at the Forks of the Road Market in Natchez. On May 7, 1840, the "Great Natchez Tornado" took 317 lives. Natchez suffered little damage after surrendering to Flag-Officer David G. Farragut in May 1862. The economy of Natchez recovered rapidly after the Civil War when river traffic was resumed and steamboats once again paddled up and down the Mississippi. When railroads replaced steamboats after the turn of the twentieth century, Natchez's economic importance diminished considerably. Today, the old city is heavily dependent on tourism. Its annual tours of the city's beautiful antebellum mansion—the Natchez Pilgrimage—draws hundreds of visitors to the city each year.

KING'S TAVERN

King's Tavern was built in 1769 of sun-dried bricks, timbers salvaged from old ships, and barge boards from flatboats that were dismantled once they had completed their journey down the Mississippi River. The imprints of a panther's paw and a bear's paw are clearly visible in the floor of the entranceway to the tavern. Evidently, the animals were attracted to the smell of cattle stabled at the tavern when the bricks had not completely dried. In 1789, Richard King purchased the building and converted it into an inn and tavern for boatmen and for weary travelers fresh from their dangerous trek down the Natchez Trace. Indian runners delivered mail to a small room on the first floor that served as a post office. People planning to travel up the Natchez Trace rented rooms on the first and second floor. A number of historical figures spent the night at King's Tavern, including Aaron Burr and Andrew Jackson. A host of unsavory characters boarded there as well, including a variety of outlaws. Richard King sold the tavern in 1820 to the Postalwaith family. Members of the Postalwaith family continued living in the old house from 1823 to 1973, when King's Tavern became a restaurant. Over the years, the walls of the old tavern have born silent witness to beatings, robbery, and murder. As a result, King's Tavern is not only one of the oldest buildings in Mississippi, but it is also one of the most haunted as well.

King's Tavern's long legacy of violence extended well into the twentieth century. In 1900, a jeweled Spanish dagger was discovered in the rubble of a chimney that had collapsed. In 1930, workmen expanding the fireplace in the main dining room were tearing out the chimney wall behind the fireplace on the first floor when they discovered three mummified bodies. The skeletons were the remains of two men and one woman. A jeweled dagger was discovered lying on the floor. The grisly find seemed to confirm Richard King's rumored affair with a sixteen-year-old girl named Madeline who worked as a server in the tavern. After Madeline disappeared, the rumor spread that Mrs. King had hired a couple of murderers to kill the girl and conceal the body behind the fireplace. The identity of the male skeletons is unknown.

Some people have speculated that they are the remains of servants or patrons of the tavern. Others believe that the same men who murdered Madeline also killed two other men and interred their corpses with hers. At any rate, many people familiar with the long history of King's Tavern trace the beginning of paranormal activity inside the old building to the renovations that were made during the Great Depression.

Madeline is usually credited with many of the disturbances that occur at King's Tavern. The image of a beautiful young woman with red hair has been seen in the ladies' restroom. The ghostly shadow of a slender woman with her hands on her hips has appeared on the third-floor landing. A reporter who was videotaping by himself on the first floor heard voices and footsteps on the second floor. He assumed that his friends and one of the servers were upstairs until he looked out the window and saw the women standing outside. She is said to be particularly fond of water. Madeline has been known to make hot water spew out of water faucets when no one is around. Water occasionally drips from the ceiling for no apparent reason. Sometimes, her footprints suddenly appear on freshly mopped floors. Madeline's ghost could also be responsible for some of the poltergeist-like activity that has been reported over the years. Burglar alarms go off for no apparent reason between five A.M. and six A.M. Lights turn off and on. Jars have fallen off shelves by themselves. Chairs hanging on the wall in the back of the main dining room start swinging, as if they are being moved by an invisible hand. Some guests have reported feeling heat coming from the fireplace on days when no fire was made. Doors open mysteriously. One night, a server who witnessed the door swing open on its own said, "All right, Madeline," and the door closed on its own.

The ghost of one of the Indian runners who delivered and picked up letters from King's Tavern seems to prefer the Tap Room, the site of the former mailroom on the first floor. Eyewitnesses have described him as an imposing figure dressed in a war bonnet. He usually makes an appearance at midnight in the Tap Room. In *Ghosts! Personal Accounts of Modern Mississippi Hauntings*, author Sylvia Booth Hubbard tells the story of a little girl who saw the image of an Indian in a mirror hanging in the old post office. When she asked her mother who the man in the red hat was in the mirror, she replied that nobody's face was in the mirror other than the little girl's.

A much younger spirit is also said to haunt King's Tavern. The story goes that one night in the late 1700s, an outlaw named Micajah "Big" Harpe was spending the night on the second floor in King's Tavern, trying to sleep off the whiskey he had drunk that evening, when he was awakened by the sound of a baby crying in the room next to his. Big Harpe staggered out of his room and knocked on the door. A harried-looking woman opened the door, a crying infant whining and wriggling in her arms. The story goes that Big Harpe took the baby from the poor woman, swung it by the ankles, smashed its head against the wall, and retuned the battered little body to its mother. He then stumbled down the steps and ordered a drink from the bar. The spectral crying of an infant has become the most common ghostly occurrence at King's Tavern. Yvonne Scott, the owner of King's Tavern, said that whenever someone goes up to the attic, the disembodied cries of the baby echo through the upper floors within a day or two.

Today, King's Tavern capitalizes on its reputation as one of the most haunted sites in Mississippi. Guests can purchase a copy of an article published in the *National Enquirer* chronicling an investigation of King's Tavern by author Sylvia Booth Hubbard. Guests are also invited to walk through the rooms on the upper floors where so much haunted activity has been reported. One might argue that ghosts do not exist, but there is no doubt that ghosts are good for business.

MAGNOLIA HALL

Built in 1858 by planter Thomas Henderson, the Magnolia Hotel is one of the most outstanding examples of Greek Revival architecture in Natchez. Henderson, who was an elder in the First Presbyterian Church, had made a fortune as a merchant and a planter. Magnolia Hall survived the Civil War virtually, but it was damaged by a cannonball fired by a Union gunboat, the *Essex*. The cannonball landed in the kitchen and did considerable damage. Like many other planters in the South, Henderson did not enjoy his palatial surroundings for very long. In January 1863, he suffered a stroke that left him paralyzed over much of his body. He died on March 6, 1863, in a downstairs bedroom. In 1984, Magnolia was purchased by the Natchez Garden Club, which furnished the fine old house with period antiques. The second floor of Magnolia Hall also houses Natchez's only costume collection. Within a few months after the house was opened for tours, the hostesses soon discovered that Thomas Henderson did not relinquish ownership of his magnificent mansion as easily as some people believed.

In 2000, a hostess named Judy Grimsley told this writer that one cool morning in October 1985, she had arrived early to turn on the lights and to make sure the rooms were straightened up, just as she always did. She walked into the downstairs bedroom where Thomas Henderson had died and was stunned by the sight of the indentation of an adult-sized head on the pillow. She was certain that no one had climbed onto the bed the night before. On another morning, Ms. Grimsley had turned on the lights in the house and was in the process of changing the signs when she felt someone staring at her. She quickly turned around and saw a shadowy figure with large shoulders standing at the top of the stairs. She blinked her eyes to make sure that she was actually seeing the apparition of a large man. Then a few seconds later, he disappeared.

On October 30, 2000, this writer participated in an all-night investigation of Magnolia Hall. I arrived at Magnolia Hall at 6:00 P.M. with two disc jockeys from radio station WOKK, Scotty Ray Boyd and Debbie Alexander, as well as a contest winner named Ashley McClearly. We were joined by disc jockeys from WOKK's two sister stations in Jackson, Mississippi, and Monroe, Louisiana. After taking a tour of the house with Judy Grimsley, the engineers, John David Ainsworth and Scott Shepherd, turned on the video and sound equipment that they had set up the day before. At 8:40 P.M., one of the engineers was staring at the video monitors when he noticed a strange ball of light hovering around the head of one of the Jackson DJs, Jerry Broadway, who was standing four feet away from the bed. A psychic we were talking to on the telephone informed us that Mr. Henderson was very fond of music. At 12:09 A.M., Jerry sat on the bed and began playing his guitar. Immediately, the ball of light began flitting around the room, almost as if it were dancing to the music.

Today, hostesses still encounter the vigilant spirit of Thomas Henderson and other ghosts inside Magnolia Hall. In an interview given to the *Natchez Democrat* reporter Julie Finley in November 2005, Judy Grimsley said that she did not believe that any of the spirits inside the antebellum home where she had spent so much time were evil. "They like to see that everything is going well, and they are pleased," she said.

THE UNQUIET SPIRITS OF SPRINGFIELD

When Thomas Marston, a wealthy planter from Virginia, built Springfield Plantation House twenty-four miles from Natchez between 1786 and 1791, Jefferson County was a part of Spanish-dominated West Florida. Building the mansion in such a remote area was extremely difficult. To make the bricks, slaves had to dig away the loose loess soil near the kilns so that the clay would be exposed. Most of the metalwork found in the house, such as the hinges, was made in the plantation blacksmith shop. Using axes and whipsaws, slaves also cut the timbers used to build the roof and floor beams of the house. Carpenters employed the tongue-and-groove method to make the ceilings and floors. The Georgian-Adam-Federal woodwork and mantels stand in stark contrast to the comparatively simple entranceway, which lacks the type of ornate staircase found in many antebellum homes. Guests accessed their rooms through an enclosed stairway. By the 1970s, Springfield had fallen into disrepair. In 1977, the owners of Springfield allowed Arthur E. La Salle to lease the old house in exchange for restoring it. Springfield is important historically, not only because it is one of the earliest plantation homes built in the Delta region but it is also one of the first houses with a full colonnade across the front to be built west of the Atlantic seaboard. Springfield is rumored to be one of the most haunted as well.

Springfield received its most famous visitor in 1791, soon after construction on the house was completed. According to local legend, Andrew Jackson married Rachel Donelson in Thomas Green's parlor. Springfield would have been the ideal site for Jackson's marriage because Thomas Green was the most prominent planter in the region. In addition two of Rachel's nieces were married to members of the

Green family. Supposedly, Jackson had brought Rachel to Natchez in 1790 to provoke a divorce from her husband, Lewis Robards. At the time of their marriage, Andrew and Rachel assumed that her divorce from Robards had gone through. Although no record of their marriage exists, documentation suggests that Rachel probably lived fifteen months at Springfield plantation and at a plantation owned by Thomas Green's brother, Abner.

In her book *Ghosts! Personal Accounts of Modern Mississippi Hauntings*, Sylvia Booth Hubbard says that when La Salle first moved in to Springfield in 1977, he and his son lived in the kitchen area while the rest of the house was being restored. One cold winter's night, La Salle's son and his son's friend were camped out in the kitchen. A couple of hours later, La Salle moved his pallet into the bathroom so that he could have a little peace and quiet. He was sleeping on the bathroom floor with a flashlight, a kerosene lamp, and a kerosene heater, when he heard the unmistakable sound of someone walking across the floor of the bedroom next to the bathroom. After a few seconds, the footsteps proceeded out of the bedroom and into the hallway. They stopped just outside of the bathroom where La Salle had been sleeping. La Salle fully expected someone to open the door and walk into the bathroom. After waiting a few tense minutes, La Salle got up off the floor and slowly opened the door. No one was there.

Over the next few years, La Salle heard a variety of spectral sounds inside Springfield. La Salle said that on Sunday afternoons when he entertained friends, they frequently heard loud crashing sounds. It sounded as if a large piece of furniture had fallen over. The source of the noise was never found. La Salle also claimed to have heard the sounds of eighteenth-century music lilting through the old house. On several occasions, he heard the phantom footsteps, which he had heard when he first moved in.

Today, Springfield is a house museum owned by the Williams family of St. Louis. It is also a working plantation, even though only two hundred acres remain. Tourists can learn about life on a Spanish colony plantation by listening to the stories told by Arthur E. La Salle and by walking down the "quarter road" to the restored slave quarters.

If they are lucky, visitors might also sense the presence of some of the people who called Springfield home.

DUNLEITH

Dunleith is a colonnade Revival temple located on the site of a house built in Natchez in the late 1700s by Job Routh and his wife. After their death, their fifteen-year-old daughter, Mary, inherited "Routhland," as it was known then. At the time, Mary was already a widow. She moved into the mansion with her second husband, Charles Dahlgren, a successful banker. However, in 1855, Routhland was struck by lightning and burned down. Mary and Charles rebuilt the house the following year and enjoyed three years of wedded bliss until Mary's sudden death. Charles sold the house and property to Alfred Vidal Davis for $30,000 to settle debts. After taking possession of the house, Davis re-christened it "Dunleith." Joseph Carpenter, a very gregarious man, purchased Dunleith in 1886. Carpenter, who loved to throw lavish parties, turned Dunleith into one of Natchez's primary social centers. Dunleith was owned by a number of different people in the twentieth century before being converted into a bed and breakfast in 1976 by Edward Worley. Twenty-three years later, Mrs. Edward Worley and her son Michael became the new owners of Dunleith. After a period of extensive renovation, Dunleith was transformed into the inn that it is today. The up-scale hostelry has twenty-six guest rooms with private bathrooms. Sixteen of the rooms feature whirlpool tubs. Some people say that Dunleith has a ghost as well.

Dunleith is said to be haunted by the ghost of "Miss Percy," to whom Mrs. Dahlgren was related by marriage. In her book *13 Mississippi Ghosts and Jeffrey*, folklorist Kathryn Tucker Windham says that Miss Percy fell in love with a dashing young Frenchman who was rumored to be a count or a high-ranking French officer. Everyone in Natchez believed that someday the handsome couple would be married. One day, Miss Percy's lover held her hands in his and told her, in a low, somber voice, that he had to return to France but that he would return for her someday soon. She waited for her lover for months without receiving even a single letter from him. Growing impatient, she announced to her friends and family that she was traveling to France to be reunited with her Frenchman. She turned a deaf ear to the pleas from the older members of her family to remain in Natchez. Instead, she boarded a ship bound for France.

Months later, Miss Percy returned to Natchez with her head bowed in shame. Her lover, it seemed, was much less attentive to her in France than he had been in Natchez. Because her family was embarrassed by the girl's humiliation, she was forced to turn to the Dahlgrens for a place to stay. They boarded her in an upstairs bedroom, where she spent most of her time. Each afternoon, Miss Percy walked downstairs and played melancholy songs on the harp. One day, several months after her arrival at Dunleith, Miss Percy was found dead in her bedroom. People said that she must have died of a broken heart. A few days after Miss Percy's burial, Mrs. Dahlgren was walking down the hallway when she heard the lilting tones of a harp coming from the parlor. As soon as she walked through the doorway, the playing stopped.

The present owners of Dunleith have gone to great lengths to restore the old mansion to its former glory. On the grounds, one can find the original dairy barn and carriage house, dating back to the late 1700s. Guest rooms are furnished with authentic antiques and ante-bellum-period replica furniture. The twenty-six stately white columns surrounding the mansion glisten in the sun, just as they did over 150 years ago. And some afternoons, guests still hear the swishing of skirts and the plucking of harp strings in the parlor where Miss Percy had tried to recapture in her music the way she had felt in the arms of her Frenchman so many years before.

LONGWOOD

In 1860, millionaire businessman and planter Haller Nutt began building what he hoped would be the most impressive octagonal Oriental Revival–style house in the United States. Nutt hired a Philadelphia architect, Samuel Sloan, to design the house that he had named "Longwood."

Early in 1861, the six-story, 30,000-square-foot house was almost finished when the Civil War broke out. Before the workers walked off the job, they had completed the exterior and nine of the mansion's thirty-two rooms. During the war, Dr. Nutt and his family lived on the first floor of the house. Even though Dr. Nutt had publicly declared himself a Federalist and even had papers verifying his claim, Union troops destroyed his steamboats and plantations in Louisiana. He died in 1864, a broken man. Following the war, Dr. Nutt's wife, Julia, won her lawsuit against the federal government, but her settlement was not nearly enough to cover the cost of finishing the mansion, which by that time was known locally as "Nutt's Folly." After years of neglect, Longwood has been restored. It is a national historic landmark and is registered on the National Register of Historic Places. The property is run by the Pilgrimage Garden Club, which gives tours of the strangely shaped mansion with the byzantine-styled dome. According to some of the tour guides, Dr. Nutt's frustrated spirit still roams the halls of his splendid home.

Longtime tour guides have been regaling tourists with weird tales about Nutt's Folly for many years. In the late 1970s, one of them told Richard Winer, author of *Haunted Houses*, that occasionally the air inside the house was permeated with the unmistakable odor of jasmine perfume, a popular scent around the turn of the century. On another occasion, a film company that was making a documentary of the city's historic homes hired a local volunteer fireman to spend the night inside Longwood and keep an eye on the photographic equipment that was stored there. Around midnight, the fireman became so frightened that the caretaker who lived on the premises had to spend the night with the terrified man.

Louise Burns, the resident manager of Longwood, told author Jim Longo that she had had a number of personal experiences during her stay at the old house. She said that one night several years after she had first moved into Longwood, she was asleep when she felt someone pulling on her hair and lifting her head above the pillow. She said that it seemed as if her head were being cradled in someone's hands. Her eyes were closed the entire time. When her fear finally subsided, Louise opened her eyes and found that her head was lying on the pillow.

Louise also said that a man she had hired to mow the grass was making erratic passes across the lawn. When he was finished, the man asked her if the house was haunted. When Louise asked him what he meant, he replied that he saw the apparition of a man who resembled Dr. Nutt standing by a tree with one hand on his hip. Dr. Nutt was wearing a white shirt and black pants. The man said that when he drove the tractor up to the tree to get a better look at the ghostly figure, Dr. Nutt disappeared.

One of the housekeepers claimed to have had a ghostly encounter with Mrs. Nutt. She said that one day she walked over to the broom closet to get a broom. When she turned around, she saw a woman standing in her way between the closet and the bedroom. She was struck by the fact that the woman was wearing a hoop skirt. All of a sudden, the woman's face began to dissipate. Then her entire body faded away.

The ghosts at Longwood also make their presence known through sound. The same housekeeper who saw the ghost of Mrs. Nutt said that she was sitting on a swing on the lawn when she heard the sound of children playing. She was the only one in the house at the time. Tour guides have also heard the sound of an invisible presence walking down the halls. Apparently, the Nutt family is not quite ready to relinquish their beloved home.

THE GHOST OF GLENBURNIE

Glenburnie is a fairly common example of a Federal-style plantation home. Today, it stands in anachronistic grandeur next to an up-scale Natchez subdivision called Glenwood. Back in the 1950s, however, another antebellum home called "Glenwood" stood where the subdivision is now located. In 1866, Reverend Dana from Alexandria, Virginia, took the position of pastor of the Trinity Episcopal Church in Natchez. Five years later, his son Richard was born. After Reverend Dana died in 1873, Richard was raised by his mother. Following his mother's death in 1885, Dick, as he was known at the time, attended Vanderbilt, where he studied music in the hopes of becoming a concert pianist. When he returned to Natchez, Dick became master of Glenwood. Dick soon became fast friends with Jennie Merrill and Duncan Minor, Jennie's wealthy cousin and lifelong friend. In the 1880s, a beautiful redheaded poet named Octavia Dockery moved in with Dick Dana at the request of her dying older sister. During the 1890s, Jennie, Duncan, Dick, and Octavia became very close friends. Jennie and Duncan eventually fell in love, but Duncan's mother discouraged them from marrying because they were closely related. After losing her family home, Elms Court, Jennie purchased Glenburnie in 1904. The stage was now set for the tragedy that would change their lives forever.

Over the next few decades, Jennie and Dick began acting very strangely. Jennie became reclusive, allowing no one to enter her house except Duncan, who began sneaking over under the cover of darkness and spending the night with her. Dick's hopes of becoming a world-renowned pianist were dashed forever after a window sash fell on his hand, breaking several fingers. He continued to play piano, despite his inability to play all of the notes. Before long, he plummeted into depression. Dick began wandering through the woods while Octavia looked on helplessly.

By the 1920s, Glenwood had fallen into disrepair. Goats wandered through the property and even into the house itself with impunity. Jennie, whose fortunes had increased while Dick's fell, tried to buy Glenwood, but Octavia blocked the sale by having herself declared Dick's guardian. One day, Jennie shot and killed one of Dick's goats that had been eating her rose bushes. Dick pressed charges against Jennie, but the judge dismissed the case. Because of the publicity the case received, neighbors began calling Glenwood "Goat Castle."

The feud between Jennie and Dick was forgotten until the night of August 4, 1932, when Duncan was driving up the drive to Glenburnie. Duncan opened the door and took only a couple of steps inside the house when he stopped dead in his tracks. Furniture was overturned and strewn over the floor. Blood was splattered on the walls. A long trail of gore led to the outside door. Horrified, Duncan followed the blood trail to the driveway. He ran all around the outside of the house in search of Jennie. After a few minutes, Duncan gave up and called the sheriff. After a while, a member of the search party found Jennie's bloodstained corpse hidden behind some bushes. Her shoes were gone, and the blue dress she was wearing was perforated with bullet holes. It turned out that Jennie had been shot several times in the chest and the head with a .32 caliber pistol. She was sixty-eight years old.

News of the grisly crime was carried by newspapers throughout the country. Octavia and Dick were the prime suspects because of their rocky relationship with Jennie, but no evidence was found linking them to the murder. Within a few days, the police discovered that Jennie had been murdered by Emily Burns, the owner of a Natchez boarding-house, and George Pearls, one of her boarders. The couple had shot and killed Jennie in an abortive robbery attempt.

Dick and Octavia were cleared, but their lives were disrupted by the publicity the crime had received. Tourists flocked to "Goat Castle" in the hopes of catching a glimpse of its eccentric occupants. Sensing that they might be able to profit from their home's notoriety, Dick and Octavia began charging visitors $.50 for guided tours of Glenwood. Octavia carried a goat in her arms and enthralled tourists with tales of the old house while Dick played melancholy tunes on the piano. Dick and Octavia continued living in squalor until his death in 1948. Octavia followed him to the grave in 1949. After their meager possessions were auctioned off, "Goat Castle" was pulled down in 1950.

Not surprisingly, Glenburnie and Glenwood rapidly acquired haunted reputations. Soon after Jennie Merrill's murder, passersby claimed to have seen her spirit roaming around the woods near her home. In *Dead Men Do Tell Tales*, author Troy Taylor says that for decades, many people living in the area refused to cut through the woods near Glenburnie for fear of confronting her ghost. Witnesses describe her barefoot spirit as wearing a bloody blue dress. Her ghost is usually on the move, running from tree to tree. Jennie's ghost also makes its presence known by moaning and screaming. Her wailing was so loud, in fact, that Dick Dana played his piano as loudly as he could to drown out the blood-curdling sounds.

Apparently, Octavia Dockery's ghost is active as well. She has appeared in different stages of life. The older version wears a straw hat and a calico hat. The younger Octavia struts around in a fine Parisian gown. As a rule, Octavia's appearances are accompanied by the playing of piano music.

Carolyn Guido, who has lived in Glenburnie since 1968, is certain that Jennie Merrill's spirit has never really left her home. For years, family members have heard a spectral voice call their name. Party guests have seen Jennie Merrill's ghost walking past the windows. Carpenters said they heard strange sounds in the basement. One day, while getting the house ready for the Natchez Spring Pilgrimage, Carolyn sensed that she was not alone. "I just felt like there was someone in the room," she said. "You know how you get that feeling that someone is standing behind you, but no one was there." The prospect of living with the ghost of a murdered woman might be daunting for most people, but Carolyn has come to terms with Jennie Merrill's spirit. "We do hear things and see things every now and then, but we feel like she's a good ghost," Carolyn said.

STANTON HALL

Like many Irish immigrants, nineteen-year-old Frederick Stanton immigrated to America from Belfast with the American Dream firmly implanted in his brain. Lured to Natchez by the promise of making a fortune in cotton, Stanton established himself in the community as a cotton broker. Stanton proved to be such a sharp investor that by the 1830s, he was a wealthy man, living in a fine mansion, Cherokee, with his wife and family. Stanton's meteoric rise was halted temporarily by the Panic of the 1830s, during which he lost much of his fortune. Stanton's financial reversals forced him and his family to leave Cherokee and move into a more modest but still impressive mansion, Glenwood.

Because of his work ethic and business acumen, Stanton recouped much of his fortune within a decade. In 1857, Stanton began construction on a magnificent mansion that was befitting a man of his standing. He commissioned Natchez architect-builder Captain Thomas Rose and local carpenters and craftsmen to build the largest mansion in the entire city. The white stucco mansion occupied an entire city block on top of a hill in the heart of Natchez. The four massive white Corinthian columns provided a mere glimpse of the luxurious furnishings inside the mansion, which Stanton had named "Belfast." Bronze chandeliers hung from every room. All of the white marble mantels were sculpted in New York.

The large gilded mirrors were imported from France. The Stanton family moved into their new home in late 1858. Ironically, Frederick Stanton had lived in Belfast for only a few months before dying on January 4, 1859. Stanton's wife, Hulda, managed to remain in Belfast with her children during the Civil War. However, in the 1870s and 1880s, the cost of maintaining her mansion was so great that she was forced to sell off most of the furnishings. Following the death of Hulda Stanton in 1893, Belfast changed hands several times. In 1938, the Pilgrimage Garden Club purchased the old house, which by that time was known as Stanton Hall. The mansion was carefully restored and opened as a tour home. The ghost that haunts Stanton Hall is definitely not as well known as the cities other spirits, but it certainly is cuter.

For many years, the staff at Stanton Hall have told stories about the ghost of a little dog that scampers down the halls and into the rooms. It is said to be the spirit of a black cocker spaniel that the Stanton family owned in the 1870s and 1880s. The children and grandchildren who lived in the house were so fond of the little canine that it was treated like a member of the family. Occasionally, guests question the tour guides about the little black dog that they saw running down the stairs or lying on the bed in one of the rooms. The dog is also said to be responsible for many of the unexplained noises in the old home.

Today, Stanton Hall is the headquarters of the Pilgrimage Garden Club. During the Spring and Fall Pilgrimages, tourists are taken through the old house by hostesses dressed in antebellum dresses. The little black dog that is sometimes seen walking behind the visitors is not an official part of the tour.

VICKSBURG

The first inhabitants of the area now known as Vicksburg were the Natchez Indians. In 1719, French colonists built Fort Saint-Pierre on the bluffs overlooking the Yazoo River. On November 28, 1729, the Indians attacked the port and massacred several hundred people. The Choctaws gained control of the area and maintained it until 1801, when the Choctaw Nation ceded two million acres of land to the United States.

In 1790 the Spanish built a military outpost called Nogales ("Walnut trees"). The Americans changed the named to Walnut Hills when they gained possession of the region in 1798. Over the next two decades, the population of the settlement grew quickly. In 1825, it was officially incorporated as Vicksburg. It was named after Methodist minister named Newitt Vick. After a forty-seven-day siege, Vicksburg surrendered to the Union army on July 4, 1863. River trade became very important to Vicksburg's economy in the postwar years. River traffic around Vicksburg was impeded in 1876 when Mississippi floodwaters cut off the large meander flowing past Vicksburg. The construction of a railroad-highway bridge in 1929 greatly improved railroad access to the west. On March 12, 1894, a local confectioner named Joseph Biederharm bottled Coca-Cola in Vicksburg for the first time. Today, Vicksburg National Military Park attracts thousands of tourists to the city. Vicksburg also hosts the Miss Mississippi Beauty Pageant every year.

ANCHUCA

Anchuca, a two-story mansion located at 101 First East Street in Vicksburg. Its architectural style is a hybrid of Greek Revival, Colonial, and Gothic features. Anchuca was built in 1830 by a local politician named J. W. Mauldin. He christened his house "Anchuca," a Choctaw Indian word meaning "happy home." In 1837, Richard Archer, an eccentric plantation owner, took up residence in Anchuca and added his own personal touches to the mansion. Victor Wilson, who was a prominent ice and coal merchant, purchased Anchuca in 1847 and added columns in the front of the mansion, making his home the first columned mansion in Vicksburg. Wilson is said to have whiled away the hours watching his barges transport coal and ice down the Mississippi River. The next occupant of Anchuca was Joseph Emory Davis, the brother of Jefferson Davis, the president of the Confederate States of America. Davis conceded defeat to the Union forces in a speech he delivered from the balcony. During the siege of Vicksburg in 1863, Anchuca served as a military hospital. Today, Anchuca's antebellum spirit permeates the old mansion, which has been converted into a bed and breakfast. Some guests claim that the spirit of Richard Archer's rebellious daughter is there as well.

One of the early owners of Anchuca, Richard Archer, had five beautiful daughters. They shared many of the same physical features, but one of them, "Archie," stood out from her sisters. She was given the nickname "Archie" because she possessed the same headstrong temperament that her father was known for in Vicksburg. Growing up, Archie enjoyed her status as Richard Archer's favorite. He asked her opinion regarding some of his agricultural experiments, such as his ill-fated plan to grow oysters in his pond. They also enjoyed reading the same novels. However, the special relationship Archie shared with her father came to an abrupt end when he discovered that she had fallen in love with Josh Melvin, the son of his overseer. The social gap between the young couple was so wide that Richard believed it could never be totally bridged. One day, Richard caught Archie and Josh sitting on a bench near the pond, absorbed in conversation. Richard strode over to the couple and ordered Josh off his land. As the young man walked away, Archie exclaimed that if Richard sent Josh away, she would never eat another meal at his table. The next day, Archie refused to sit at the dinner table with the rest of the family. Instead, she stood by the fireplace and ate from the marble mantel. She continued to dine in this way for the rest of her life as a show of defiance against the father who had run off the only man she had ever loved.

The first ghostly activity in Anchuca was reported by Mr. and Mrs. Jack Lavender, who moved into the old mansion in 1966. In *13 Mississippi Ghosts and Jeffrey*, folklorist Kathryn Tucker Windham said that one day the Lavenders' teenage daughter, Mel, was walking through the parlor when she saw the slender form of a beautiful young woman dressed in a brown nineteenth-century dress standing by the fireplace. Mel stared at the apparition for several seconds before it finally dissipated. At the time, Mel was unfamiliar with the story of Archie Archer.

Archie's ghost has been sighted many times since Mel's first encounter with the spirit. In *Haunted Inns of the Southeast*, innkeeper Loveta Byrne told author Sheila Turnage that in 2001 she felt a presence in the house that upset her greatly. Byrne said that guests have also seen a ghost inside the slave quarters.

Southern folklore contains many stories in which houses that have been witnesses to tragedy still resonate with sorrowful emanations. In the case of Anchuca, many residents of Vicksburg choose to believe that Archie's ghost remains in Anchuca because she is still waiting for Josh to return for her. A much less romantic possibility, though, is that Archie Archer's spirit still stands by the mantel as a sign that she will never forgive her father.

LAKEMONT

Judge William Lake was unique among Mississippi politicians in that he had held political office in the North as well as in the South. Born near Cambridge, Maryland, on January 6, 1808, Lake matriculated at Jefferson College, Pennsylvania, where he majored in classical studies. In 1831, Lake was elected to the Maryland House of Delegates. After his term in office had ended, Judge Lake moved to Vicksburg, Mississippi, with his wife, Ann, to study law. In the early 1830s, he built a beautiful Greek Revival home at 1103 Main Street, which he called Lakemont. After being admitted to the bar in 1834, Judge Lake began practicing law. Even though Lake had a successful law practice, politics was still in his blood. In 1838, Lake was elected to the state senate. Between March 3, 1855, and March 3, 1857, he served as an American Party candidate to the Thirty-fourth Congress. He ran unsuccessfully for reelection the Thirty-fifth Congress in 1856 but was elected to the state house of representatives between 1859 and 1861. Not long after the outbreak of the Civil War, Judge Lake's decision to run as a candidate for the Confederate Congress changed his life, and his wife Anne's, forever.

On October 15, 1861, Judge Lake told his wife to have a lovely afternoon and walked through the front door, just as he did every morning. While he worked in the office, Ann enjoyed calling on her friends or walking in her garden. On this particular day, however, he was on his way to fight a pistol duel with his opponent for the Confederate Congress, Colonel Chambers. The site of the duel was De Soto Point, a sandy strip of land where dueling was legal because it was beyond the Mississippi border. By the time Ann found out from one of her servants what her husband was about to do, she grabbed her opera glasses and climbed the stairs to the second-floor veranda so she could see for herself what was about to transpire. Gazing through the opera glasses, she

saw her husband and his opponent select their pistols from their sec-
onds, walk ten paces, turn, and fire. A gasp escaped her throat as Judge
Lake crumpled to the ground. The doctor who was kneeling by Judge
Lake's prostrate body looked up at Lake's second and shook his head.
Ann dropped her opera glasses and walked slowly downstairs. Judge
Lake's body was placed on a boat and transported to City Cemetery in
Vicksburg for burial.

Subsequent owners of Lakemont have detected a considerable
amount of paranormal activity in the old house. In *13 Mississippi Ghosts
and Jeffrey*, folklorist Kathryn Tucker Windham said that the transparent form of a woman has been seen strolling through the garden where
Ann Lake often went to rest her mind. People have heard the rustling
of silk skirts on the porch and in the garden. Residents of Lakemont
have detected the presence of Ann Lake when the scent of jasmine
perfume drifts through the house. One of the owners of Lakemont,
Becky Jabour, said that in 1978, she was giving a tour to Lakemont during Vicksburg's Pilgrimage Tours. She had finished talking about the
death of Dr. Lake and was in the process of talking about the spirit she
referred to as "The Perfume Lady" when there was a loud crash. She
walked into the front parlor and was shocked to find that a beautiful
Federal mirror hanging on the walk was cracked. Later that day, Becky
and her husband were sitting outside on the gallery when they detected
the strong scent of lavender perfume. Ann Lake, it seems, is reluctant
to leave the house where she had shared so many fond memories with
her husband, the judge.

CEDAR GROVE MANSION

John Alexander Klein was born in Virginia. When he arrived in Mississippi in the 1830s, he became one of the nineteenth-century entrepreneurs who perceived the economic potential of Vicksburg. His
business interests included lumber, cotton, and banking. He was also
an architect and jeweler. In 1840, he fell in love with fifteen-year-old
Elizabeth Bartley Day, who had come to New Orleans to visit relatives. Convinced that he had found his one true love, the young man
set about building a mansion that was worthy of her. John married

Elizabeth in 1842 and gave her Cedar Grove as a wedding present, even though the mansion was still under construction. At the time of their marriage, John was thirty, and Elizabeth was sixteen. The couple spent their honeymoon in Europe, where they purchased many of the furnishings that still grace the interior of Cedar Hall, such as the Italian marble fireplaces, Bohemian glass for the doorway, French empire gasoliers, exquisite clocks, gold-leaf mirrors, and paintings. The Kleins also traveled to New Orleans and commissioned Prudent Mallard to make several pieces of furniture. For the first ten years of their marriage, John and Elizabeth lived in a poolside cottage while workmen finished Cedar Grove. In 1852, the couple was finally able to move into their elegant mansion.

John and Elizabeth's marital bliss was briefly interrupted by the Civil War. While John rode off to fight for the Confederacy, Elizabeth remained at Cedar Grove, awaiting the birth of their child. Cedar Grove survived the siege of Vicksburg relatively unscathed, primarily because Elizabeth was related to General Sherman, who had her safely escorted behind Union lines so the she could give birth in relative safety. After her son was born, Elizabeth expressed her gratitude to the general by naming him William Tecumseh Sherman Klein. In her absence, Cedar Grove was used as a Union hospital. When Elizabeth finally returned to her beautiful home, she removed all traces of the Union occupation of Cedar Grove with the exception of a cannonball that is still embedded in one of the parlor walls.

By the time Ted and Estelle Mackey purchased Cedar Grove in 1983, the fine old Greek Revival mansion was just a shadow of its former self. They filled the house with period furnishings and cleaned and painted the rooms in an attempt to make the house look the way it did when John and Elizabeth Klein lived there. Some people say that Ted and Estelle did such a good job that the Klein family has moved back in.

The high levels of paranormal activity reported in Cedar Grove Mansion over the years can most likely be attributed to the young people who have met untimely ends in the house. Four of Elizabeth's ten children did not live to adulthood. Their first child died in the nursery when she was two years old. Several years later, an infant son died in the nursery at the age of two months. A young daughter died of a childhood disease in a second-floor bedroom. The Kleins' seventeen-year-old son, Willie, died when he was sitting on the back step with a friend after a hunting trip, and his rifle accidentally discharged. Some residents of Vicksburg believe that Elizabeth inadvertently cursed her son by naming him after William Tecumseh Sherman, who stayed at the house during the Civil War. Years later, the sister of a doctor who purchased Cedar Grove Mansion shot herself in the ballroom.

Testimony from guests and staff suggest that the spirits of all of the young people who died in Cedar Grove are reluctant to leave. Many people have heard the sound of children playing and laughing. Several people have heard the sound of a ball bouncing down the stairs and through the halls. People have heard the cries of a baby in the former nursery on days when no babies were in the bed and breakfast. The ghost of a little girl has been seen running up and down the steps leading to the second floor. Some staff members have speculated that the ghostly footsteps heard walking up the outside stairs are made by the ghost of Willie, who is still trying to enter the house after his fatal accident. Sometimes, a gunshot is heard in the ballroom where the young woman killed herself. A tour guide said that one morning she saw the apparition of a beautiful young woman standing in the ballroom. After a few seconds, she faded away.

According to eyewitnesses, the ghosts of John and Elizabeth Klein are also occupying Cedar Grove Mansion. Employees of the bed and breakfast say that the presence of pipe smoke in the gentleman's parlor is a sign that John Klein's ghost does not approve of the person smelling it. Guests and staff claim to have seen the ghost of Elizabeth Klein walking down the front stairs.

Unexplained noises echo through the house as well, usually at night. Many times, staff members have heard crashing noises coming from the basement. A former manager of the house was standing behind the desk when she heard the unmistakable sound of a body falling down the stairs. She rushed into the stairway and ran up the stairs. At first, she was relieved to find that no one was injured. Then it dawned on her that if a real person did not fall down the stairs, she must have heard a ghost.

The owners of Cedar Grove promote the beautiful old mansion as the perfect site for a romantic getaway. Indeed, the home that once entertained the likes of Jefferson Davis and Ulysses S. Grant offers visitors a taste of nineteenth-century elegance that is rarely found in the twenty-first century. They might also, if they are particularly sensitive to the paranormal, meet the spirits of the first family who lived there.

DUFF GREEN MANSION

In 1856, businessman Duff Green built his mansion as a wedding gift for his bride, Mary Lake. Prior to the Civil War, Duff and Mary threw lavish parties at the beautiful home, which had been designed for entertaining. The parties ended during the siege of Vicksburg. In 1863, the Duff Green Mansion was struck five times by Union cannon. The damage inflicted by one of the cannonballs is still visible in one of the ceiling beams of the mansion. To prevent the Yankees from destroying their beautiful home, the Greens surrendered the mansion to the Union army for use as a hospital. While Duff and Mary lived in two caves built in a side yard, both Union and Confederate soldiers received medical treatment in their home. Bloodstains on the main floor and the basement floor offer mute testimony to the surgical procedures that were performed in the house at this time. While she was living in the caves, Mary gave birth to a son, whom she named William Siege Green. Duff and Mary were finally able to move back into their mansion in 1866 after all of the Yankees had gone. The Green family continued to live in their home until Duff Green's death in 1880. That same year, Mary sold her home to the Peatross family. In 1910, the mansion was sold to Fannie Vick Willis Johnston, the great-granddaughter of Reverend Newet Vick, the founder of Vicksburg. After her new home, Oak Hall, was completed in 1913, Fannie donated the mansion for use as a boys' orphanage. Years later, the mansion was also used as a retirement home for elderly widows. In 1931, the Salvation Army purchased the Duff Green Mansion for $3,000. The Salvation Army served daily meals and offered temporary housing to transients in the historic home until 1985, when Mr. and Mrs. Harry Carter Sharp of Coral Gables, Florida, bought the Duff Green Mansion. With the money from the sale of the mansion, the Salvation Army was able to move into a much larger building.

Under its new ownership, the Duff Green Mansion was transformed into an inn. To ensure the accuracy of the renovation of the mansion, the Sharps and local architect Skip Tuminello consulted the U.S. Department of the Interior and the Mississippi Department of Archives and History. Over a two-year period, workers restored thirteen fireplaces and added fifteen bathrooms. Magnificent chandeliers hang from the ceilings of the fifteen-and-one-half foot tall public reception rooms. The Duff Green Mansion also features a swimming pool and a complimentary bar. Today, the Duff Green Mansion stands as one of the finest examples of Palladian architecture in Mississippi. Some of the visitors who spent the night in one of the five guest rooms have discovered very quickly why the Duff Green Mansion is featured in Vicksburg's ghost tours.

The psychic residue from the pain and suffering of the soldiers hospitalized at Duff Green Mansion has manifested itself in a number of different ways over the years. One of the basement rooms, the Dixie Room, was used as a makeshift operating room during the Civil War. The most common operation at the time was amputation. Routinely, amputated arms and legs were thrown out of the basement window to be carted away and disposed of later on. Many days, the pile of amputated appendages was several feet high before it was removed. In the 1980s, workmen who were remodeling the mansion found evidence that not all of the limbs were carried off. A few feet under the ground, workers found a number of skeletal arms and legs bearing the unmistakable marks of a surgical saw. The owners notified the police, who identified the bones as Civil War–era remains. The police, in turn, contacted a local funeral home, which interred the bones. Since that grisly discovery, a number of guests have reported seeing the apparition of a Confederate soldier with one leg standing by the mantel or rocking in a chair. Doctors and nurses who have stayed in the Dixie Room have detected the strong odor of ether. Only medical personnel seem to be able to smell it.

The spirits of two of the original occupants of Duff Green Mansion have also been sighted. Several members of the staff have seen the apparition of Mary Duff Green. She is usually described as a beautiful blonde woman in a green dress. Owner Harry Sharp said that one night he caught a glimpse of someone out of the corner of his eye. When he turned around, he saw the back of a woman wearing a green antebellum dress. She faded away after only a couple of seconds. A few weeks later, a cook named Brian Riley was standing over the stove stirring a pan full of grits when he felt small, female hands rubbing his shoulders. Riley has had over ten encounters with the ghost of the lady of the house. The ghost of the Greens' daughter, who died young, has also been seen running through the house and bouncing a ball. Several times, David Sharp and employee Lib Galloway have heard the patter of small feet running down the hallway when no children were present.

On October 31, 2009, the members of Mississippi Paranormal Research conducted an investigation of the Duff Green Mansion. One of the investigators named Angela saw a dark, shadowy form just as she crossed the threshold of the Confederate Room. When she was standing in the Dixie Room, Angela felt someone touch her. At the same time, another investigator named Amanda took a photograph of Angela. The resulting photograph clearly showed an orb hovering around Angela's side. The group caught a few hours sleep in the Camellia Room. Angela said that at 4:00 A.M., she felt a heavy pressure on her chest, as if someone or something were weighting her down. A few minutes later, Angela saw the image of a black woman in a navy-blue dress with an apron standing over her. The apparition dissipated in just a matter of seconds.

Visitors flock to Duff Green Mansion for several different reasons. People fascinated with antebellum architecture and period furnishings marvel at the richly decorated walls, the magnificent chandeliers, and the fifteen-and-one-half-foot reception room. Amateur historians pause to gaze at the impression of a cannonball in the ceiling beams and the bloodstains on the main floor and the basement floor, which bear mute witness to the operations that were performed there. Ghost hunters, however, are drawn to Duff Green Mansion by the legends and by the eyewitness testimony of guests and employees.

VICKSBURG NATIONAL MILITARY PARK

Situated atop a high bluff overlooking a hairpin turn of the Mississippi River, Vicksburg is a sleepy little river town, known for its antebellum homes, quaint gift shops, antique stores, fine restaurants, and the casino. However, in the early years of the Civil War, taking Vicksburg became the Union army's top priority. President Abraham Lincoln was keenly aware that as long as the Confederacy controlled Vicksburg, and by extension, the lower Mississippi River, the agricultural produce of the Northwest could never reach world markets. If Vicksburg fell into Union hands, the states of Texas, Arkansas, and Louisiana would be cut off, thereby depriving the southern states of desperately needed supplies and recruits.

In October 1862, Major General Ulysses S. Grant, commander of the Union Army of the Tennessee, was ordered to capture the city that President Lincoln called the "key" to winning the war. Grant recognized that this would not be an easy task. Vicksburg was protected by swamps to the north and south, by a ring of forts, and by a battery of artillery positioned along the riverfront. Following a series of failed attempts to take Vicksburg by amphibious operations and by digging a canal to bypass the city's batteries of artillery, Grant realized that the most prudent course of action would be to march down the west side of the Mississippi River and cross the river south of the city on naval transports. His army would then attack the city from the south or the east. To keep his army supplied, the Union navy would have to silence the Confederate's shore batteries.

On March 29, Grant's army of 45,000 men left their encampment on the Louisiana side of the Mississippi River and marched from New Carthage to Hard Times, building corduroy roads and bridges along the way. At 9:15 P.M. on April 16, the Union fleet under the command of Rear Admiral David Dixon Porter proceeded to run the Vicksburg batteries stationed along the Mississippi River. Suffering multiple hits and the loss of only one transport, Porter's fleet rendezvoused with

Grant south of Vicksburg. On April 30, 24,000 federals, under the command of Major General John A. McClernand and Major General James B. McPherson, gained the east bank of the Mississippi and proceeded to penetrate deep into Mississippi. Following Union victories at Port Gibson and Raymond, Grant's forces captured Jackson on May 14, thereby preventing General Joseph E. Johnston's forces from assisting with Lieutenant General John C. Pemberton's defense of Vicksburg. On May 16, General Pemberton's army made a last ditch attempt to stop the advance of General Grant's army at Champion Hill, but Grant prevailed. On May 17, the Federals drove the Confederates back to Vicksburg at Big Black River Bridge. The door was now open for the federal army to move into Vicksburg.

The siege of Vicksburg began on May 19. While Porter's fleet held the river, Grant's army lobbed shells into the city. To compensate for the lack of mortars, the Federals made mortars out of hollow logs wrapped in iron bands. The citizens of Vicksburg sought refuge in cellars and caves. On May 22, Grant's army sustained losses in excess of 3,000 men in two attempts to take the city by storm. Realizing that Vicksburg could not be taken by force, Grant decided to lay siege to the city. On May 26, Grant's forces dug a line of trenches fifteen miles long, virtually sealing off the city. Waiting for Vicksburg to surrender was almost as hard on Grant's tired, dirty, bored troops as it was for the citizens of Vicksburg, who were subsisting on whatever food they could find. Their stubborn resistance convinced Grant that another tactic would be needed to take the city. He decided to dig tunnels under the Confederate fortifications and blow them up with charges of black powder. The resulting explosion would enable the Federals to surge through the breaches and pour into Vicksburg. Grant's engineers proceeded to dig the tunnel in the direction of the Third Louisiana Redan through the first three weeks of June. Finally, on June 25 at 3:30 P.M., the fuse was lit. A great geyser of dirt rose in the air. When the dust and smoke cleared, the federals poured into the crater, only to be repulsed by the Confederates, who had thrown up an interior earthwork across the gorge of the Third Louisiana Redan. A second mine was exploded on July 1, but it was not followed by a second assault.

On July 3, General Pemberton and an escort of Confederate horsemen bearing white flags rode out from Vicksburg on the Jackson Road.

Pemberton met General Grant under the shade of a stunted oak tree not far from the Third Louisiana Redan to discuss the terms of surrender. Unable to reach an agreement, the two men returned to their respective camps. The men met again at 10:00 P.M. This time, Grant's terms were acceptable to the Confederates. Grant was offering parole to all of the defenders of Vicksburg. The next day at 10:00 A.M., the Confederates marched out of their fortifications and furled their flags. Their valiant defense of Vicksburg had ended.

The most commonly reported paranormal activity reported at and around the battlefield is fog. Jim Wilson, a Civil War buff, said that one cloudy winter's day he was walking near the area where over 3,000 federal soldiers died in a futile attempt to overtake the Confederate defenders of the city on March 22, 1863, when he spotted a cloud of fog appear from the woods. He could not help noticing that the fog seemed to follow the same route that the Union army took in its assault on the Confederate fortifications. Wilson described the fog as being between thirty yards long and ten yards wide. After the fog dissipated, Wilson realized that the fog was moving against the wind and that this particular spot was the only place in the battlefield that was foggy. At the time, Wilson was the only person at the site and the only witness to the strange cloud of fog.

A friend of Jim Wilson's had his own bizarre encounter with fog at the national cemetery. He was jogging near the cemetery as he was accustomed to doing after getting off work at the casino when he noticed a strange cloud of fog hovering over the graves. The fog appeared to be only about a foot high. No other part of the cemetery was blanketed by the fog.

McRAVEN

In 1797, Andrew Glass built a way station in the little town of Walnut Hills for pioneers traveling on the Natchez Trace. The brick house acquired the name "McRaven" because it was located on McRaven Street. The middle dining room and the bedroom above it were added by Sheriff Stephen Howard, who purchased the home in 1836. Howard's wife, Mary Elizabeth, died in childbirth in the middle bedroom that same year. In

1849, John H. Bobb built the Greek Revival section of the house. During the siege of Vicksburg in 1863, McRaven served as a field hospital and as a camping ground for Confederate soldiers. A number of the wounded soldiers who died in the house are rumored to have been buried on the grounds behind the house. McRaven was struck by cannonballs fired by both Union and Confederate forces during the siege.

In 1864, during the Union occupation of Vicksburg, Bobb returned home one day and discovered a band of drunken Union soldiers picking flowers from his garden. Bobb told the men to leave, but they refused. He picked up a brick and threw it at one of the soldiers, hitting him in the head. Bobb then went to the headquarters of General Henry W. Slocum, the federal commander of Vicksburg, and complained about the behavior of his men. When Bobb returned home, he was greeted by twenty-five angry Union soldiers, who dragged him one hundred yards from the house to Stout's Bayou and shot him. Bobb's widow, Selena, sold the house in 1869.

In 1882, William Murray and his wife, Ellen Flynn, purchased McRaven. He and his wife raised seven children in McRaven. William died in the house in 1891, and Ellen followed him in death ten years later. William and Ellen's spinster daughters, Annie and Ella, continued living in the house well into their old age. The Murray sisters refused to furnish the house with modern conveniences like electricity. Ironically, the sisters' refusal to enter the twentieth century preserved most of the house's eighteenth- and nineteenth-century features. After they entered their dotage, they chopped up some of their antique furniture and used it as firewood to keep warm. After Ella Murray died in 1960 at the age of eighty-one, her sister Annie sold McRaven and then moved into a nursing home.

The new owners of McRaven, the Bradway family, renovated the historic home and converted it into a tour home. In 1884, Leyland French purchased the home. He made additional improvements to the old house, such a bathroom and a modern kitchen, and reopened it as a tour home. French had no trouble attracting visitors eager to walk through one of the most famous haunted houses in the entire state.

The first reported haunting in McRaven took place during the Civil War. Following the fall of Vicksburg, the Union commander in charge of the city, Colonel J. H. Wilson, designated Confederate defector Captain James McPherson to act as liaison between the Union army and the citizens of Vicksburg. McPherson mysteriously disappeared while making his rounds one night and was never heard from again. *Late one evening, Colonel Wilson, who was staying at McRaven, entered his bedroom and was shocked to see McPherson's wet, dripping body sitting in a rocking chair. McPherson informed Wilson that he had been murdered by a mob who threw his body in the Mississippi River.*

Several ghosts have been sighted outside. The ghost of John Bobb has been sighted at Stout's Bayou where he was murdered. Bobb's apparition has also appeared in a corner of a room by McRaven's main foyer. The specters of Confederate soldiers who died in the old house and were buried on the property are said to wander around the trees and flowers in the yard.

Various members of the Murray family also make an occasional appearance at McRaven. The spirits of William Murray's unmarried daughters, Annie and Ella, have been sighted in different rooms inside the house. The ghost of their father, William, is said to be the most terrifying ghost currently haunting McRaven. *One evening in 1985, Leyland French was walking up the great flying-wing staircase when he turned around and saw a man standing on the landing. French recognized the face of the man he was staring at as belonging to William Murray, whose photographs are still in the house. As chills crept over his body, French ran up the stairs to Bobb's bedroom and slammed the door shut. A few weeks later, he was walking through the parlor to answer the phone and was pushed to his knees with such force that his glasses were pushed into his nose. The cuts on his face were so deep that he had to drive to Parkview Hospital, where he received five stitches. French was still not very concerned about his safety until a door inexplicably slammed shut on his hand, causing serious injury. The next day, he contacted an Episcopal priest, who performed an exorcism in an effort to cleanse McRaven of its negative energy.*

Sheriff Howard's wife, Mary, is said to haunt the middle bedroom upstairs where she died in childbirth at age fifteen. Her funeral notice hanging on the wall of the bedroom serves as a melancholy reminder of her tragic fate. Her ghost has been seen lying on the bed where she died and standing in a corner of her room. Mary Elizabeth's spirit has also manifested in the dining room and on the staircase. Tour guides say that her lamp has been known to turn itself on. Mary Elizabeth's wedding shawl also exhibits bizarre behavior at times. Some people say that it seems to be struggling to escape their grasp when they are holding it. Others say that the wedding shawl feels unusually warm at times.

Tour guides are a good source of information regarding paranormal activity at McRaven. Brian Riley worked as a tour guide at the antebellum mansion from May to December 2001: "We collected money for tours, we gave tours, and, if needed, we cleaned up a little. I'd grab the dust mop or broom and sweep in the carpeted area in the entranceway." Brian had has first ghostly encounter in McRaven shortly after he started working there. *"I was giving a tour one time to a high school group," Brian said. "Some of the people in the group kept saying that they were being touched. I saw them look around and ask, 'Who touched me?'"*

Shortly after this incident, Brian began noticing unusual sounds in the old house. "I heard footsteps a lot," Brian said. "That was a continuous thing. I heard them all over the house. That place had some kind of activity that went on around the clock. Mr. French told me that the activity continues all through the day and night, but at night, it's three times worse. I was there a couple of times by myself at night, and I heard a lot of strange noises."

None of McRaven's odd sounds really bothered Brian until July 4 when a couple of ghost hunters arrived at the mansion for an investigation. *"These two ladies were going through the house, and I was able to go with them," Brian said. "We left the dining room and were about to head up the stairs to the Frontier Bedroom, and it sounded like somebody was pressing a piano key a couple of times. I said, 'I think I heard something. I think it's coming from the parlor.' We went into the parlor, and there was nobody there. All of us heard the plinking of the piano key."*

Brian's most startling encounter occurred in August 2001. It was late in the evening, and he was getting ready to turn off the lights in the 1836 Bedroom, where Mary Elizabeth spent much of her time. *"I walked in there, and Mary Elizabeth was standing right there in the window, looking out on the balcony," Brian said. "I could see the form of a woman from head to toe. She was transparent. At first, chills traveled all across my arms. As she faded away into thin air, I just stood there, frozen. Then I rushed through the room. I turned out the lights and ran out the door. This was the first full-bodied apparition I had ever seen. That incident will always stay with me."*

In 2007, Leyland French put McRaven up for sale. As of this printing, the old mansion stands vacant, waiting for the next intrepid owner who is willing to share his home with the spirits of the former occupants. After all, McRaven is not just a place where one can get in touch with history. As Leyland French and others would testify, sometimes the past at McRaven touches back.

Missouri

NEW MADRID

Two French brothers, Francois and Joseph Lesieur, started the settlement that eventually grew into the town of New Madrid. They were followed by hundreds of French settlers from Canada. In 1789, Colonel George Morgan from New Jersey brought fifty to sixty immigrants from Maryland and Pennsylvania to a tract of land he had purchased from the Spanish government one mile below New Madrid. The area was devastated by over one thousand earthquakes that struck between 1811 and 1812.

THE HUNTER-DAWSON HOUSE

New Madrid is located in southeast Missouri's Bootheel region, on a bend of the Mississippi River, and it was an ideal location for trade. During the first half of the nineteenth century, New Madrid became a thriving river port. One of the city's most prosperous businessmen was William Hunter, whose large dry-goods store, the Crystal Palace, earned him a fortune. Hunter also ferried goods to towns along the Mississippi River and operated a gristmill and lumber mill. In the years just before the Civil War, William and his wife, Amanda, became so wealthy that they were able to buy 15,000 acres of land in four states. In 1859, the Hunters began planning a magnificent mansion fashioned in the Georgian, Greek Revival, and Italianate architectural styles. It was constructed of yellow cypress that was milled in their own sawmill. Some of the Hunters' slaves served as workers on the house. Before work on the house was completed in April 1860, William Hunter died of yellow fever. William's widow and her seven children moved into the mansion between 1860 and 1861. Amanda's brother managed her husband's business interests.

Unlike many antebellum homes, Amanda Hunter's mansion did not really feel the impact of the Civil War. According to family folklore, during the battle of Island No. 10 and the siege of New Madrid, Union troops under the command of General John Pope occupied the Hunter plantation. Miraculously, both the Hunter family and the house itself passed through the Civil War unharmed. In fact, only one son fought in the war—for the Confederacy.

The post–Civil War years brought some important changes to the Hunter family. In 1874, Amanda's youngest daughter—Ella—married William Dawson. Following Amanda's death in 1876, Ella and her new husband inherited the plantation. William went on to an illustrious career in politics. He served three terms in the Missouri State Legislature. He was also elected to the U.S. House of Representatives in 1884. In 1898, William was appointed to the planning committee for the World's Fair Exposition in Chicago.

Descendants of the Dawson family continued living in the family home until 1958. In 1966, the house was purchased by the city of New Madrid, which, in turn, sold the Hunter-Dawson House to the state for one dollar in 1967. After the house was completely restored, it was opened for tours in 1981. The fifteen-room antebellum mansion survives as a remnant of the luxurious lifestyle of the Bootheel's wealthiest families. Some people believe that the spirits of the occupants of the Hunter-Dawson House have survived as well.

Rumors about the ghostly inhabitants of the Hunter-Dawson House began to circulate around New Madrid soon after the mansion became a house-museum in 1981. Just a few days after the mansion opened its doors to visitors, people began hearing footsteps on both floors. They also detected the distinctive smell of lavender water and cigar smoke. One day, a longtime resident of the area was talking in the front yard with a female tour guide when he happened to look up at one of the windows in the ladies' sitting room. He clearly saw a woman dressed in a nineteenth-century dress, staring into the distance. Later, the man said that the woman had a very distracted look on her face, as if her mind were a million miles away. One day, while he was staring at a portrait of Amanda Hunter in the ladies' sitting room, the man realized that this was the woman he had seen staring out the window.

The paintings in the ladies' and the men's sitting rooms also appear to be imbued with the spirits of William and Amanda Hunter. William's portrait hangs over the fireplace in the men's sitting room, and a portrait of Amanda and her infant son, Harvey, hangs over the fireplace in the ladies' sitting room. Tourists have noticed that Amanda's and Harvey's eyes seem to follow them around the room, regardless of where they are standing. The two rooms are separated by pocket doors. Not long after the house was opened for tours, the tour guides had difficulty keeping them from falling off the walls. One day, one of the tour guides who had become tired of re-hanging the fallen portraits propped them up on the floor against one of the walls in the men's sitting room and told William and Amanda that there was no reason for them to express their displeasure at being separated. She explained to the married couple that even though their portraits hung in separate rooms, the rooms were interconnected. She told the portraits to behave themselves and hung them back on the walls. The portraits have been hanging in the sitting rooms without incident ever since.

A restless spirit is said to occupy the guest room. Tour guides straighten up the bed every afternoon just before closing. The next morning, the bed in the guest room appears to have been slept in. The covers are in disarray, and the impression of a sleeping body is clearly visible in the mattress.

For the most part, the spirits of the Hunter-Dawson House are kindly spirits who mean no harm to those who encounter them. However, the very close encounters with the paranormal have proven to be particularly unnerving. For example, one of the tour guides was standing in the hallway on the second floor, talking to a tour group, when he felt a hand grasp his elbow. He said it felt as if someone was trying to get his attention. The tour guide turned around and was shocked to see that none of the tourists were standing behind him.

Tourists have had terrifying experiences on the second floor. One afternoon, a lady on one of the tours informed the tour guide that she was a clairvoyant and that she sensed a presence in the house. After the tour, the lady walked upstairs while the tour guide was saying goodbye to the rest of the group. Suddenly, the people downstairs heard a blood-curdling scream. Then the sensitive woman ran downstairs, obviously very distraught. When she regained her composure, she explained that she had seen something in one of the rooms, but she would not say what it was.

A twenty-one-year-old tour guide also had a horrifying experience on the second day. Late one afternoon, she unlocked the front door and began walking into the house when she heard a very loud female voice say from the top of the stairs, "I'm back here." Knowing that she was the only person inside the house at the time, she ran back out of the front door and across the yard to the office. As she sat in the office, shaking uncontrollably, she informed one of the tour guides that she was not going back into the house for the rest of the day.

The first floor has also had its share of paranormal occurrences. One morning, two tour guides were standing in the kitchen talking when they heard a thumping sound coming from the side porch just off the kitchen. They looked out the window and were amazed to see one of the three rocking chairs rocking by itself. It was rocking so forcefully that it was banging against the outside of the kitchen wall. There was not a breeze in the air at the time. They tried to get the attention of one of the more skeptical administrators, but by the time he walked into the kitchen, the rocker had stopped moving.

A few months later, the Hunter-Dawson House was hosting a special occasion. All of the tour guides and even the administrators were dressed up in period dress for the event. Two of the tour guides were talking in the kitchen when one of the administrators walked through the door. He was dressed in a long black coat and a top hat. One of the tour guides had just said "Hello" when, out of the corner of his eye, he caught a glimpse of another male figure wearing a black coat and hat walk into the kitchen. Within two or three seconds, the apparition was gone.

Some tourists have inadvertently collected support for the mansion's ghost stories. In the sitting room on the first floor, tourists who have taken digital photographs of an antique bookcase have captured the images of faces in the glass. The daughter of one of the tour guides filmed a spectral woman walking across the room in front of the bookcase with her video camera. In the children's room, tourists have caught the image of a blue dress in a mirror. The body of the woman wearing the dress is barely visible. On December 29, 2009, my wife, Marilyn, was taking pictures in the oldest boy's bedroom. In one of her photographs, three orbs are clearly visible. In the largest of the orbs, one can see what appears to be a face.

Despite the fact that most of the original plantation behind the Hunter-Dawson has been converted into a subdivision, the old mansion maintains much of its nineteenth-century splendor. Three of the outbuildings—a grain shed, the carriage house, and an outhouse with six seats—are still standing. Eighty-five percent of the furnishings inside the house belonged to William and Amanda Hunter. Perhaps this is the reason why the ghosts of the original owners seem to be reluctant to leave.

ST. LOUIS

Colonial French traders Rene Auguste Chouteau and Pierre Laclede founded St. Louis in 1764 just south of the junction of the Mississippi and Missouri Rivers in 1764. They named the city after King Louis IX of France. After the Seven Years' War, Spain took control of St. Louis, but the city was returned to French control in 1800. In 1803, Napoleon Bonaparte sold the city to the United States. The arrival of the *Zebulon M. Pike* on July 27, 1817, ushered in the steamboat era in St Louis. In the 1840s, waves of immigrants from Ireland, Germany, and Bohemia flooded into St. Louis. Primarily because St. Louis sided with the Union, the city survived the Civil War virtually unscathed, except for the loss of its lucrative markets in the South. On August 22, 1876, St. Louis seceded from St. Louis County and became independent. In the twentieth century, a number of large companies grew up in St. Louis, including Anheuser-Busch, the Brown Shoe Company, Ralston-Purina, and the St. Louis division of the Curtiss-Wright Aircraft Company. Because St. Louis was the fourth largest city in the country in 1900, it was chosen to host the World's Fair of 1904. The city's revitalization efforts included the building of the new Busch Stadium in 2006.

THE LEMP MANSION

America's Gilded Age in the second half of the nineteenth century is known for the rise of entrepreneurs like Cornelius Vanderbilt and Andrew Carnegie. Some of the wealthiest of these enterprising businessmen were the German immigrants who made their fortune brewing beer. In the early nineteenth century, most of the German brewers were producing only top-fermented English styles and stouts. However, after the arrival of bottom-fermented lager beer yeast from Europe in the 1840s and 1850s, German brew masters were able to brew the type of Bavarian-style lagers and golden pilsners that reminded the thousands of German immigrants of home. By the mid-1870s, the number of breweries in America had risen to 4,000. By 1900, the nation's beer production had grown from approximately 10 million barrels per year to 40 million barrels per year. Beer-making dynasties took root all over the United States. One of the most prosperous—and tragic—of these German dynasties was the Lemp family in St. Louis, Missouri.

In 1838, Johann Adam Lemp arrived in St. Louis from Eschwege, Germany. His first business enterprise, a small store on Delmar and Sixth Street, sold household items, but his best-selling item was beer that he brewed himself. Lemp's beer was a light, golden lager that offered a pleasing alternative to the dark, English ales that the German immigrants were drinking. In 1845, Lemp founded a small factory at 112 Second Street, very close to the site where the Gateway Arch now stands. He transported the beer to a cool cavern at Cherokee and De Merill Place to allow the lager to run its course. By the 1850s, the Lemp's Western Brewing Company was one of the largest breweries in St. Louis. After Adam Lemp died on August 25, 1862, his son William Sr. took over the family business. William Sr.'s expansion plans for the brewery included absorbing a five-block area around the lagering caves. The Lemp Western Brewery Company achieved a national reputation in the 1890s with the production of its immensely popular Falstaff beer. In fact, Lemp's company was the first brewery to distribute its beer coast to coast.

Flush with money, William Sr. decided to purchase a house suitable for a man of his wealth and standing. In 1876, he bought a mansion that his father-in-law, Jacob Feickert, had built in 1868. Because the mansion was just a short distance from the Lemp Brewery, William intended to use it as an auxiliary brewery office and as his private residence. His thirty-three-room showplace included a tunnel leading to the cave that Johann Adam Lemp had discovered. One large chamber was transformed into an auditorium and theater. Just twenty-two feet from the auditorium was a large concrete lagering pool that William converted into a swimming pool.

Despite the fact that the Lemp family had acquired many of the trappings of wealth, their personal lives were anything but pleasant. In 1901, William Sr.'s favorite son, Frederick, died of heart failure at the age of twenty-eight. Many people close to the Lemp family believed that Frederick, who was being groomed to take over the family business, worked himself to death. In 1904, William Sr.'s best friend, Frederick Pabst, passed away. Devastated by the loss of the two most important people in his life, William Sr. shot himself in the head on February 13, 1904.

In 1904, William Jr. inherited the brewery and the family's legacy of suffering and tragedy. He and his wife, the former Lillian Handlan, filled the family home with priceless works of art, closets stuffed with expensive clothes, and lavish furnishings. William's happiness as heir apparent of the family fortune was short-lived, however. In 1906, William Jr.'s mother died of cancer. Three years later, William Jr. was involved in a bitter divorce from Lillian. Lillian not only charged him with entertaining prostitutes in the caves below the mansion, but she also accused him of fathering a son with Down syndrome by another woman. The child, known in the neighborhood as "Monkey Boy," was said to be kept in the attic, safely tucked away from public scrutiny. In 1911, William Jr. made a number of structural changes to the mansion, including the addition of an immense bay window on top of the atrium. The front part of the mansion was converted into private offices and rooms for clerks.

Most of America's breweries incurred tremendous losses during World War I, but the Lemp Brewery suffered the most because William Jr. had not made technological improvements in the brewery's antiquated machinery. Prohibition finished off the Lemp Brewery for good. Convinced that Congress would never repeal Prohibition, William decided to close the plant without notifying the workers. He also sold the Falstaff brand name to brewer Joseph Griesedieck for $25,000. In 1922, William Jr. sold the brewery to the International Shoe Company for only $588,000.

Now that he was rid of the family business, which he had never shown much interest in, William was prepared to live the rest of his life in luxury. However, not even his immense wealth could insulate William Jr. and his family from suffering. In 1920, his sister, Elsa Lemp Wright, shot herself in her bedroom. For some mysterious reason, her husband did not contact the police for two hours. William Jr. sank into depression soon after the sale of the family brewery and shot himself in the heart with a .38 caliber revolver in his mansion office on December 22, 1922, shortly after speaking to his wife on the telephone. William Jr.'s brother, Charles Lemp, who had distanced himself from the brewery, was not immune to the "curse" that seemed to have singled out the Lemp family. Charles, who had forged a successful career in politics and banking, remained in the family mansion with only two servants and William Jr.'s illegitimate son. On May 10, 1949, Charles shot himself in his bedroom with a .38 caliber Army Colt revolver. He was buried on his farm, the location of which has never been determined. Edwin Lemp, who had a pathological fear of being alone, lived in his estate in Kirkwood, Missouri, from 1911 until he died of natural causes at the age of ninety in 1970. Before his death, he burned all of the Lemp family's paintings, documents, and artifacts.

Today, all that remains of the Lemp family is the brewery and the mansion. The fourteen-acre Lemp Brewery complex continued development through the 1950s under the ownership of the International Shoe Company. Following Charles's suicide in 1949, the mansion was converted into a boardinghouse. In the 1970s, the house began to deteriorate. Dick Pointer and his family purchased the old house in 1975 and rescued it from its imminent decline. Today, the Lemp Mansion is one of the most popular bed and breakfasts in Missouri.

Rumors about the ghosts in the Lemp Mansion first surfaced during its years as a boardinghouse in the 1950s. Boarders complained about hearing disembodied footsteps and knocking sounds on doors and walls. However, the mansion's haunted reputation was not cemented until the new owners, Dick and his sister, Patti Pointer, began renovating it between 1975 and 1977. Workers reported hearing doors slam, gunshots, laughs, cries, and voices calling their names. They also felt as if they were being watched by unseen eyes. Occasionally, tools that the workers placed in a specific spot before leaving were inexplicably moved to a different location the next morning. In his book *Lemp: The Haunting History*, Stephen P. Walker tells the story of a painter named Claude Breckwoldt, who was working on the ceiling in the parlor when he was overcome by the feeling that an invisible entity was looking at him. One day, Breckwoldt was restoring the parlor ceiling when he heard someone call his name. After working on the house for a few days, the usually reclusive painter encouraged people to watch him work. In an interview with Steve Mainer of the Southern Illinois University-Edwardsville *Focus* in 1981, Dick Pointer said that one of the men who worked on the ceilings stayed in an apartment in the mansion. One morning, he told the Pointers that he had heard the sound of horses' hooves on cobblestones during the night. The Pointers did not take him very serious because they had no knowledge of any cobblestone walkways or roads on the property. A few weeks later, patches of dead grass began appearing in the back yard. When Pointer dug up the grass, he discovered cobblestones leading to the carriage house.

Patti Pointer said that when the old house was being renovated, her mother and father and her brothers said that they often felt like someone was watching. However, because no one was ever there when they turned around, they believed that their minds were playing tricks on them. *One night in 1976, Dick was in the house by himself on the second floor. "He was pretty much locked in except for the back door," Patti said. "My brother had a Doberman Pincer named 'Shadow' because she was his shadow. She followed him everywhere. He couldn't shake her. So one evening, we had all gone home, and Dick went to bed. He was an avid reader, so he was reading in bed. The house was in shambles. Shadow was lying at the end of the bed when she suddenly started growling. Then she started barking. Her ears went up, and she hopped off the bed and ran to the door. She was really upset. Dick didn't hear anyone break in, but he figured he had better investigate anyway. All he had was Shadow*

and an umbrella. Dick went down the servants' staircase to the base-
ment and checked all of the doors and windows on the first floor. Noth-
ing was awry. Shadow was still barking, so he went back upstairs to the
second floor. He looked in all the rooms and checked the windows. Noth-
ing. He thought he had them trapped in the attic, so he went up to the
first landing. Shadow was still with him. He made his way to the second
landing, and Shadow stopped. She lay down. Her ears were down. She
was moaning and crying. She wouldn't get up, so he left her and checked
the attic. There was nothing, so he called home and told the story."

·After the restaurant opened, the Pointers began getting more and
more news coverage. *In 1979, a television show called* Real People *fea-*
tured the Pointers and their spooky old house. After the show aired, the
Pointers were inundated with requests from people eager to investigate
the Lemp Mansion. One of the best applicants was a psychic. "She was
able to back up what some of the researchers had found," Patti said. "She
went up the back stairs and into the attic. She walked up to the first
landing, but she stopped at the second landing. She asked Patti's mother
if they had any pets in the house. She said no. The psychic replied, 'It's
so terrible. I have an impression of a short-haired German dog that
died here.' We didn't know what she was talking about. Six years later,
the granddaughter of Charles Lemp's manservant stopped by the Lemp
Mansion. She had just left the Charles Lemp Room on the second floor.
She and Patti were about to step on the landing when the granddaughter
said, 'It's so terrible what [Charles Lemp] did to his dog. He had the most
beautiful red Doberman called Serva. He shot him here right here on the
landing, just before he killed himself.' When I heard that, the hair on the
back of my neck stood up." Since then, a number of guests have heard the
panting of a dog and the clicking of its nails in the back stairway. A few
have even felt a dog brushing up against them. This is possibly the spirit
of the dog that Charles Lemp killed shortly before killing himself.

The ghosts became even more active after the Pointers opened up
the mansion as a bed and breakfast. Doors lock and unlock by themselves. The lilting notes from a ragtime piano echo through the first
floor late at night. Lights flicker on and off. Some guests have been
awakened during the night by an invisible hand that strokes their head
in a comforting manner. Others have had personal possessions like cell

phones turn up in strange places. Occasionally, guests receive phantom telephone calls late in the evening. In the dining area in the living room, staff members have encountered a strange man sitting at a table who disappears when asked what he is doing there. Some people have been touched there as well. The ghost of Lillian Lemp, known as the "Lavender Lady" because of her fondness for lavender dresses, has been seen gliding down the hallways on the second and third floors. In the downstairs women's restroom, women have caught the sight of a ghostly face peering down at them from the top of one of the stalls. A few guests dining in the Atrium Room, where the Lemp family once housed exotic plants and birds, have heard phantom bird songs. Many guests have complained about hearing someone banging on the door to their room early in the morning. Dick Pointer discovered the reason when he read in an old newspaper interview with William Lemp Sr. that he kicked on the doors to his sons' rooms every morning because they were too lazy to get up on their own. Even the current owner, Paul Pointer, has had strange experiences in the mansion. One day, his sister asked him to shut a door in a drawing room on the first floor. Seconds after he did so, the door slowly opened by itself.

Ghostly sightings have occurred on two of the suites on the second floor as well. In the William Lemp Suite, guests have seen the ghost of an old man sporting a two-inch beard in the sitting room by the window. The specter has also appeared close to the sliding door leading to the bedroom. Guests have also sensed the presence of an entity near an antique clothes closet. Sometimes, guests hear a man running up the staircase and kicking the door. In the Lavender Lady Suite, guests have detected the odor of lavender perfume. At times, the aroma is so strong that it even permeates the furniture. People using the bathroom claim to have seen a shadowy figure slip through a crack in the bathroom door. Some guests told the management that they locked up the room before they left for the evening, but when they returned, they found the door standing wide open.

Most of the reports of ghostly activity center around three areas in the old house. In the basement dining room, which the staff refers to as "The Gates of Hell," psychics have reported the presence of an angry spirit that walks back and forth in front of the sealed entrance to the caves running beneath the mansion and the brewery. Tablecloths have flown off the tables when patrons and guest have turned their backs. Tables that have been arrayed have been disrupted and moved as well. Staff and guests have seen glasses rise off the bar and fly through the air. Swizzle sticks have been seen stirring drinks by themselves. *Stephen P. Walker recounts the story of a bartender in the restaurant who was on his way downstairs to clean up. When he reached the bottom of the stairs, he noticed a well-dressed, middle-aged man standing there with a peaceful smile on his face. The bartender could tell immediately that the man was not real because of his translucent appearance.* During a paranormal investigation of the basement, an investigator who tried to photograph a wispy shape near an archway was surprised to find that his digital camera had captured an orb instead. Unseen eyes seem to follow patrons and staff around the basement. The main stairway also seems to be a hot spot of paranormal activity. A number of people have photographed orbs on the stairway with still and video cameras. People standing on the first floor have felt as if someone standing on the stairway was watching them. The most haunted room in the entire house is the attic. Supposedly, it is haunted by the pathetic spirit of Billy Lemp's illegitimate son, the "Monkey Boy." People passing by outside the house have seen the sad face of a Down syndrome child peering from the attic window. Paranormal investigators who left a few toys in the room in specific places found that the little toy soldiers and animals and little balls had been moved. One of the investigators felt an unseen hand pulling on his hair. The little ghost, who is obviously starved for love and attention, has aroused both fear and pity in guests who have heard his spectral voice plead, "Come play with me" in the attic.

Not surprisingly, Patti Pointer has had her own share of ghostly encounters over the years. *One Sunday night in 1990, she and Dick were sitting in the bar, which was located in what is now the main dining room on the first floor. "On Sundays, we had a real casual dinner—fried chicken, all you can eat. Dick was telling me how I should be running the kitchen," Patti said. "So I was listening and nodding, but not really paying attention. I was looking right past him. We had candles on either side of the mantel in the main dining room. They weren't lit because this was an informal Sunday night. Suddenly, one of the candles lit up by itself. My face was flush, and he asked me what was wrong. I told him that the candle lit up thirty seconds ago. He told me to go blow it out, but I said, 'I'm not going in there. You blow it out!' So we both went in, and there was no melted wax that would have collected if the candle had been burning for a while. We said, 'Well, good night. We'll see you tomorrow,' and we left."*

Patti had another bizarre experience in the bar one night when she was alone in the house with her brother Paul and her boyfriend at the time, who worked as a waiter in the Lemp Mansion. *She was on the first floor, and Paul and her boyfriend were upstairs in the office. Suddenly, she heard someone moving around on the first floor. She yelled up to her boyfriend that someone else was inside the house.* "My boyfriend came down and looked around," Patti said. "There was nobody here. I thought it was trucks from the highway causing the place to vibrate, so we sat in the bar, waiting for my brother to come. For whatever reason, we were both seated in the bar, facing straight ahead and talking. All at once, I looked away from him, and he said, 'What's wrong?' I said, 'I saw somebody walk by the door.' He looked toward the door, but he couldn't see anyone. So we switched seats, and then after a few minutes, he saw someone walk by the door. It was like a Three Stooges' routine. Five minutes later, there was a very quiet whoosh of air. Then complete silence. The next day, my boyfriend and I were talking, and he said, 'Did you feel anybody walk behind you in the bar last night?' I said, 'Yeah, did you?' He said, 'Yeah, but I thought you'd think I was a weirdo for saying it.'"

One of Patti's most terrifying experiences inside the Lemp Mansion occurred in 2003. *She and her nephew Matthew were getting ready to lock up the house for the night.* "Generally, when we leave, we lock everything up. Then we go through the kitchen and out the back door," Patti said. "I was on the front porch, and I said, 'Where's my purse?' Before I could even lock the door, I spun around and went right back through the doors. When I crossed the threshold of the front door, I felt this cold chill. It was overpowering. The hair on my arms stood up. It terrified me. My nephew asked me what was wrong. I told him to go inside and get my purse. I went right back outside. That never happened again to me. It was really unnerving."

The local media has also been involved in the investigations of the Lemp Mansion in recent years. One of the local radio stations broadcasts from the old house every Halloween. *One year, the radio station brought over ten people the week before Halloween. They had all submitted e-mails stating whey they wanted to spend the night with no electricity in the Lemp Mansion. "They sent them all on little missions," Patti said. "I was here with one of the servers. We took care of them. Finally, the DJ picked the winner. She was excited and happy. He told her that if she got too scared, so could only leave by the back door. Before leaving, he and the rest of the crew unscrewed all of the light bulbs. Then the maintenance guy cut the power. I thought it was weird that the radio was still on, so I yelled down at the guy to cut the power. He said, 'There is no power.' I said, 'The radio's still playing.' He came upstairs, and the radio continued playing for about a minute and a half. Now this poor woman was really, really scared. I felt bad about having to leave her there all alone. About 3:30 A.M., she called the radio station and said, 'Guys, I gotta get out of here. There's somebody up here with me. I'm telling you, I'm terrified. I don't know what to do. Can you send someone?' They said they could, but if they did, she wouldn't win the prize, so they talked her into staying. When the radio guys returned to the Lemp Mansion at 6:00 A.M., the woman was huddled up by the back door in one of the comforters she had dragged off the bed."*

A few years later, a television crew inadvertently recorded evidence of the paranormal at the Lemp Mansion. Patti Pointer said, *"One year around Halloween, there was a real estate show in town. This was on a Saturday morning. A camera crew arrived to interview my mother about buying and selling real estate. The interviewer began by asking her a few questions about the history of the house. Then he asked her to tell some ghost stories. She told them the story about Shadow and my brother Dick. After a couple of minutes, the producer of the show turned to the soundman and said, 'Play that back. I want to hear the audio.' So he played it back, and it was just a dog barking. My mother—the biggest nonbeliever who ever lived—said, 'What's that?' The producer said, 'That's the audio from your story.' She said, 'It can't be. That's a dog barking.' The whole interview was nothing but a series of barks."*

In recent years, the Pointers have invited people to investigate the Lemp Mansion for a twenty-five-dollar fee. The event is held every other Thursday night. *"The guests go through the house with infra-red cameras that a paranormal group supplied us. We turn off the lights downstairs and on the two floors upstairs. The guests search for orbs or mists or whatever else they might find,"* Patti said. *"On April 2, 2010, one of the researchers came downstairs and asked me, 'Is somebody smoking a cigar?' I said no. She said, 'Come upstairs.' So I went upstairs, and it smelled like someone had started smoking a cigar. It was so overwhelming."*

Even though a few guests have been too frightened to spend the entire night at the Lemp Mansion, Paul Pointer, the current owner, is not overly concerned that his bed and breakfast is haunted. In fact, Pointer is proud of the fact that in 1980, *Life* magazine listed the Lemp Mansion as one of the nine most-haunted places in America. He believes that the presence of ghosts in his house has been good for business. "People come here expecting to experience weird things," he said, "and they have not been disappointed."

THE EDGEWOOD CHILDREN'S CENTER

The St. Louis Association of Ladies for the Relief of Orphan Children was founded in 1834 by Episcopal, Methodist, and Presbyterian women to care for the large number of orphans produced by the cholera epidemic of 1832. In 1848, the orphanage changed its named to the St. Louis Protestant Orphans' Asylum after expanding its services. In 1865, the orphanage merged with the Soldiers' Orphans' Home of Webster Groves. The St. Louis Protestant Orphans' Asylum moved from its north St. Louis location to the Rock House in Webster Groves, a southwest St. Louis suburb. Reverend Artemus Bullard built the Rock House in 1850 as a seminary for young men. Bullard, an ardent abolitionist, was rumored to have used the Rock House as a way station on the Underground Railroad. Local legend has it that a tunnel running under the Rock House served as a hiding place for slaves. Supposedly, the exit was closed off in 1890 after two children perished in the tunnel when they were unable to find their way out. In 1910, a devastating fire roared through the St. Louis Protestant Orphans' Asylum; one child died in the blaze. Although the interior of the building was completely destroyed, the stone exterior remained intact. After a period of extensive renovation, the orphanage once again took up residence in the former Rock House. In 1944, the St. Louis Protestant Orphans' Asylum changed its name to Edgewood Children's Center to reflect its shifting focus toward meeting the needs of emotionally disturbed children. Some say that the childish laughter that echoes off the walls of the former orphanage might be ghostly in origin.

One of the ghosts in the Edgewood Children's Center is the spirit of a little girl the staff has christened "Rachel." Her disembodied footsteps have been heard in empty hallways of the old Rock House. Her footsteps have also been heard running up a staircase that was removed years ago. Adults living on the second floor of the building claim that objects are sometimes relocated in a different place by an unseen hand. Some of the more "sensitive" residents report feeling very uneasy in several of the rooms.

Ghostly activity has also been reported outside of the Edgewood Children's Center. The ghost of a ten-year-old girl has been sighted in the vicinity of an old cottonwood tree. In recent years, the ghosts of several children have been seen playing tag in the vicinity of the cottonwood tree as well.

Most people who are familiar with the history of the old orphanage have identified the ghosts as the spirits of the little girls who died in the tunnel in 1890 and the child who burned to death in 1910. If they are correct, then these spirits might have returned to the school because it was the only home they ever knew.

THE GEHM HOUSE

Webster Groves is an upscale suburb in southwestern St. Louis. In 1890, Bart Adams built his two-story house on the 300 block of Plant Avenue as a summer retreat. In 1906, a German immigrant named Henry Gehm rented the house. Gehm was an eccentric loner who never associated with his neighbors. Gehm worked for a railroad car company that leased cars to traveling circuses. Because Gehm never spoke to anyone about himself or anyone else, rumors spread that he was connected with the circus somehow. People also said that Henry Gehm hoarded gold coins and hid them in the house because he did not trust the banks. In 1944, Henry Gehm died of cancer of the spine in a hospital, not in the house, as many people have said.

The ghost stories began in 1956 when the S. L. Furry family bought the house. Fanny Furry was the first member of her family to sense that something was not right about the house. She said that soon after she and her family moved into the house, she was shaken awake every night at 2:00 by an unseen presence. One night, she was awakened by someone banging a hammer against the headboard of her bed. When she turned on the light, she was surprised to find that the headboard was not damaged at all. A few days later, a sconce fell off the wall. Over the next few weeks, she began hearing disembodied footsteps walking up and down the stairs.

Before long, the other family members began having weird experiences that supported Fanny's stories. One night, her husband woke up and saw a milky-white shape pass through the door into the hallway. He leaped out of bed and followed the entity to his youngest daughter's bedroom. When he entered the room, the ghostly shape was gone. The couple's three-year-old daughter also had an encounter in the house. At breakfast one day, she told her parents that an old lady in a black dress walked into her room every night with a little boy. On one occasion, the old lady spanked the little girl with a broom, but the child said the spanking did not hurt. Eventually, the ghost of the old lady appeared to everyone in the family.

In 1965, the Furry family moved out of the old house, and the Walsh family moved in. One evening, the family dog began shaking uncontrollably. Claire Walsh, who was cooking dinner at the time, walked over to comfort the dog. She glanced over at the doorway and saw a blurry white form the same size as a human being. The shape floated into the living room and disappeared. In the next few months, other strange things happened in the house: footsteps were heard stomping up and down the stairs; soft, indistinct voices were heard in certain parts of the house; dresser drawers were pulled out; clothing was strewn about; a typewriter began typing on its own; a broken music box started playing music; the attic door opened and closed on its own.

After a few months, the Walsh family became familiar with specific spirits within their house. The ghost of a little girl made her presence known by crying in the middle of the night. The family also found the handprints and footprints of a child in the attic around a dollhouse. On March 1, 1966, Claire came face to face with Henry Gehm himself. She said that the ghost showed her a hidden doorway in the attic, which led to a secret chamber. When the family decided that enough was enough, they contacted the man who had the rented the house to them and told him that they were going to leave as soon as construction of their new house was completed.

The next—and last—family to occupy the Gehm House was the Wheeler family. June and Robert Wheeler are convinced that the old house is haunted. Their German shepherd, Andy, was often seen standing at the top of the stairs with his tail straight up, staring at something only he could see. One night, June opened the door to the walk-in pantry and almost walked into a white figure. She quickly shut the door and collected her thoughts. June concluded that one of her children was covered with flour from playing in the pantry. Angry, she reopened the door. Nothing was there, not even loose flour on the floor.

In an interview conducted with Robbi Courtaway in 1999, June Wheeler said that she had an even closer encounter with the ghost one night when she was trying to fall asleep in the room next to her bedroom. At 2:00 A.M., she pulled the blanket up to her face, only to feel it being pulled back a few seconds later. It felt as if someone was trying to tuck in the blanket at the foot of the bed. After pulling the blanket back up to her head the fourth time, June felt a hand pushing on her back. Terrified, she fell off the bed, but her legs were paralyzed; she fell to the floor. June tried to scream, but no sounds came from her throat. After a few minutes, she was able to crawl across the floor. By the time she reached the door, her voice returned, and she called to her husband, who was annoyed at being awakened in the middle of the night.

Despite the fact that the peace of their happy home has been disrupted on numerous occasions, the Wheelers do not feel that their ghosts are malicious. Referring to the ghosts' tendency to disrupt his office and scatter his books and papers around, Robert Wheelers believes that at least one of their spirits enjoys reading books. Consequently, June believes that their ghosts are more respectable than the garden variety of spirits.

THE CUPPLES HOUSE

Samuel Cupples was born in Harrisburg, Pennsylvania, on September 13, 1831, to James and Elizabeth Cupples, who emigrated from County Down, Ireland. Even though his father ran a school in Pittsburgh, Cupples had very little education. In 1846, Cupples traveled to Cincinnati, Ohio, where he secured employment at a woodware company. While traveling down the Mississippi River on a barge bound for New Orleans, he was advised by river men that St. Louis would be an ideal location for a branch office of his company. His bosses back at Cincinnati agreed, so he returned to St. Louis with a barge loaded with wooden spoons, baskets, and broom handles. Business was so good that he expanded his company to include the manufacture and distribution of wooden utensils. In 1856, Cupples took on two partners, Robert and Harry Brookings, whose business savvy initiated a period of rapid growth. By 1893, the company owned twenty-two warehouses next to the rail lines. Over forty companies stored their goods in Cupples's warehouse complex, known as Cupples Station. The warehouses, located south of Busch Stadium, brought in approximately $100 million annually.

In the 1880s, Cupples decided to build a mansion appropriate for a man of his wealth. Although he and his family loved their new home, their lives were wracked by sadness and tragedy. His first wife and three daughters all succumbed to diphtheria. Before Cupples died in 1912, he stipulated that his house could not be sold for at least eight years after his death. He also said that the house could not be sold to St. Louis University because he hated the Jesuits. Cupples's family sold the house to the American Railroad Telegraphers' Union, which retained possession until it was sold to St. Louis University in 1970. In 1973, Friar Maurice McNamara saved the Cupples House from the wrecking ball. He initiated efforts to remodel the old house, which was open to the public in 1975. The house was listed on the National Register of Historic Places in 1976.

Today, employees claim that the restless spirit of Samuel Cupples is very active at his former home. They hear voices and strange noises in the house after the lights have been turned off, especially down in the basement. His ghost also seems to enjoy turning the lights off and on. Bridget White, who is secretary to the director of the house, says that many times she has turned off the light in the second-floor library, but by the time she has locked up the house and walked to her car, the light is turned back on. Interestingly enough, the library was Samuel Cupples's favorite room. Wright also said that several times, she has returned to the house in the morning and found a chest moved to a different place. The chest is so heavy that it takes two or three people to lift it. She has also seen spectral figures running down the upstairs hall. White is so afraid of the house's resident ghost that she never stays there by herself.

Why has Cupples's ghost chosen to remain in his mansion? One theory lies in his desire that the third floor of his mansion not be used as a ballroom, as was the custom in those days, because he detested dancing. However, following his death, his relatives threw champagne and oyster parties at the house on New Year's Eve. Many of the revelers danced all night long. It is also possible that his ghost is unhappy because his house was sold to St. Louis University against Cupples's wishes. As any folklorist knows, there is a price to pay for not respecting the wishes of the dead.

THE WHITTEMORE HOUSE

When thirteen-year-old Heinrich Christian Haarstick arrived in St. Louis in 1849, the city was in the grip of a severe cholera epidemic. In addition, a devastating fire had destroyed the riverfront area. He learned at a young age that people, like cities, have the power to recover from adversity. When the distillery he purchased in his twenties burned down, Haarstick rebuilt it and sold it. By the time he was thirty-one, he had already made his first fortune. Haarstick was also one of the first entrepreneurs to realize the business opportunities that lay in barges.

He purchased the only barge in St. Louis and eventually founded St. Louis & Mississippi Valley Transportation, which became the largest barge line in the United States in 1874. Later, Haarstick expanded his business interests to include banking and chemical production.

In the early 1900s, the Haarsticks were one of St. Louis's most prominent families. Heinrich co-founded the Veiled Prophet Ball, one of St. Louis society's most prestigious annual events. Because of his growing stature within the community, Haarstick decided that he and his family should have a mansion worthy of people of their wealth and status. In 1912, architect James P. Jamieson, who had designed Washington University's earliest Gothic buildings, built two houses for Haarstick at a cost of $47,049 each. Haarstick gave one to his younger daughter, Emma, and her husband, Clinton Whittemore. Haarstick and his wife took up residence in the other house, along with his older daughter, Ida, and her husband, Oscar Herf, who founded the Herf and Frerichs Chemical Company in 1886. After Oscar Herf died in 1928, Haarstick's grandson, stockbroker Henry Haarstick Whittemore, moved in with his bride, Margaret ("Maggie") Anne. According to local historians, the parties the Whittemore's threw for St. Louis's elite in the 1920s were legendary. In 1966, Henry Whittemore's widow donated the house at 6440 Forsyth Street to Washington University. After serving for many years as the Alumni Club, the Whittemore House was converted into the Faculty Conference Center.

The ghostly aura that surrounds the Whittemore House was most likely generated by the five deaths that took place in the house. Haarstick, his wife, Ida Herf, and Oscar Herf all died of natural deaths within the mansion. The fifth death was an infant adopted by Henry and Maggie Whittemore. The baby, Leigh, had been tucked in too tightly by the nanny and choked to death on her own vomit on New Year's Day 1937. Another person might have died on the property as well. In 1969, workmen excavating around the house found the skull and leg of a child. The bones were placed in a plastic bag and moved to an undisclosed location. No records of the discovery of human bones at Whittemore House exist.

People whose memories go back to the renovation of the old house say that the ghosts became active when the house was being refurbished in the late 1960s. Workers digging in the old wading pool in the back yard discovered a variety of toys, such as a doll and a toy baby carriage. Not long thereafter, tools were moved from one place to another. Footsteps echoed through hallways where no one was present. Soon, the workmen reached the uneasy conclusion that they were not alone, even when no human beings were present.

The reports of ghostly encounters escalated right after the Alumni Club opened in 1969. Art Keine, the former manager of the club, said that late at night after closing time, he and his assistant, Shirley Sweeney, often heard children laughing and balls bouncing. Sometimes, they heard angry voices in the lobby. A former caretaker, Willie Holt, said he had trouble falling to sleep some nights because of the voices. He also heard the clinking of glasses and the playing of a piano late one night. The ruckus was so loud that a passerby peered in one of the windows. Some nights, the ghosts were so noisy that he was forced to sleep outside on the back lawn.

Over the years, other staff members and managers began talking about the weird "goings on" in the Whittemore House. Wedges had to be inserted under open doors to prevent them from slamming shut on their own. The sounds of disembodied footsteps became commonplace. A few people saw a male apparition in the Whittemore House. The male figure wore a beard and a plaid shirt. As a rule, he was visible only from the waist up.

The ghost—or ghosts—responsible for the eerie occurrences in the Whittemore could be the spirits of any of the five individuals who died there. However, the spirit of the child whose buried bones were discovered on the property could also be trying to gain attention. Perhaps the ghost is restless because he—or she—was not interred in hallowed ground.

JEFFERSON BARRACKS

The post that was to become Jefferson Barracks was established south of what is now downtown St. Louis by Major Stephen Watts Kearny on July 10, 1826. In October of that year, the name of the post was changed to Jefferson Barracks in honor of President Thomas Jefferson. Three years later, soldiers stationed at the barracks began escorting merchants along the Santa Fe Trail. Between 1846 and 1848, Jefferson Barracks served as the jumping-off point for military units participating in the Mexican War. In 1861, troops from Jefferson Barracks defeated the pro-secessionist troops from Camp Jackson in St. Louis. In 1862, the Army Medical Department took control of Jefferson Barracks, making it the largest federal medical facility in the United States. After several of the old stone buildings were razed in 1892, a number of brick officers' quarters and barracks were built in their place. Most of these buildings are still in use today by an assortment of Missouri Army and National Guard units. In 1898, Jefferson Barracks was the stepping-off point for soldiers participating in the Spanish-American War. Between 1917 and 1918, Jefferson Barracks served as the largest induction and demobilization center during World War I. During World War II, the barracks served as an induction and separation center. In 1946, all but 135 acres of the post were closed. In 1950, the St. Louis County Parks and Recreation Department took over 500 acres of the closed post, creating Jefferson Barracks Park. Not surprisingly, the spirits of some of the soldiers and civilians who were part of the post's long history are said to be still on duty.

First Lieutenant David Goodwin, who was appointed detachment commander of the HHD 1138 Engineer Battalion in Building 27, interviewed a number of military personnel for his book *Ghosts of Jefferson Barracks*. According to the people he spoke to, almost all of the buildings erected at and before 1900 are haunted. Constructed in 1900, Building 1 serves as the post's headquarters. One of the ghosts in this building is the spirit of an elderly Confederate general, seated in the post's commander's office with a feather quill pen. The ghostly peck-peck-peck of an antique typewriter has also been heard in the building late at night. Building 27 was built in 1860 as the post's water works, but it was converted into the guardhouse and jail in 1883. Today, the building is used as the dining facility for the post. In 1992, a female Air Guard soldier said that the ghost of a woman in a long, trailing skirt passed in front of her as she walked down the hallway. Building 27 served as the enlisted soldiers' quarters when it was built in 1896. In September 2000, a personnel clerk for the 235th Engineer Company sighted a Civil War–era cavalry scout in the main foyer of Building 27. He wore striped uniform riding pants, carried a sword, and had shoulder-length brown hair. Later, she saw the same apparition on the landing stairs leading to the second floor. Built in 1896, Building 66 is so haunted that an employee posted a sign on the stairway leading to the third-floor attic. The sign states, "Resident Ghost Quarters, Do not Disturb." For years, National Guardsmen have heard banging noises from the third-floor attic. Others have heard the sound of papers being shuffled and furniture being moved around on the second floor.

Almost all of the hauntings reported at the Jefferson Barracks are residual in nature. These are entities whose actions are being replayed over and over again like a loop of film. One could surmise, though, that it is their sense of dedication that keeps these spirits at their post.

ZOMBIE ROAD

Zombie Road is a two-mile stretch of road that runs through a heavily forested valley near the Wildwood and Glencoe area where the Old State Road meets Highway 109. Nicknamed Zombie Road by teenagers in the 1950s, it was constructed in the late 1860s to provide access to the Meramec River and to the railroad tracks that ran parallel to the river. Listed on maps as Lawler Ford Road, it was used after the Civil War by the Glencoe Marble Company, whose trucks hauled quarry stone on the road. Sometime in the early twentieth century, the gravel and dirt road was paved over with asphalt. It eventually fell into disrepair and was abandoned. By the 1950s, Zombie Road became a favorite hangout for teenagers looking for a place to "make-out" and party.

At least two legends have been created as a means of explaining the origin of the name of the road. One variant has it that the road was named after a homicidal maniac nicknamed "Zombie" who escaped from a local insane asylum. He was never found, but his bloodied gown was discovered on the road that bears his name. According to another legend, railroad workers who once worked in the area rise from their graves and stumble along the road.

Zombie Road's haunted reputation has its source in a number of ghost legends. Some say that the strange, shadowy figure that has been seen on the road is the ghost of a man who was hit by a train in the 1970s. Because no record of this accident exists, this death is probably apocryphal. However, in 1876, Della Hamilton McCullough actually was run over by a railroad car on the spur line from the Rockwoods Reservation. Therefore, her spirit could be the ghost that haunts Zombie Road. Others say that the ghost of a boy who fell from the bluffs along the river walks the old roadway. The ghost could be the spirit of a pioneer who was struck by a train in the late 1800s. It has also been suggested that the ghost of a man who lost his wife in a poker game and committed suicide afterward could be scaring travelers along the road. Many people claim to have heard the screams of an old woman who holds a gun and stands in the doorway of one of the ramshackle houses that were part of Glencoe's resort community until 1945. Many of these clubhouses became permanent homes; others were simply left to rot. The ghosts of Indians who lived nearby have also been cited as possible candidates for the ghosts.

Zombie Road can be reached by taking Manchester Road west of the city to Old State Road South. Curiosity seekers should then turn down Ridge Road to the Ridge Meadows Elementary School. The road is just to the left of the school. The entrance is marked by a chained gate. A sign identifying the road as Lawler Ford Road was stolen years ago. The road is not accessible by automobile. People interested in going down Zombie Road should be aware that "No Trespassing" signs are posted everywhere and that the local police patrol the road on a regular basis. According to the police, trespassers are more likely to be harmed by human beings on Zombie Road than by ghosts.

CALVARY DRIVE

Calvary Drive, also known as Calvary Avenue, separates Bellefontaine Cemetery and Calvary Cemetery. Bellefontaine Cemetery had its inception during the cholera epidemic of 1849. A number of famous people are buried there, including Thomas Hart Benton, Sara Teasdale, General William Clark, William S. Burroughs, and the Lemp family. On the other side of the roadway from Bellefontaine Cemetery is Calvary Cemetery. It was started in 1857 because most of the other cemeteries were filled to capacity with cholera victims. Ironically, neither cemetery has generated any ghost stories. However, the road that runs between them, Calvary Drive, is said to be haunted.

One of the ghost stories centering around Calvary Drive is that of "Hitchhiker Annie," a variation of the Vanishing Hitchhiker story. The earliest version of the tale dates back to the 1940s, when more and more people were driving, especially soldiers home from the war. Her ghost usually appeared at the vicinity of Calvary Drive at sunset. In the standard version of the story, a young man was on his way to a dance when he is flagged down by a pretty girl with long brown hair and pale skin. She usually told the young man that her car broke down and she was trying to make her way home. She asked the young man to drive her home, and he agreed. On the drive home, the girl was surprisingly quiet. As the young man drove past the gates of Bellefontaine Cemetery, the girl vanishes from the front seat of the car.

By the early 1980s, the Hitchhiker Annie story had died out. It was replaced by the story of a little boy dressed in nineteenth-century clothing. Many drivers claimed that they were driving along Calvary Drive when the figure of a little boy suddenly appeared in the middle of the street. The drivers slammed on their brakes and swerved to miss the boy. When they drove back to see if they had hit the boy, he was nowhere to be found.

A third ghost who haunts Calvary Drive is the spirit of a lady in a long, black Victorian dress. She wore a hat and a veil over her face. The woman appeared to be dressed for a funeral. Drivers reported seeing her walk across or stand in the middle of the road, like the little boy. She usually vanished just before the cars struck her.

By the late 1990s, all of the ghost stories connected to Calvary Drive have faded away. One can only hope that the ghosts have found their way "home," wherever that home might be. One thing is for certain: driving along Calvary Drive is much more uneventful than it used to be.

BISSELL MANSION RESTAURANT

Lewis Bissell was born in Connecticut on October 12, 1789. His father, Major Russell Bissell, was the first commander of Fort Bellefontaine.

General Daniel Bissell, who was the first commandant of the U.S. Military Department of Missouri, was his father. When Lewis Bissell was nineteen years, President Thomas Jefferson sent him to what was then the Western frontier. He fought in the War of 1812 and was promoted to captain in 1815. He served as commander of Fort Clark in Peoria for three years before becoming part of the Yellowstone Expedition up the Missouri River in 1818. When Lewis returned home in 1821, he married Mary Woodbridge. He then purchased 1,500 acres, which later became known as Bissell's Point. His property spread east to the Mississippi River and north to Fort Bellefontaine. After Bissell built his home on a heavily wooded hill, a number of other homes were built on Bissell's Point. Bissell's wife, Mary, died in 1831; six years later, he took a second wife, Mary Jane Douglass. Lewis and Mary Jane lived together in the mansion for almost forty years before his death in 1868. One of the later owners, Frederick Kraft, built the northwest wing of the house. By the time I-70 was constructed in the 1950s, the Bissell Mansion was slated to be razed. It was rescued by the Landmarks Association, which, unwittingly, saved the spirit of Lewis Bissell as well.

One would expect the oldest brick residence in St. Louis to be haunted, and this is certainly true of the Bissell Mansion Restaurant and Murder Mystery Dinner Theater. The ghostly activity really began after the mansion was renovated in the 1980s. The ghosts of two former residents of the mansion refuse to leave. One is the ghost of a woman in a long, flowing white evening gown. Apparently, she is a friendly ghost who turned and smiled at a waiter while she was walking up the stairs. People familiar with the history of the mansion believe that she is the ghost of one of Captain Bissell's two wives. The other ghost is the spirit of Captain Bissell himself. He has been seen standing in the parking lot, staring at the house. One—or perhaps both—of the restaurant's ghosts enjoys playing with the wine glasses. Robbi Courtaway, author of *Spirits of St. Louis*, reports that after the dinner theater got under-way, the manager began noticing that one or two wine glasses turned up missing. She was in the habit of counting every glass, so she became concerned when the glasses she ended up with at the end of the day was smaller than the number of glasses she started with. The manager assumed that the spirits were punishing her for some reason by making off with the glasses.

Today, customers get more than they usually receive at a restaurant. Everyone receives an "Identity" when they arrive and participate in the murder mystery. A four-course dinner is served between the acts of the show. If the legends can be believed, occasionally, a ghost or two gets into the act as well.

POWELL SYMPHONY HALL

The building known today as Powell Symphony Hall was originally called the St. Louis Theater. Built in 1925 by the architectural firm of Rapp & Rapp, the St. Louis Theater was originally used for vaudeville acts. When movies replaced vaudeville in the 1920s, it became a movie palace. In 1966, the St. Louis Theater showed its last movie—*The Sound of Music*—and closed. That same year, a gift of $500,000 from Oscar Johnson Jr. enabled the Symphony Society to purchase the building. After the theater was extensively renovated at a cost of $2 million, the St. Louis Symphony Orchestra acquired its first permanent home, as well as one of the most elegant concert halls in the entire world. The theater officially opened on January 24, 1968. The theater is named after Walter S. Powell, a St. Louis shoe manufacturing executive and patron of the arts. By the end of the 1980s, Powell Symphony Hall had become the focal point of the city's revitalized art district. In 2001, Powell Symphony Hall was entered in the National Register of Historic Places. Today, music lovers in St. Louis flock to the Powell Symphony Hall to enjoy fine classical music and, perhaps, to meet George, the ghost.

Witnesses describe George as a middle-aged male in a white suit and hat. George's true identity has never been clearly determined. Some say that he is the ghost of a stagehand who simply stopped coming to work one day and was never heard of again. Others say that he is a vaudeville performer whose aspirations of becoming a star on Broadway never materialized. Today, he mopes around Powell Symphony Hall, venting his frustration by disrupting tours and performances. He has been blamed for causing the stage lights to flicker. He also seems to enjoy riding the elevators up and down the floors. When an elevator door opens and no one is inside, people familiar with the ghost legends say that George is playing around again.

In the book *Spirits of St. Louis,* marketing manager Joan Fan tells of her encounter with George's ghost during a tour she was giving of the old theater at 11:30 A.M. She and a family of tourists were standing in front of one of the false rooms behind the walls when they heard a loud hammering sound on the wall behind them. She turned around and was shocked to see that no human being was making the sound. When no one could give a plausible explanation for the weird sound, Fan quickly hustled her group out of the room.

According to conductor David Robinson, George also likes to hang around the part of the stage that is covered by the canopy. He said that one evening, renowned conductor Leonard Slatkin was strolling through the area when the door suddenly slammed shut, locking him in. Slatkin banged on the door until somebody heard him and came to his rescue. Robinson said that Slatkin banged so hard that the marks he made on the door are still visible.

Ghostly activity is reported in Powell Symphony Hall on a fairly regular basis. To most people, George is, at worst, an annoying spirit, but not really malicious. This playful ghost takes the old saying "the show must go on" very seriously.

HANNIBAL

Moses Bates founded Hannibal, Missouri, in 1813 on land that had previously been occupied by Native American tribes. The city's population rose from 30 people in 1830 to 2,020 by 1850, due in large part to river and railroad transportation. In the nineteenth century, Hannibal's economy depended heavily on grain, livestock, and the production of shoes and cement. Author Mark Twain is the city's most illustrious native son, and thousands of his fans visit his birthplace each year. However, other notables also hail from Hannibal, such as the "Unsinkable" Molly Brown and Chicago White Sox baseball player "Shoeless" Joe Jackson.

ROCKCLIFFE MANSION

John J. Cruikshank was a Scottish immigrant who made a fortune in the lumber industry in Missouri. In 1898, he set about to build an American castle high on a rocky knoll, a residence worthy of a man of his means. The total cost of building the mansion was $125,000. In 1900, Cruikshank, his wife, and their four daughters moved into their 13,500-square-foot palatial mansion, consisting of nine bedrooms and seven bathrooms. Only the finest quality oak, mahogany, and walnut building materials were used in the construction of the four-story house. The interior was furnished with hand-carved pieces at the cost of $50,000. The landscaping costs, which included the construction of a rock wall that encircled the house, totaled $75,000. Rockcliffe Mansion was resplendent with palladium windows and ten carved marble and tile fireplaces. The contractor built the home with double-brick walls to ensure that the house would stand for decades. In 1902, the *St. Louis Post Dispatch* dubbed Rockcliffe Mansion as "The Finest Home in Missouri."

The Cruikshanks lived in their magnificent home until 1924, when John Cruikshank died in his bed. His wife and daughters left Rockcliffe and moved to the house next door. Rockcliffe Mansion stood deserted for forty-three years. Children and teenagers who broke into the house spread the rumor that it was haunted. In the late 1960s, the old mansion was saved from the wrecking ball when three local families got together and restored Rockcliffe to its former glory. Miraculously, the interior of the house was not severely damaged, aside from graffiti on the walls and a few bent chandeliers. All of the lavish furnishings were intact, including the impressive Tiffany stained-glass window on the landing of the staircase. Today, Rockcliffe Mansion is a bed and breakfast. Rockcliffe's thirty rooms are filled with family heirlooms, antique furniture, period clothing, and, some say, a number of ghosts.

Mary McAvoy, who was caretaker at the mansion between 1993 and 2005, lived on the property for two years before actually meeting the ghost of John Cruikshank. *In an interview conducted by James Offutt in 2007, Mary said one night in 1995, she spent the night alone in the second-floor guest room while her husband was attending a class reunion. She was sleeping until 2:00 A.M., when she awakened and heard someone open the door to the servants' entrance, walk up the back staircase, and go down the hall to John Cruikshank's second-floor bedroom. Mary was certain that she was the only one in the mansion at the time. Evidence suggests that Cruikshank's ghost might still be sleeping in the large canopy bed where he breathed his last breath. Tour guides have fluffed the mattress before leaving for the night. When they return the next morning, they have found the impression of a person in Cruikshank's bed.*

John Cruikshank's spirit has manifested itself in corporeal form on several occasions. Guests have seen his spectral figure floating through the grand music room. His ghost has also been seen standing by the bar in the ground-floor kitchen. His apparition is usually described as being the ghost of a small man with a goatee and mustache, wearing a brown felt hat and an old-fashioned suit.

Another male spirit in the house might be the ghost of Hannibal's most-famous resident. In 1902, author Mark Twain gave his "Farewell to Hannibal" speech at Rockcliffe Mansion. The heavy odor of Twain's favorite smoke—a cigar—has been detected in the room on many occasions. At times, the smell has been so strong that tour guides have had to leave the room to catch their breath.

Ken and Lisa Marks purchased Rockcliffe Mansion in September 2009. After the Chrysler plant closed in St. Louis and Ken lost his managerial position, they found themselves at a crossroads, pondering their future. "We were asking ourselves what we were going to do next. We decided to save Rockcliffe," Lisa said. After they took possession of the house, it became readily apparent why the children who believed the house to be haunted got that impression. In the Reception Room on the first floor are two framed photographs of J. J. Cruikshank and his wife. Lisa noticed that as she passed by the portrait of Mr. Cruikshank, his eyes seemed to follow her. "This is why we think the kids told their parents that the house was haunted," Lisa said.

They soon discovered how difficult it was going to be to have any privacy in Rockcliffe, even when they were the only ones there. "We constantly have people driving around up here," Lisa said. "They park and take pictures. They walk their dogs and walk around the property.

So we became very careful when we went to bed on the second floor to lock all of the first floor doors to keep curiosity seekers out of the house." Almost immediately after moving in, Ken and Lisa began hearing doors slamming downstairs, even though they were certain that all of the doors were locked. "How do you slam a door that is already locked?" Lisa asked, rhetorically. "It's not lightly shutting the door. It's opening it as wide as you can and slamming it shut. It's loud enough that when we are sleeping in one of the rooms on the third floor, we bolt up in bed because of the doors slamming on the first floor."

Before long, they began having weird experiences that seemed to verify the stories that they had heard about the old house. *One winter night, they were sitting in the dining room at 9:00 or 10:00 P.M., watching a DVD on their laptop. Suddenly, they started hearing noises coming from upstairs. "We heard furniture scraping and footsteps," Lisa said. "It would last for ten seconds, and then it would go away for twenty minutes. It almost sounded like someone crunching through the snow. We looked out the window, and there was no one there. As the night wore on and the sounds continued, we realized that they were coming from the ballroom."*

A few weeks after they moved in, the Marks heard a different kind of noise inside the house. *"We were in the office one night," Lisa said, "and we heard a crashing sound. It took us twenty minutes of searching to find out what had happened. In the girls' bedroom is a closet containing a lot of dresses. We had placed a vase of artificial flowers on a shelf in the closet. When we walked into the room, we saw where the vase had shattered. But it wasn't like it had just fallen off the shelf in the closet. It fell into the room several feet away from the closet. I picked up the pieces of glass and put them at the base of the oak tree just outside the door, almost like an offering."*

Footsteps are frequently heard in the house as well. *At 6:00 one evening, Ken and Lisa were eating dinner in the kitchen when they heard footsteps in the stairwell. "We could tell the footsteps were moving up and away because they were getting quieter and quieter," Lisa said. "Finally, the footsteps stopped at the second-floor landing. My husband asked, 'Are you nervous?' I said, 'No.' He said, 'O.K.,' and we started eating again. Within a few seconds, we heard the footsteps walking on the second floor."*

One night, Ken had a particularly unnerving experience with some porcelain dolls' heads that had been donated to the mansion. Most of the dolls' heads were stored in a cabinet in the ballroom, but four broken heads were kept on a shelf in the back of the office. Ken was working in the office when one of the heads crashed right in front of him. He immediately called up Lisa, who was in St. Louis at the time, and asked her if the dolls' heads were valuable. She said no. "That's good," Ken said, "because we lost one."

One of the tour guides they hired to lead visitors through the house told Ken and Lisa that she saw the ghost that she believed was disturbing the peace and quiet in the old mansion. Lisa said, *"One of our tour guides was walking into the kitchen one day, and she saw Mr. Cruikshank standing by the pantry door. I asked her if it was a ghost she saw or a man. She said it was a ghost because he slowly disappeared. She claimed to have seen him two other times as well, but they were just fleeting glimpses."*

Soon, guests also began sensing the paranormal activity in the mansion. *On Halloween night 2009, a couple checked into the mansion.* "We got up the next morning for breakfast, and they were gone," Lisa said. "They left us a note stating that they had left about 1:30 in the morning. They left the key too. So we called them the next morning and asked them why they left so suddenly. The man said, 'I woke up in the middle of the night and heard music playing downstairs, and that was it. We left.'"

Five ladies who booked a night at Rockcliffe Mansion in the hope of seeing a ghost got their wish. *"They were in their twenties and thirties,"* Lisa said. *"They stayed on the second floor. They hooted and hollered all night long. They had the most fun. They said they were having paranormal experiences. I don't know if they really were or if they were just playing tricks on each other. Before they left, they asked us to take pictures of them on the Grand Staircase,"* Lisa said. *"Three of them sat on one step, and two sat on the other. Before I took the photograph, I pointed to the step where the two ladies were sitting and said that that is where J.J. would be sitting. When I took the photo, it turned out that there was an orb right where I said J.J. would be."*

On April 3, 2010, this writer and his wife, Marilyn, spent the night at Rockcliffe Mansion. We were spending the night in the Sage Room on the third floor. At 2:00 A.M., Marilyn left the room and went into the bathroom in the hallway. After she returned to bed a few minutes later, she distinctly heard footsteps out in the hallway. She said that the person had a "light" step, like that of a woman or a child. The entity took only seven or eight steps down the hallway. Then Marilyn heard the sound of someone shaking a doorknob. Although she was not really frightened, Marilyn decided not to open the door. The next morning, Lisa Marks told us that we were the only guests in the house at the time. She and her husband were sleeping in their room on the second floor.

When we told Lisa what had happened, she said that another couple had had a strange experience in the Sage Room. *A woman was asleep in the bed when she felt someone take her hand. Her first thought was that her husband was holding her hand. She looked over at him and was shocked to find that he was sleeping on the other side of the bed. Lisa said that all of the ghostly experiences seem to be especially tailored for the individual guests. None of them has had exactly the same type of encounter.*

Lisa said that her scariest moment in the house happened in late December 2009. *"A paranormal group came here in late December 2009," Lisa said. "It had snowed. I hung out with them until 3:00 A.M. My husband wasn't here. He had to go to St. Louis. So I went into the office and lay down. About an hour later, I looked out the window, and the group's cars were still there. I knew I wasn't alone in the house, so I went back to sleep. About an hour later, I was awakened by a very loud door slam. I sat straight up in the bed and looked out the window. The cars were all gone. I was all alone in the house. It couldn't have been them leaving. That's when panic washed over me. Then I thought, 'Thank God, it was a ghost and not a man!' It happened about 4:30 A.M."*

Like a number of other businesses in Hannibal, the owners of Rockcliffe Mansion have tried to capitalize on the house's haunted past. In recent years, they have offered tours and cemetery walks of Hannibal every weekend in September and October. Tour guides demonstrate the proper use of copper dousing rods to guests in Rockcliffe

Mansion. Ghosts, it seems, can be an asset as long as their antics are playful.

GARDEN HOUSE BED AND BREAKFAST

In the late nineteenth century, Millionaire's Row as Hannibal's most exclusive residential district. In 1896, Albert Pettibone Jr., the wealthy son of the founder of the Hannibal Saw Mill Company, built a lovely Queen Anne Victorian home at 301 North Fifth Street. Albert had not lived in the house for very long before he died at the age of twenty-nine. The house changed owners several times in the twentieth century. In the 1920s, Albert's son Charles lived here. In recent years, Will Griswold, the proprietor of a local hardware store, owned the house. The old Queen Anne mansion is now one of Hannibal's most popular bed and breakfasts. Sometimes, workers at the bed and breakfast get the distinct impression that Albert Pettibone Jr. still roams the upstairs rooms and hallways at night.

The owners of the Garden House Bed and Breakfast do not really downplay the presence of ghosts in the old house. In fact, in the dining room, one can see a photograph on the wall that is best described as "ghostly." It is a photograph of a man sitting at a table. Leaning into the photograph from the side is the spectral image of a little boy's face. Apparently, he could not pass up the opportunity to have his picture taken.

Guests claim to have heard the unmistakable sound of piano music from the first floor. Others have heard spectral voices echoing through the hallways. Sometimes, people hear the sound of someone sawing wood down in the basement. At least two guests have had terrifying personal experiences in the house. *In 2006, a ghost hunter who was taking readings in an upstairs bedroom said he saw a shadowy figure walk in front of the television set. In 2008, a married couple was celebrating their eleventh wedding anniversary at the Garden House Bed and Breakfast. That night, the wife was asleep when she felt her body being taken over by a spirit she identified as the ghost of Albert Pettibone Jr. The ghost's hold on her was broken only after her husband roused her from her sleep.*

One of the waiters at the LaBinah Bistro has had personal encounters with the spirit—or spirits—inhabiting the Garden House Bed and
Breakfast. Between 2006 and 2010, Arif Dagin, a native of Turkey,
rented a room at the bed and breakfast. When this writer interviewed
Arif on April 3, 2010, he had moved out of the Garden House Bed and
Breakfast and was renting a room in the LaBinah Bistro. During the day,
he was doing his student teaching at an elementary school in Hannibal.
Arif said that a former manager of LaBinah Bistro also roomed at the
bed and breakfast before he arrived at Hannibal. He said that her Sibe-
rian Husky occasionly acted perturbed, as if an unwelcome presence
was in the room.

Arif's first brush with the paranormal inside the Garden House
occurred shortly after he moved into his room in 2006. *He said that
every evening before closing time, the staff set the plates, silverware, and
glasses on the table in the Iris Dining Room. One morning, he walked
into the dining room and was surprised to find the table settings in complete disarray. Arif assumed that one of the staff members was not doing
his job. He rearranged the plates and silverware and went to work at
LaBinah Bistro. The next morning, he walked through the dining room
and once again discovered that the dining room table was a complete
mess. He began to wonder if maybe the ghost stories he had heard about
the old house were true. When Arif discovered the plates and silverware
scattered all over the table a third time, he was starting to believe that
the Garden House Bed and Breakfast really was haunted.*

*Arif became convinced that he was sharing the bed and breakfast
with ghosts one cold winter's night when he was awakened after midnight by the sound of someone walking around on the first floor. When
he heard the footsteps make their way up the stairs, he grabbed an
empty bottle and waited by the door. He clearly heard someone walk
into the room next to his. After a few moments, he threw open the door
to his room and barged into the neighboring room, hoping to catch the
intruder with his guard down. The room was completely empty.*

The guest rooms on the second floor offer more than just a spec-
tacular view of the Mississippi River. The oak and mahogany paneled
walls are adorned with artwork from local artists and photographs
from the house's past. Guests are treated to old-fashioned featherbeds

and hand-embroidered comforters as well as satellite televisions and WiFi wireless Internet. The paranormal activity in the old house seems to fit in nicely with the innkeepers' efforts to mesh the old with the new in the Garden House Bed and Breakfast.

Tennessee

MEMPHIS

When Spanish explorer Hernando De Soto arrived in the Memphis area in 1541, he encountered the original inhabitants, the Chickasaw Indians. In 1682, French explorer Rene Robert Cavelier, Sieur de la Salle, built Fort Prud'homme and claimed the area for France. By the late 1700s, the United States had taken control of the Tennessee region. In 1818, the U.S. Government purchased much of western Tennessee from the Chickasaws. In 1819, General Andrew Jackson, Judge John Overton, and General James Winchester organized a settlement of five thousand acres, which they christened "Memphis." Cotton planters moved in during the early 1800s. Hundreds of slaves were brought to Memphis from New Orleans to work on the plantations. By 1860, Memphis had become the sixth-largest city in the United States. In 1862, Memphis was taken by the Union army. In the 1870s, the population of Memphis was decimated by a series of yellow fever epidemics. Over half of the residents of Memphis moved out. The increase of the river trade in the 1880s helped boost the city's population. The building boom of the 1960s brought a number of factories and skyscrapers to Memphis.

GRACELAND

The most famous house in Memphis was built on property originally owned by the publisher of the *Memphis Daily Appeal*, S. E. Toof. He named his farm after his daughter, Grace, who eventually inherited the land. Grace passed down 13.8 acres of the farm to her niece, Ruth, and her husband, Dr. Thomas Moore, who constructed the present

Colonial-style mansion on the property in 1939. In 1957, Elvis Presley purchased the house and property and moved in with his mother, Gladys, and his father, Vernon Presley. Priscilla Presley moved into Graceland in 1962 and continued living there for five years after she and Elvis were married in 1967. On August 16, 1997, Elvis was found dead in his bathroom, apparently of a drug overdose. His body was originally interred at Forrest Hill Cemetery, but it was moved to Graceland after a botched attempt to steal his corpse. Ever since Graceland opened to fans and tourists in 1982, many people have sworn that Elvis has not really "left the building."

Sightings of Elvis Presley's ghost began soon after Graceland was open to the public. Over the years, many people have seen the image of his face staring out of a window at Graceland. In *Strange Tales of the Dark and Bloody Ground*, author Christopher K. Coleman writes of a tourist from Great Britain who took a photograph of the exterior of Graceland in 1985. When she examined the photograph closely, she found the face of someone resembling Elvis Presley staring out of a downstairs window. In 1987, a couple from Missouri had just finished touring Graceland and were about to leave when the husband decided to run around the front of the house and take a quick photograph. When he raised the camera to take the picture, he saw Elvis peering out of a second-story window.

The ghost of Elvis Presley has been seen in other parts of Graceland as well. For many years, people standing outside of the gates of Graceland have reported seeing Elvis sitting inside a black limousine that drives up to the gates of Graceland at 2:30 A.M. The car always vanishes before it passes through the gates. A few people have seen Elvis inside Graceland as well. In 2005, a young woman was staring at an exhibit of Elvis's sequined jumpsuits inside a glass case when she saw the reflection of Elvis Presley's face. Her first impression was that Elvis was standing behind her. When she turned around, he was gone. A few minutes later, she was walking through the Mediation Garden. The girl stopped to read the plaque dedicated to the Presley family when, once again, she saw the reflection of Elvis's face.

The ghost of Elvis Presley even seems to like the Chapel in the Woods, a small church in the woods adjacent to Graceland where hundreds of couples go to get married each year. Oddly enough, people claim to have seen Elvis's ghost taking wedding vows with actress Marilyn Monroe inside the Chapel in the Woods, even though the two never met. In 2007, a woman standing outside of the chapel said she heard Marilyn Monroe's voice singing "Diamonds Are a Girl's Best Friend" coming from inside the chapel. A history teacher who witnessed the two apparitions inside the chapel claimed that Elvis was "sweating a lot."

When sightings of Elvis Presley were first reported soon after his death, many of his die-hard fans took these appearances as proof that he was still alive. However, the fact that he always looks the way he did just before he died suggests that the eyewitnesses have actually seen the ghost of Elvis Presley. The orbs and mists visitors have captured on cameras in the basement rooms have also lent credence to the belief that Graceland is indeed haunted. In 1991, a frequently observed phenomenon at Elvis Presley's former home—the ghost of Elvis walking down Union Avenue and through the gates of Graceland—was memorialized in Marc Cohn's 1991 song "Walking in Memphis." Who knows how many of the faithful who make pilgrimages to Graceland drive hundreds of miles in the hope of catching a glimpse of the late, great King of Rock and Roll?

HEARTBREAK HOTEL

Heartbreak Hotel is a 128-room boutique hotel located across the street from Graceland. Since the unabashedly retro hotel first opened its door in 1996, devotees of Elvis Presley's have gotten their "Elvis fix" by staying in one of the four themed suites: the Graceland suite, modeled after Elvis's dining room and billiard room; the Gold and Platinum Suite, dedicated to Elvis's record-breaking albums; the Hollywood Suite, honoring his career as a movie star; and the Burning Love Suite, complete with red and pink rugs, furniture, and bedspreads. Guests can also indulge their hunger for "everything Elvis" by taking a dip in the heart-shaped pool and watching back-to-back Elvis movies on television. Some say that the ghost of Elvis Presley, who was an avid fan of kitsch, occasionally gets in a romantic mood at the Heartbreak Hotel.

A number of witnesses claim to have seen Elvis's ghost in the lobby of the Heartbreak Hotel, usually in the company of Marilyn Monroe. In 2007, a clerk was in the lobby all by himself when he saw Elvis and Marilyn kissing on the purple couch. That same year, a teacher who was a fan of Marilyn Monroe's was escorting a group of sixth-grade students into the dimly lit lobby when several students peering through the fogged glass doors noticed Elvis and Marilyn "making out" on the couch. The clerk, who was checking invoices in the manager's office, heard the students talking and turned up the lights. At that very moment, Elvis and Marilyn vanished.

Memphis is not the only city where the ghost of Elvis has been seen. His ghost has also been sighted in a white-sequined suit at the Las Vegas Hilton and at the site of the former RCA studios just off Nashville's Music Row. It just seems fitting, though, that his ghost prefers the city that he called home for twenty years. The vision of Marilyn Monroe and Elvis Presley, two of the most tragic celebrities of the twentieth century, finding love in an Elvis-themed hotel in his favorite city may be nothing more than wishful thinking on the part of their fans. Who can say?

TENNESSEE BREWERY

The Tennessee Brewery, which sits atop a bluff overlooking the Mississippi River, was founded by G. H. Herboro in 1877. Originally known as "The Memphis Brewing Company," the brewery was purchased by J. W. Schoor, Casper Koehler, and Associates in 1885. It began operations in its present site at the intersection of Butler and Tennessee Streets in 1890. The first beer brewed here was Pilsener. By 1903, it had become the largest brewery in the entire South, with an annual production of 250,000 barrels. At its height, the Tennessee Brewery employed over 1,500 workers. The brewery closed down during Prohibition. The Tennessee Brewery resumed production following the repeal of Prohibition in 1933. It began producing a variety of beers, including "Jockey Club," "Faultless," and "Pearl of Memphis." Its most popular brand, "Goldcrest," was renamed "Goldcrest 51" in 1938 in recognition of the brewery's fifty-one years of operations. The Tennessee Brewery closed down in 1954 and is now vacant.

Today, the Tennessee Brewery is better known for its ghostly activity than it is for its beer. Locals talk about hearing disembodied footsteps and crashing sounds in the empty building. Some people claim to have been pinched or pushed as they climb the iron stairways. Michael Espanjer, founder and director of the Memphis Paranormal Investigations Team, has conducted fifteen investigations of the Tennessee Brewery. "I'm friends with one of the owners, and we have spent the night there many times," Espanjer said. "The brewery has these elaborate staircases everywhere. We'd be walking up the stairs, and I'd tell everyone to freeze. We'd be really quiet, and we'd hear footsteps walking behind us." Memphis Paranormal has collected some intriguing evidence during its investigations, including moving orbs, energy rods, ectoplasm, EVPs, and odd reflections in a metal mirror. Espanjer insists that nothing he and his group have encountered in the brewery is malevolent. Laura Cunningham, author of *Haunted Memphis*, speculates that one of the ghosts haunting the Tennessee Brewery could be the ghost of a boxer who was killed in the ring back in the days when boxing matches were held there.

Despite the fact that the old brewery is listed on the National Register of Historic Places, its future remains in doubt. Developers have proposed converting the building into a shopping center, but the plans have fallen through. While Memphis decides what it is going to do with the Tennessee Brewery, efforts have been made to shore up the slowly disintegrating building. Hopefully, the day will come when ghost hunters are not the only ones who appreciate the historic importance of the Tennessee Brewery.

THE UNIVERSITY OF MEMPHIS

The Tennessee Legislature established the University of Memphis in 1909 as West Tennessee State Normal School. The college opened its doors to students in 1912. During the college's first ten years of existence, the first library was housed in the administration building, and the first dining hall and dormitory were erected. The college changed its name to West Tennessee State Teachers College in 1925. Its name was changed again in 1941, this time to Memphis State College. The graduate school was established in 1950. Seven years later, the college received full university status. The first African American students were admitted in 1959. During the 1970s, an extensive building program was initiated under the supervision of President Cecil C. Humphreys. Another building boom took place on the campus in the 1990s. In 1994, the college became the University of Memphis. Today, the University of Memphis houses 21,000 students and, legend has it, at least a couple of ghosts.

The two most haunted buildings on the campus of the University of Memphis are also the oldest. Mynders Hall, built in 1912, is said to have been named after Elizabeth Mynders, the daughter of Seymour Mynders, the first president of the university. According to campus lore, president Mynders constructed the building in memory of Elizabeth, who died at the age of twenty-one. This story was probably generated from the building's resemblance to a giant "E." In the early years, Mynders Hall served as both a women's dormitory and as an infirmary and dining hall. During World War II, soldiers were housed in Mynders Hall. For approximately one hundred years, students have claimed to have had paranormal experiences in the old dormitory. Elizabeth Mynders is said to be a firm but affectionate spirit who has the best interest of the girls in mind. Some girls say that when they were walking in the hallways late at night, a female apparition floated toward them and ordered them to get back to their rooms. Because of the belief, passed down by generations of students, that Elizabeth hates mirrors, many girls still hang their mirrors in their closets and keep the doors shut.

Brister Library, which was built in 1928, is home to a much more agitated spirit. Students say that late one night many years ago, a female student was raped and murdered in the tower of the library. Ever since, students and janitors have reported seeing a wispy female form that dissipates when they attempt to talk to it. The piercing screams that occasionally emanate from the two have been so loud that campus police have run up the tower stairs, expecting the worst. The source of the screams has never been discovered.

The ghost stories students still pass around at the University of Memphis contain motifs that are found in ghost stories all over the world. In

The Encyclopedia of Ghosts and Spirits, author Rosemary Ellen Guiley says that one of the reasons why a ghost returns is to avenge its wrongful death. Apparently, the spirit haunting Brister Library is still searching for her murderer, who was never apprehended. Elizabeth Mynders illustrates an entirely different motif. Guiley says that ghosts also return to complete unfinished business. Because Elizabeth's young life was cut short, it could be that she is trying to live through the girls who are enjoying all of the pleasures of young womanhood that she was denied.

THE MEMPHIS CONVENTION AND VISITORS' BUREAU

The Memphis Convention and Visitors' Bureau was created in 1925 to promote the city as an attractive destination for conventions and tourists. Beginning in the 1970s, tourism has become one of the city's major industries. Over 50,000 tourism-related jobs have been created to accommodate the thousands of visitors who flock to Memphis each year. Today, this not-for-profit membership organization is housed in the Woolen Building, the oldest commercial building in Memphis. Constructed of bricks made on the site in the 1840s, the Woolen Building was used as a hospital by federal troops during the Civil War. The horrors of nineteenth-century battlefield medicine seem to have left an indelible imprint on the fabric of this old building.

The most common type of surgery performed in the Woolen Building was amputations. Wounded soldiers had their limbs removed without the benefit of any anesthetic at all. The lucky ones were given a shot of whiskey before the surgeon got to work. Employees at the Memphis Convention and Visitors' Bureau claim that they still hear the ghosts of the soldiers screaming and moaning before and during their operations. Most of the paranormal activity in the Woolen Building occurs in the basement and in a large room behind two white doors on the first floor. Not surprisingly, surgeries were performed in both of these areas.

Passersby have also witnessed strange phenomena inside the Woolen Building, even after it is closed. Some people claim to have heard strange noises inside the bureau by standing outside the front of the building and pressing their ear against the window. In November

2009, this author's daughter, Andrea Reynolds, said that she heard a weird humming sound coming from somewhere inside. Ten of us were present at the time, and only one other young woman heard the same sound. Some people have also captured ghostly faces in the front window. That same year, a young man walking past the Memphis Convention and Visitors' Bureau stopped long enough to take a photograph. He was amazed to see the shadowy form of a figure standing by the white doors.

Experts in the paranormal refer to ghostly activity like that which occurs inside the Memphis Conference and Visitors' Bureau as residual hauntings. Troy Taylor, author of *The Ghost Hunter's Guidebook*, defines a residual haunting as events that "are often replayed as smells, sounds and noises that have no apparent explanation. Often, the mysterious sounds or images that are recorded relate to traumatic events that have taken place and that have caused some sort of disturbance (or 'impression') to occur there" (78). Buildings that were the scenes of great suffering, like the Woolen Building, are prime candidates for this sort of "unintelligent" haunting.

SAUCES RESTAURANT

In the nineteenth century, a number of different epidemics, such as smallpox, cholera, and dysentery, raged across the South. People living in Memphis were particularly susceptible to yellow fever, owing to the city's close proximity to the Mississippi River. Transmitted by the female Aedes aegypti mosquito, the disease induces jaundice, headaches, a high protein content in the urine, and liver and renal failure. The most noticeable symptom of yellow fever was black vomit, consisting of stomach acids and blood. Yellow fever was carried up the Mississippi from New Orleans, where the disease was spread by infected sailors on ships from the Caribbean or West Africa. Memphis was also an ideal breeding ground for mosquitoes because of the town's swampy location. Bayou Gayoso, a winding creek that fed into the Mississippi River by way of the Wolf River, became nothing more than a sewer in the second half of the nineteenth century as a result of the city's tremendous growth. Outbreaks of yellow fever were reported in Memphis in 1828, 1855, and 1867. However, no one was prepared for the severity of the yellow fever epidemic of 1873. Over 2,000 people succumbed to the disease after the physicians originally declared the outbreak an epidemic on September 14, 1873. To make matters worse, Memphis was still reeling a smallpox and a cholera epidemic that struck the city at the beginning of the year. When an outbreak of yellow fever was reported in Vicksburg in July 1878, city officials in Memphis halted travel to Memphis from the South. However, a steamboat worker named William Warren who was infected with yellow fever made his way into Kate Bionda's restaurant on August 1, 1878. The next day, he began exhibiting the unmistakable symptoms of yellow fever, and he was quarantined on President's Island, where he died a few days later. He infected Kate Bionda, who became the next yellow fever casualty on August 13. Yellow fever spread like wildfire throughout the city. With the memory of the previous yellow fever epidemic still fresh on their minds, over 25,000 people fled Memphis, leaving devastation in their wake. During the entire month of September 1878, an average of 200 people died each day. Those few people who were still healthy cared for the sick. By the time cold weather arrested the progress of the disease in early October, 20,000 people in the Southeast were dead. Because African Americans seemed to possess a genetic resistance to the disease, only 7 percent of the blacks who contracted yellow fever died. Ninety percent of the citizens of Memphis who contracted the disease were white; 70 percent of these victims died. The next year, Memphis city leaders initiated a massive project to improve the city's sewer system. Today, the yellow fever epidemics of 1873 and 1878 are a fading memory, kept alive by the thousands of yellow fever victims in the local cemeteries and in ghost stories generated in and around the makeshift hospitals that were quickly set up to treat the victims.

One of these field hospitals is the Barbaro Building at 95 South Main Street. At the time of the yellow fever epidemic of 1878, an Italian immigrant named Anthony Sebastian Barbaro operated a wholesale grocery at this site. Sebastian, who had contracted yellow fever in 1873, converted his store into a clinic five years later. Cots were set up in the first and second floors of the building and the basement. As many as a hundred people were treated in the store each day between August and September.

Unfortunately, hundreds of yellow fever victims died as well. As a result, the alley next to Barbaro's store served as a kind of morgue. The bodies were piled up in the narrow space for days at a time in the sweltering heat, which caused the corpses to putrefy even faster. The stench was intolerable. Not surprisingly, the alley is said to be haunted. When this author visited Sauces Restaurant in November 2009, I took photographs of my daughter and son-in-law standing in the alley. When we examined the pictures, two orbs were clearly visible over their heads. My wife, Marilyn, also captured a number of orbs in that location.

Barbaro's company was still in business until 2003, when Sauces Restaurant took over the building. In recent years, employees at the restaurant have had a number of paranormal experiences there. Chairs have fallen over by themselves. In the basement, furniture has scooted across the floor, pushed by an unseen hand. Several employees have heard their names called. Like many places that were scenes of great suffering, Sauces Restaurant seems to be inhabited by the spirits of those victims of the yellow fever epidemic of 1878.

THE WOODRUFF-FONTAINE HOUSE

Victorian Village is an area along Adams Avenue between Danny Thomas Boulevard and Manassas that was once considered one of the most exclusive residential districts in Memphis. In the mid-1800s, many of the city's wealthiest layers, judges, merchants, cotton factors, and businessmen built townhouses and mansions in architectural styles ranging from neoclassical through late Greek Revival. Most of the houses built on this street in the late 1840s and 1850s were comparatively modest. However, by the 1890s, a number of lavish Victorian homes lined Adams Street. Most of these treasures are gone now, but a few remain. One of the most intriguing of these old homes is the Woodruff-Fontaine House.

In 1845, a carriage maker named Amos Woodruff came to Memphis from New Jersey. He rapidly became one of the city's most successful entrepreneurs, earning a fortune in banking, cotton, lumber, and insurance. By the late 1860s, Woodruff began thinking seriously about building a residence that would reflect his status in the community. He paid $12,000 for a lot in "Millionaire's Row," now known to locals as Victorian Village. In 1870, construction of his opulent home at 680 Adams Avenue was completed. Amos Woodruff lived there until his death in 1883. The first gala to be held at the mansion was the marriage of Amos Woodruff's nineteen-year-old daughter, Mollie, to Egbert Woodridge on December 18, 1871. After their lavish wedding, the couple moved into a suite of rooms on the second floor of the family home.

Unfortunately, the happiness of married life eluded Mollie. Her first son died soon after birth on March 13, 1875, in her bedroom at the northwest corner of the house. Two months later, Mollie suffered another crushing blow when her husband, Egbert, drowned in a boating accident from "swallowing too much swamp water." Egbert, who had also contracted pneumonia, breathed his last in the Cabbage Room of the Woodruff home. For the next eight years, Mollie lived the life of a widow in her parents' house. Then on June 14, 1883, Mollie married again, this time to James Hennings just before Amos sold the house at 680 Adams Avenue to Noland Fontaine. Two years later, the couple's only child died at birth in 1885. Mollie herself died while visiting her sister's home on September 14, 1917.

Noland Fontaine and his family lived in the Woodruffs' former home for the next forty-six years. The Fontaines, who loved to entertain, transformed the home into one of the city's primary social centers. Their guest list routinely included the rich and famous. Grover Cleveland, John Philip Sousa, and Adlai Stevenson all attended parties there. After Noland died in the home of kidney failure in 1913, his widow, Virginia, continued living in the mansion until her own death at the age of eighty-two. The old mansion housed the James Lee Art Academy from 1930 until 1959. The house, which had been deeded to the city, stood vacant for several years until it was rescued from demolition by the Association for the Preservation of Tennessee Antiquities in 1962, which restored the Victorian showplace to its former grandeur. The mansion opened as a house museum two years later. The Woodruff-Fontaine House is now one of the best-known mansions in Victorian

Village. The possibility that Mollie Woodruff's melancholy spirit might have returned to the family home has undoubtedly enhanced its allure.

Stories of the haunting of the Woodruff-Fontaine date back to the three decades when it housed the art academy. Students told the director of the academy, Rosa Lee, that they sensed a presence and heard sighs and whispers in Mollie's bedroom, known as the Cabbage Room because of cabbage-rose print wallpaper that covers the walls. On a few occasions, students said that they heard a woman crying in the room. For some strange reason, the Cabbage Room always seemed to be colder than any other part of the house.

More ghostly incidents were reported in Mollie's bedroom after her home became a house museum in 1964. Visitors and volunteers have heard the sound of a baby crying, possibly the spectral cries of Mollie's first-born son, who died there. People have also heard a mournful voice saying, "Oh, dear. Oh, dear" in the Cabbage Room. In the mid-1980s, a tourist was walking into Mollie's bedroom when she found it difficult to breathe. She immediately walked out of the bedroom and asked the tour guide who died there. On May 26, 1984, tour guides Ted Hinson and Scarlett Cavagnaro were working on the first floor at 10:00 A.M. when they heard a woman's muffled crying coming from the second floor. They listened for about twenty minutes before deciding to investigate. As they were walking up the stairs, they could tell that the crying was coming from Mollie's bedroom. When they reached the first-floor landing, the crying stopped. The pair went into Mollie's bedroom and found everything was normal. Scratching their heads, Hinson and Cavagnaro walked back downstairs. After a few minutes, the crying resumed. Later, the tour guides discovered that they had had their weird experience just one day before the anniversary of Egbert Woodridge's death in the house.

In the early 1980s, a professor from the University of Alabama had an even stranger experience in the Cabbage Room. He and a tour guide had just walked into the bedroom when both of them saw the bed sheets visibly smoothen, as if by an invisible hand. Later that evening, the professor and his family returned to the Woodruff-Fontaine House after closing hours. They just happened to gaze up at Mollie's bedroom window, and they noticed that the shutters were flapping wildly. The window was shut at the time, so the disturbance could not have been caused by the wind. The professor and his family piled back into their car and left.

Mrs. Elizabeth Dow Edwards, the great-granddaughter of Mollie's sister Sarah, has heard doors slamming in the house, usually when the volunteers are preparing for a party. However, in 1979, something happened that almost made her believe that the house is haunted. Elizabeth was cataloging the costumes with a friend, Margo Ramsey, on the first floor when her daughter, Michelle, came down the stairs. Margo could tell by the stricken look on the girl's face that something was wrong. Michelle said that while she was walking down the stairs, she had the feeling that someone was following her. When she turned around, no one was there. Margo had a similar experience a few days later when someone standing behind her said, "My dear." She looked behind her, and there was no one there.

Martha Griffin, a former volunteer at the Woodruff-Fontaine House, believes that Mollie's ghost is not the only spirit haunting the old house. The second entity, an aggressive, masculine spirit, usually manifests on the third floor of the house. Several visitors have sensed a malevolent presence on the third floor. This ghost is said to be much more threatening than Mollie's benevolent spirit. Griffin was leading a group of tourists on the third floor when she realized that something evil was nearby. "He didn't want me up there. I knew that," Griffin said.

Volunteers are at a loss to explain all of the ghostly occurrences at the Woodruff-Fontaine House. However, an explanation for the paranormal activity inside the Cabbage Room might have been provided by a medium who was taking a tour of the house. When the medium walked into the Cabbage Room, she grew pale, and her entire body began to tremble. After she regained her composure, she informed Mrs. Edwards, the tour guide, that Mollie's bedroom had been arranged incorrectly. She said that the big half-tester bed covered with a crocheted bedspread should have been placed on the staircase wall on the east, not on the south wall. One wonders if Mollie's ghost will continue to express her displeasure in her bedroom until her bed is moved back where it belongs.

SLAVE HAVEN / BURKLE ESTATE

Little is known of Jacob Burkle, the builder and owner of the Burkle Estate. In the mid-1840s, Burkle fled Germany to escape conscription on Bismark's army. Within just a few years of arriving in Memphis, Burkle became the wealthy owner of a stockyard and a bakery. In 1849, he built a comparatively modest cottage at 826 North Second Street on what was then the north edge of the Gayoso Bayou. In 1849, Jacob married Mary Frecht, who bore him three children. Following Mary's death in December 1859, Jacob married Rebecca Vorwort three months later. Jacob and Rebecca had two children. The house was passed down to one of his daughters, Rebecca, who married a salesman named John Lawless. Rebecca and John had three sons and one daughter, Mrs. Townes Compton. Mrs. Compton was the last member of Jacob Burkle's family to live in the old house. She died in 1978, and in 1997, this small, white clapboard house become a museum. Today, the Burkle Estate is remembered for the legends Mrs. Compton told about the house and for the ghostly experiences that tour guides and ghost hunters have had there.

Were it not for the historical marker placed in front of the house by the Tennessee Historical Society, the Burkle Estate would appear to be nothing more than a spooky-looking old house with a sagging front porch, peeling paint, and cracked columns. However, underneath a thick wooden door in the parlor are steps leading to a small cellar, with a ceiling less than six feet high. Three brick steps lead into a wall of the cellar. Even though the cellar is no bigger than a department-store elevator, legend has it that as many as fifteen runaway slaves once took refuge there. They then crawled through tunnels leading from the Burkle Estate to the Wolf River, which, according to maps dating back to 1860, was only 1,500 feet from the house. According to stories told by Catherine Compton, her grandfather left a sack of gold on a fence post at the river. The captain of a passing steamboat would then pick up the runaway slaves. The escaped slaves then went to Cairo, Illinois, and eventually made their way to Canada.

People interested in the South's tragic legacy of slavery are not the only visitors to the Burkle Estate. In recent years, the old house has attracted the attention of local ghost-hunting groups. Michael Espanjer, director of the Memphis Paranormal Investigations Team, said that his group has taken some eerie photographs at the house during the daylight hours. Espanjer became interested in the house after hearing a story told by a former employee who worked at the gift shop. Late one afternoon when he was the only person in the building, he was standing behind the counter when the front door slowly opened by itself. A few seconds later, he heard two other doors open and slam shut in other parts of the house. The man was so startled that he ran out the front door and never returned. Some visitors have reported being overcome by a chilly feeling while walking through the house. The cellar is also unusually cold at times.

Because of its legendary past, the Burkle House has become a stop on tours conducted by an African American history foundation called Heritage Tours Inc. Inside the house, one can find not only nineteenth-century furnishings, but also such grim reminders of slavery as slave auction materials, slave trader handbills proclaiming "Negroes wanted!" and a photograph of a half-naked male whose back was crisscrossed with scars made by an overseer's whip. A map hanging in the east central hall details the routes of the Underground Railroad. However, no hard evidence supporting the house's storied past as a stop on the Underground Railroad has been found. In fact, an archaeological survey of the property revealed the existence of no tunnels at all. Apparently, a letter written to Burkle by a grateful fugitive slave and other documents were burned by his great-granddaughter years ago. Only the mute testimony of the mysterious cellar and the uneasy spirits trapped inside the house supports the legend.

RALEIGH CEMETERY

In the early years of the nineteenth century, Raleigh, established at Sanderlin's Bluff over the Wolf River, was one of the few thriving cities in Shelby County. In 1825, Raleigh became the county seat of Shelby County because it was more centrally located than neighboring Memphis. For the next few decades, Raleigh, not Memphis, seemed destined to become the largest city in the county. By 1840, Raleigh was a thriving city with academies, churches, and a mineral spa. However, in the 1840s, Memphis experienced a growth boom that eventually eclipsed that of the county seat. Raleigh's decline escalated after the courts moved back to Memphis. After World War II, Raleigh was incorporated into the city of Memphis.

The most significant remnant of the old town is the seven-acre Raleigh Cemetery on Old Raleigh Lagrange and East Streets. The earliest burial in the old cemetery dates back to 1841. The inscriptions on the tombstones bear mute witness to the wide variety of social classes and cultural groups buried there. Isaac Rawlings, the second mayor of Memphis, was buried at Raleigh Cemetery because he did not wish to be interred in a town as rough and uncultured as Memphis was at the time. The children of the philanthropist Wade Bolton are buried there as well. However, one can also find the graves of former slaves and victims of the city's yellow fever epidemics of the 1870s.

Old Raleigh Cemetery has been almost entirely overshadowed by Elmwood Cemetery, the oldest active cemetery in Memphis. Its ghosts are not nearly as well known as those at Elmwood Cemetery, probably because Old Raleigh Cemetery is much less accessible. In recent years, the abandoned cemetery has become popular with local paranormal investigators, who have photographed orbs and mists floating among the tombstones. *In the early 2000s, Michael Espanjer, founder and director of the Memphis Paranormal Investigations Team, conducted a late-night investigation of Old Raleigh Cemetery on Veterans Day. While one of Michael's investigators, Ginger, took photographs of the grave of a veteran of World War II, Michael saluted and said, "You served your country well." When Michael examined Ginger's photograph, he was surprised to see in one of the photographs a beam of light shooting down from the sky at a ninety-degree angle right into the veteran's tombstone. The other pictures of the same grave, taken just seconds apart, revealed nothing unusual.*

Today, only a small section of Old Raleigh Cemetery has been cleared. The rest of the cemetery is so overgrown that many of the tombstones are barely visible. Erosion created a huge ravine, which has engulfed many of the graves. Erosion has also exposed a number of caskets on the south side of the cemetery. A number of the vaults have caved in, exposing their contents. The neglect, which began in the 1940s, continues to this day because of disputes over landownership. Folklore contains many stories of the supernatural consequences of not honoring the dead. Perhaps this is the reason why the spirits of Old Raleigh Cemetery are so restless.

THE ORPHEUM THEATER

The Orpheum Theater stands on the site of the Grand Opera House on the corner of Main and Beale Streets. When construction was completed, it was one of the most elegant theaters outside of New York City. In 1906, the Grand Opera House changed its name to the Orpheum Theater. For the next sixteen years, vaudeville acts from all over the United States performed at the Orpheum Theater. In 1923, tragedy struck. A fire broke out during the performance of a stripper named Blossom Seeley and burned the theater to the ground. A few months later, a Chicago architectural firm by the name of Rapp and Rapp was hired to design a new theater, similar to the larger Orpheum in Omaha, Nebraska. In 1928, the Orpheum was rebuilt at a cost of $1.6 million. Twice as large as the old theater, the new Orpheum was resplendent with enormous crystal chandeliers, tasseled brocade draperies, and gilded moldings. The new theater had three balcony structures: a mezzanine, a large main balcony, and an asymmetrical uppermost section known as the "gallery." In an effort to conform to the Jim Crow laws of the 1920s, the designers divided the gallery into an "Upper Gallery" and "Lower Gallery" so that black and white patrons would not sit together. A Mighty Wurlitzer organ was installed as the centerpiece of the theater.

In 1940, as movies were replacing vaudeville as America's primary form of entertainment, the Malco movie theater chain purchased the Orpheum Theater and transformed it into one of the South's premier movie palaces. The number of black patrons grew to the point that the upper gallery was no longer large enough to accommodate all of them. A wall was erected down the middle of the main balcony so that blacks could sit on the north side of the theater and whites on the south side. When Malco announced that it was selling the Orpheum Theater in

1976, rumors spread around Memphis that the old theater would be razed to make room for an office complex. The Orpheum Theater was saved from the wrecking ball in 1977 when the Memphis Development Foundation became the new owners of the building. Once again, concerts and Broadway productions were featured at the Orpheum. The former movie palace closed on Christmas Day 1982 for renovations. Two years later, the Orpheum Theater was fully restored at a cost of $5 million. Today, patrons can enjoy Broadway musicals like *Cats* and Las Vegas performers like Tony Bennett, singers like Gladys Knight and the Pips, musicians like Kenny G., and figure skaters like Dorothy Hamill at the Orpheum Theater. If they are lucky, patrons might also catch a glimpse of a little girl who haunts the Orpheum.

The ghost who haunts the Orpheum Theater is the spirit of a little twelve-year-old girl who has come to be known as Mary. The story goes that in 1921, she was crossing Beale Street in front of the Orpheum when she was struck and killed by a car. For some unknown reason, she has made the Orpheum Theater her adopted home. She has been described as a little girl wearing a white dress, long black stockings, and pigtails, who is usually seen sitting in seat C-5. She has been seen walking through the uppermost aisles of the balcony and running through the dark hallways. People who have seen her up-close remember her blank stare and her otherworldly appearance. She is a mischievous little sprite who has been known to play the organ and open and slam dressing-room doors backstage. Many people have heard her muffled footsteps all over the theater after it was closed.

Many attempts have been made to contact the shy little ghost over the years. In 1977, the New York Company of *Fiddler on the Roof* became so convinced that the Orpheum Theater was haunted that they held a séance in the upper balcony in an attempt to contact the ghost. Two years later, a parapsychology class from the University of Memphis used a Ouija board and séances to make contact with Mary. The students concluded that Mary was actually killed in a fall that occurred outside the theater. They also detected the presence of other spirits in the theater.

In the early 1980s, Yul Brynner appeared at the Orpheum Theater for a production of *The King and I.* Brynner, who had an abiding interest in the paranormal, was elated when he was told about Mary's ghost and was eager to communicate with her. He went to the mezzanine and sat next to C-5, Mary's seat, in the hope that she would talk to him. Several hours later, Brynner emerged from the theater with a wide smile on his face. Later, he told a reporter that he had talked to Mary's ghost for several hours, but he refused to divulge the specifics of their conversation.

In 2005, the Memphis Paranormal Investigation Team visited the Orpheum Theater. At the time, the investigators were followed around by a film crew with The Learning Channel. Michael Espanjer, the director, said that when the researchers were on the fourth-floor mezzanine, something growled at them. "It was kind of like the *Poltergeist* movie," Michael said. "The other spirits tried to keep the girl [Mary] protected."

Mary reappeared once more during the 2006 production of *The Lion King*. Almost immediately, the stagehands complained that objects they had set down in a specific place had been moved to a different location an hour later. When the last of the twenty-seven trucks was being unloaded, three burly men ran down the stairs yelling, "We saw her! We saw her!" After they calmed down, the stagehands explained that they had seen Mary's ghost standing at the end of a hallway.

Admittedly, most of the people who have encountered Mary's ghost have not enjoyed the experience. For example, Vincent Astor, the former building supervisor organist, said that in 1972, he was changing a light bulb when he was overcome with the feeling that someone was watching him. He was alone in the building at the time. "Then I felt that cold, eerie feeling many have described," Astor said. "It was like getting into a bathtub of cold liver. Once you feel it, you never forget it." Other people who have heard Mary's spectral cries at night are moved to pity for the little girl who seems to crave human company.

ERNESTINE AND HAZEL'S

Ernestine and Hazel's at 531 South Main Street has the most colorful past of any bar in Memphis. In the early 1900s, it housed a pharmacy and dry-goods store. Abraham Plough, the founder of the Schering-Plough Corporation, sold St. Joseph's Aspirin and other pharmaceuticals from the building. From the 1920s to the 1950s, the first floor was converted into a saloon. The bar itself was originally used to serve up ice cream sodas back when a drugstore was located here. The second floor was a brothel. During World War II, the establishment was very popular with military personnel, who arrived in Memphis at the train station just across the street. In the late 1950s, the building was purchased by two cousins, Ernestine and Hazel, whose husbands had connections with Stax Records. They purchased the building and transformed it into a hotel for travelers who had just disembarked from the train. At this time, the hotel was popular with rowdy musicians and bluesmen. Elvis Presley is rumored to have spent the night here in the 1950s. By the 1960s, Ernestine and Hazel's had become a hangout for Otis Redding, Ike and Tina Turner, and Solomon Burke. Stax musicians also called Ernestine and Hazel's home. Today, Ernestine and Hazel's shabby ambience has made it a popular setting for movies. As of this printing, three movies have been filmed here: *21 Grams* (2003), *Black Snake Moan* (2007), and *My Blueberry Night* (2008).

Ernestine and Hazel's signature hamburger—the Soul Burger—as well as the drink, music, and atmosphere are undoubtedly responsible for the bar's popularity. In recent years, however, more and more people walk through the doors in the hope of making contact with the paranormal. The best source for ghost stories is part-time bartender Nathaniel Moore, who has lived in Memphis since 1947. Resplendent in his vest, shirtsleeves, and fedora, Moore tells late-night patrons about the haunted jukebox, which plays songs that reflect the tenor of the conversations of people sitting nearby. For example, several years ago, some women were celebrating their divorces at the bar when the jukebox started playing Tammy Wynette's "D.I.V.O.R.C.E." People sitting in the rooms upstairs have heard the mournful strains of blues music. Spectral music has been known to filter down to the bar area from the piano upstairs. Moore also speaks of spectral figures that people have seen at the bar. The janitor, who reports to work at 6:00 P.M., has seen apparitions walking up and down the staircase. Lured to the old bar by the countless ghost stories, a group of paranormal researchers named Memphis Ghosthunters investigated Ernestine and Hazel's in the early 2000s. The group's photographic evidence included the image of a woman's face on a door. They also captured the face of a man on the staircase. The group's most impressive "catch" was the videotaped image of a full-bodied apparition.

Walking through the front door of Ernestine and Hazel's is like stepping back into the past. Couples dance to the songs of Elvis Presley and Al Green on the jukebox. The tables are covered with magazines from the 1950s. Visitors walking through the warren of rooms on the second floor can easily envision ladies of the evening lounging on the gritty vinyl couches. Upstairs, one can also see the old claw-footed bathtub in which a prostitute committed suicide. Thousands of locals and tourists visit Ernestine and Hazel's every year, despite the rather harsh rules so colorfully expressed in a sign in an upstairs hallway: "No dope smoken No Cursin No freeloaden." These days, the thrills ghost hunters seek at Ernestine and Hazel's are more legitimate—and some would say more enjoyable—than the pleasures desperate men sought on the second floor so many years ago.

THE NATIONAL ORNAMENTAL METAL MUSEUM

In 1881, bricks from a military hospital destroyed by a flood in Napoleon, Arkansas, in the mid-1800s were brought to Fort Pickering in Memphis. In 1884, the U.S. Public Health Service constructed the U.S. Marine Hospital, consisting of six buildings. For sixty-seven years, it was run by the U.S. Army and the Army Reserve. In 1951, the government changed the name of the complex to the United States Public Hospital, which was operated by the National Guard until 1965. In 1970, the City of Memphis acquired the western half of the property. Three of the buildings were leased to the National Ornamental Metal Museum, which opened its doors on February 5, 1979. The museum itself is housed in the Nurses' Residence, which was built in 1937. The Doctors' Residence, which was built in 1884, is now used as housing for metalworker interns and for apprentice blacksmiths. All three buildings are clustered around a beautiful garden. Even though most of the traces of the old military hospital have been removed, the misery endured by many of the patients admitted there is still embedded in the walls and floors of the facility.

Paranormal activity has been reported in all three buildings. Over the years, workers at the Ornamental Metal Museum have reported hearing ghostly voices and footsteps in empty corridors. Objects placed in a specific spot at night have been moved to an entirely different location the next morning. Mists and even full-bodied apparitions occasionally make an appearance here as well. Laura Cunningham, author of *Haunted Memphis*, reports that in the former Officers' Residence, an intern sleeping in her dorm room was awakened by the sound of bottles and jars sliding off her bathroom shelf between 3:00 and 4:00 A.M. The poltergeist activity ceased only after the room was painted. The most commonly sighted apparitions, though, are the ghosts of soldiers and nurses who have been seen walking the grounds.

The most haunted of the three buildings is undoubtedly the metallurgy library. In the 1880s, a tunnel connected the building to the main hospital. When the former Doctors' Residence was remodeled, the tunnel was blocked. During the yellow fever epidemic of 1873, the basement of the building served as the morgue for the hospital. A chute was installed to facilitate the moving of the corpses down the stairs. Workers recruited from a local prison are said to have run out of the building during the daytime because of something they saw down there. Just before the museum opened in 1979, an employee standing on the first floor of the metallurgy library peered up through a hole in the ceiling and saw a face staring down at her. One night, several interns saw the ghostly image of a man in a wheelchair on the second floor of the building. In 2008, during an all-night investigation of the metallurgy library, members of the ghost-hunting group Paranormal Inc. heard a ghostly voice say "Hey!" from one of the back rooms. A half hour later, they saw black, shadowy figures block out the light seeping through the cracks in the door leading to the stairwell. One of the EVPs the group recorded that night was a faint voice saying, "Hi."

The National Ornamental Metal Museum is the only American institution devoted to the promotion and preservation of fine metalwork. Tourists travel thousands of miles to watch the museum's skilled artisans and blacksmiths create beautiful jewelry and household utensils. Classes offered at the museum teach budding young metal artisans the centuries-old craft of metalworking. One wonders, though, how many people visit the National Ornamental Metal Museum because of its reputation as one of the most haunted places in Memphis.

Wisconsin

WEST SALEM

A Baptist minister named Elder Card platted West Salem, Wisconsin, in 1856 on ten acres of land donated by a railroad company. A New Englander named Thomas Leon had built the first log cabin there in 1851. Card named the fledgling settlement "Salem" because it is the Hebrew word for "peace." The word "West" was added later on to alleviate the confusion caused by having two towns in the state named "Salem." A train station was erected on the original Milwaukee–La Crosse Railway. The nearby town of Neshonoc lost out on its bid to have the depot constructed there, so a number of homes and buildings were relocated from Neshonoc to West Salem. On July 1, 1911, the town was nearly destroyed by a fire that broke out near the railroad tracks. Today, West Salem is a sleepy little midwestern town with a population that hovers around 5,000 people. The town is of particular interest to architects because of the Palmer brothers octagonal houses. They were built in 1856 and 1857 by Dr. Horace Palmer and Monroe Palmer.

THE HAMLIN GARLAND HOMESTEAD

Hamlin Garland (1860–1940) was a Pulitzer Prize–winning American novelist, short-story writer, poet, essayist, and memoirist. He is best known for *Main Traveled Roads* (1891), a collection of short stories that chronicle the rigors of living on the prairie in the Midwest in the second half of the nineteenth century. His autobiography, *A Son of the Middle Border*, is an account of his life growing up in a succession of homesteads in Iowa and South Dakota. Garland was born in a small log cabin in West Salem, Wisconsin, on September 14, 1860. The next year, he and his family moved to Green's Coulee near Onalaska, where they stayed until moving to Iowa in 1869. In 1893, Garland returned to West Salem and purchased the site that is now the Garland Homestead with royalties he had received from the publication of *Main Traveled Roads.* He spent most of October renovating his new house so that his family could move in by Thanksgiving. Garland's house, known in the 1890s as "Maple Shade," was the first home in the area to have indoor plumbing, a room-sized fireplace, and a tennis court on the lawn. The house partially burned in 1912, but Garland rebuilt it quickly. He used the homestead as a retirement home for his parents and as a summer home for his family between 1893 and 1915. Garland's first daughter was born in the Homestead House in 1903. His mother passed away in the house in 1900; his father followed her in death in 1914. Garland also wrote a number of novels in the house. He moved to New York in 1915 to be closer to his publisher. The house was sold in 1938 and remodeled to accommodate two-person occupancy. In 1972, the Hamlin Garland Homestead was declared a historic landmark by the Department of the Interior. Restorations of the old house to its pre-1915 appearance did not begin until 1975.

People began talking about the ghosts in the Hamlin Garland Homestead in 1940, shortly after the author's death. Children passing by the house told their parents that someone who resembled Mark Twain was standing in the doorway of the empty house. The strange man was also seen looking out one of the upstairs windows. Actually, many people believed that Mark Twain and Hamlin Garland resembled each other, so the confusion the children experienced is understandable.

The paranormal activity inside the Hamlin Garland Homestead escalated after it became a house museum. Many people who walk through the front door immediately feel a presence in the house. In an interview with Jim Longo in the book *Ghosts along the Mississippi*, Errol Kindschy said that when he and his father were restoring the house in 1975, a beautiful floor lamp standing in the middle of the floor suddenly toppled over, smashing the globe. In 1976, Errol and the museum treasurer had just locked the front door and were walking down the sidewalk when he remembered that he had to get something from the gift shop. When he returned to the front door, it was standing wide open. No one was in the house at the time. On a number of different occasions, after Errol turned off the lights and locked up the house, he returned to his little house behind the Homestead House and was shocked to find that the lights were turned back on. As a rule, at the end of the tourist season, the staff turns off the heat in the building to save money. One cold winter's night, Errol walked into the house and was surprised to find that the house was warm. There is no way the heat could have turned on by itself.

Errol Kindschy is not the only person who has had ghostly encounters in the Hamlin Garland Homestead. Late one afternoon just before closing, a couple of volunteers checked the house to make sure that all of the chairs were pushed back under the tables, that the floors were clean, and that the bedspread was smoothed out. When they returned the next morning, they were shocked to find the impression of a body on the bed in Hamlin Garland's bedroom.

Anyone who is familiar with Hamlin Garland's life and work should not be surprised by ghostly occurrences in the Hamlin Garland Homestead. Garland spent the last ten years of his life studying psychic phenomena. He wrote five books on the subject. His last book, *The Mystery of the Buried Crosses* (1939), recounts his attempts to verify the legitimacy of a medium who led him to several buried objects. When Garland died in 1940, his ashes were not scattered along West Salem's hillside. Instead, they were buried in a local cemetery. Could it be that Garland's spirit is expressing its displeasure at not being buried the way he had wished?

LA CROSSE

Fur traders were already living in the area now occupied by the city of La Crosse when New York native Nathan Myrick established a temporary trading post at the junction of the Black, La Crosse, and Mississippi Rivers in 1841. In 1844, a small community of Mormons moved to the new settlement. By the end of the decade, the settlement included a hotel, stores, and a post office. It was incorporated as a city in 1856. The construction of the La Crosse & Milwaukee Railroad in 1858 brought even more growth to the city. In the second half of the nineteenth century, La Crosse became the second-largest city in the state. Its economy was boosted by the development of the lumber industry and the brewing industry. Three colleges and universities were founded there between 1890 and 1912.

THE FIRST LUTHERAN CHURCH

The roots of the First Lutheran Church in La Crosse can be traced back to a small group of believers organized on April 22, 1859, called "The German Evangelical Lutheran Church." Because the members of the church did not have a preacher, they had to worship by means of "reading Services" and Sunday School classes. The fledgling congregation acquired its first pastor when a traveling minister named Gottlieb Fachtman arrived in La Crosse on August 1, 1859. The members worshiped in a rented school until April 1860, when they moved an old wooden church to Fifth and Jay Streets. In 1867, a new church was built at Fifth and Cass. This was the home of the First Lutheran Church for thirty-seven years. The congregation moved to its present location at West Avenue and Cameron in 1905. At the time, no one realized that what they thought was the perfect location for their new church actually had a very dark history.

In 1848, an arrogant English immigrant named John Barlow bought a tract of land now bounded by West Avenue from Market Street to State Street with the intention of becoming a gentleman farmer. However, Barlow overestimated his knowledge of agriculture, and his property was reduced to what is now the southwest corner of Cameron and West Avenues. Barlow's fortunes seemed to be on the up-swing when he received a letter informing him that his father had died in England and had left him an inheritance of 10,000 pounds. A messenger traveled to Wisconsin to deliver the money to John Barlow. However, a week after the messenger arrived, both he and John Barlow were stabbed to death in Barlow's small house. Neither the culprit nor the money was ever found.

Not long after Barlow's murder, locals reported seeing his ghost walking around his small tract of land. Decades later, his ghost was seen walking down Cameron Avenue, usually around 10:00 P.M. After the specter crossed the street at the corner of West Avenue, he uttered several strange, unintelligible words and vanished. People continued seeing Barlow's ghost for fifty years. However, after the cornerstone of the First Evangelical Lutheran Church was laid on a corner of what used to be his farm, his ghost was never seen again. Perhaps the founding of a church on Barlow's property convinced the greedy man that his search for his stolen money, even after death, was preventing him from entering Paradise.

THE BODEGA BREW PUB

In the 1890s, Paul Malin opened the Malin Pool and Sample Room at 120 South Fourth Street. After Malin died in 1901, the building changed hands several times over the next few years. Nobody really knew why no one stayed in the building very long until the owner, a German immigrant named A. J. "Skimmer", Hine, made a startling confession to his friends in 1907.

In the early 1900s, Hine ran a bar called the Union Saloon in the building. He told his friends that ever since he moved in, the ghost of former owner Paul Malin appeared to him every night. The ghost also made its presence known at night by making weird noises. Finally, by 1907, Hine had lost so much sleep that he decided to sell his business for the sake of his health.

In 1994, Jeff Hotson opened the Bodega Brew Pub in the old building. His bar was not open long before employees began having strange experiences. Several of these encounters were recorded in *The Wisconsin Road Guide to Haunted Locations*, by Chad Lewis and Terry Fisk. One night after the bar closed, an employee saw a male ghost walking through the bar. The man did not acknowledge the presence of the employee. On another occasion, an employee who was working in the basement moved a pile of bricks in front of a door. He then went upstairs for a few minutes. When he returned to the basement, the bricks were in a different location entirely. Some employees and customers have heard the clicking sounds of a woman in high heels walking across the basement floor.

Today, the Bodega Brew Pub is one of the most popular eating places in La Crosse. The bar offers customers fifteen tap beers and four hundred bottled beers. At lunchtime, people flock to the Bodega Brew Pub to sample such fare as braunschweiger, onion, and bleu cheese sandwiches, tacos, and Thai spiced chicken. The pub is also a good place for people who simply want to relax by playing board games and talking about the ghost of the former owner who refuses to leave.

THE HYDRITE CHEMICAL COMPANY

Established in 1929, the privately owned Hydrite Chemical Company is a manufacturer and distributor of chemical products. The company's diverse business segments include food sanitation, waste management, organic processing, food ingredients, pulp and paper, and processed sulfur. In recent years, the Hydrite Chemical Company has entered the graphic arts Market, producing solutions resins that have a long-established history in the water-based ink and coating market. The chemical plant might not be haunted, but the site on which it is located certainly was.

Around the turn of the century, an old factory stood on the site of the Hydrite Chemical Company. Former night watchmen and managers said that for many years the presence of a poltergeist made working there almost intolerable. They could tell when the entity was about to become active when the wind began howling in the distance. The roaring of the wind was amplified as it approached the factory. Then, suddenly, the sound would cease altogether. It was replaced a few minutes later by the maniacal laughter of an invisible entity. After announcing its arrival, the poltergeist began throwing objects across the plant. It then made its way through a boarded-over door in the wall and up the stairs to a vacant place above the offices where an employee was said to have killed himself.

The poltergeist tormented the employees of all three companies that were housed in the building: the George Pierce Sash and Door Factory, the Packers' Package Company, and the Vought-Berger Plant. In 1903, one of the plant owners, George Pierce, told his employees that he had so much work to do that he was going to spend the night in the building. He was found dead the next morning. The paranormal activity stopped only after the old factory was razed. Occasionally, spirits that haunted a building that has been torn down move into the next structure that occupies the site. If the poltergeist is tormenting the employees of the Hydrite Chemical Company, no one seems to be talking about it.

MINERAL POINT

In 1827, the first settlers arrived in what is now Mineral Point, Wisconsin. In 1828, the discovery of large quantities of galena, or lead ore, transformed Mineral Point into the focus of lead mining operations in present-day Wisconsin. Hundreds of immigrants flocked to the region in the hope of making a fortune. In the 1840s, so many Cornish miners flocked to Mineral Point that by 1845 half of the town's inhabitants had Cornish ancestry. By the end of the decade, however, the lead deposits were becoming depleted. A large number of miners left Mineral Point in 1849 after gold was discovered in California. By the end of the nineteenth century, zinc mining and smelting had replaced lead mining in importance. Zinc mining continued on a large scale in Mineral Point until the 1920s.

THE WALKER HOUSE

The old building that is known today as the Walker House was created in 1836 when an addition was made to an old miner's stone house. Originally established as an up-scale inn, the handsome three-story building had a pub on the first floor. The dining rooms were on the second floor. Guests slept in the bedrooms on the third floor. For over 120 years, the old inn attracted miners, tourists, gamblers, and railroad workers. After the inn closed in 1957, it stood vacant for seven years. Then in 1964, Ted Landon and his partners purchased the old house and devoted the next decade to renovating it. In 1974, the Cornish Pub opened its doors in the old structure. However, four years later, the pub was sold to Dr. David Ruf, who changed the name of the business to "The Walker House." A few years later, the new owners changed the name once again, this time to "The Walker-Gruber House." By 2002, the restaurant was closed, and the Walker House was placed on the list of the most endangered properties in Wisconsin. Joseph and Susan Dickinson came to the rescue of the Walker House, which they purchased in 2005. In 2008, they reopened the Cornish Pub in the Walker House and remodeled the dining rooms and kitchen on the second floor. The Dickinsons soon discovered that the rumors they had heard about the ghosts in the Walker House were true.

One of the two apparitions that haunt the Walker House is said to be the ghost of William Café, who was known to have a fiery temper. One day, he became embroiled in an argument with an acquaintance. Café became so angry that he produced a gun and shot the man. Café was found guilty of the crime and sentenced to hang in front of the Walker House. Café was delivered to the makeshift gallows in a horse-drawn wagon. Supposedly, he sat on top of his coffin and played a kind of funeral dirge with two beer bottles, which he banged on the sides of the wagon. He was determined not to go quietly to his grave.

Evidence suggests that William Café has still not quieted down. He enjoys annoying staff and guests by throwing plates, glasses, and silverware across the room. He also delights in terrifying patrons by moving chairs around. Door handles turn by themselves, as if by an invisible hand. Café's apparition has been seen in the dining rooms on the second floor. Witnesses say he wears a wrinkled gray suit and sometimes appears without his head. His headless ghost has also been sighted sitting on a bench on the back porch. Some people swear that they saw Café's wheezing ghost stumbling down the hallway on the second floor.

The identity of the second ghost who haunts the Walker House is unknown. The ghost of a man wearing clothes of the 1800s seems to enjoy strolling around the pub on the first floor. He has also been blamed for the disembodied voices that have sent countless shivers up the spines of employees since it was renovated in the 1960s and 1970s.

By December 2009, the Walker House had closed again. At that time, the proprietors were accepting donations to help them keep the Walker House open for at least six more months. People who contributed to the cause received a monthly newsletter that included the most recent sightings. They also began selling a book on the ghosts of the Walker House titled *The Spirits of Walker House: Top 10 Encounters of 2009* to help raise money. If the owners' fund-raising efforts do keep the Walker House open, it will join an elite group of houses that have actually been saved by the ghosts who haunt them.

GENOA

David Hastings built the first house in Genoa, Wisconsin, in 1853. In the early years, Genoa was known primarily as a steamboat landing. By the end of the nineteenth century, the town's economy was boosted by the limestone quarry and by two clamshell button factories, which set up business in Genoa. The Chicago, Burlington & Northern Railroad completed its first route through Genoa in 1884. The first public school in Genoa was housed in what is now the American Legion Club. A convent was erected for two Franciscan sisters in 1925. In 1930, Congress authorized the construction of Lock and Dam #8 in Genoa. In 1940, the Dairyland Power #1 coal-fired power plant was built. The La Crosse Boiling Water Reactor was built in Genoa in 1967, but it was shut down in 1987.

THE HAWG CHASIN' GHOST

The Hawg Chasin' Ghost first appeared on a farm just south of Genoa, Wisconsin, in 1901. A farmer named Ellis was inside his house one hot summer day when he heard a commotion coming from his barn. Thinking that some of the local children were harassing his livestock, Ellis plowed through the back door and hurried over to his barn. To his amazement, a woman dressed in the finery of an upper-class lady was waving her arms and running after the hogs. Concerned that the pigs would overheat and die, he yelled at the woman to stop. She looked at him for a brief moment, then she ran out the door and ducked into the woods.

The next time the woman was seen, she targeted another type of barnyard "critter" on a farm just east of Genoa. A farmer named

Alderson was working in a field with his son when they heard a noise coming from the chicken house. The first thought that came to mind was that a fox was killing their chickens. When they arrived at the chicken coop, they discovered a well-dressed woman inside the chicken coop. For a few seconds, Alderson and his son just stood in the doorway, dumbfounded. Then Alderson pulled the door shut. The farmer was satisfied that he had trapped the strange intruder. Instead of showing fear or guilt, as any normal trespasser would have done, she simply walked through the rear wall.

For the next few months, several attempts were made to trap the "Hawg Chasin' Ghost." People riding wagons and horses were unable to catch the fleeing woman before she disappeared. One ingenious farmer tried to lure the ghost with food and music, but she would not take the bait. Meanwhile, the farmers were becoming desperate. The obnoxious entity was now tormenting all kinds of livestock. One farmer said that she killed several of his calves one hot July afternoon by chasing the poor animals back and forth across a small pasture. By the time fall arrived, reports of the Hawg Chasin' Ghost had ceased altogether.

For the next few weeks, people living in and around Genoa came up with a number of explanations. Some people said that the farmers who had lost the livestock had made up the story to garner sympathy. Others said that the woman was a farmer's wife who took her anger out on barnyard animals because her husband paid more attention to his pigs and chickens than he did to her. Bruce Carlson, author of *Ghosts of the Mississippi River from Minneapolis to Dubuque*, theorized that the woman was actually a ghost who found lying in a box under the ground to be dreadfully boring.

Works Cited

BOOKS

Asfar, Dan, and Edrick Thay. *Ghost Stories of the Civil War.* Canada: Ghost House Books, 2003.

Ballard, Michael B. *The Campaign for Vicksburg.* Ft. Washington, PA: Eastern National, 2007.

Brown, Alan. *Ghost Hunters of the South.* Jackson: University Press of Mississippi, 2006.

———. *Haunted Places in the American South.* Jackson: University Press of Mississippi, 2002.

———. *Stories from the Haunted South.* Jackson: University Press of Mississippi, 2004.

Buxton, Geordie. *Haunted Plantations: Ghosts of Slavery and Legends of the Cotton Kingdom.* Charleston, SC: Arcadia Publishing, 2007.

Carlson, Bruce. *Ghosts of the Mississippi River: Dubuque to Keokuk.* Fort Madison, IA: Quixote Press, 1988.

———. *Ghosts of the Mississippi from Minneapolis to Dubuque.* Fort Madison, IA: Quixote Press, 1988.

Chaneles, Janine. *Prisons and Prisoners: Historical Documents.* Abingdon, UK: Routledge Press, 1985.

Christenson, Jo-Anne. *Ghost Stories of Illinois.* Canada: Lone Pine Publishing, 2000.

Coleman, Christopher. *Strange Tales of the Dark and Bloody Ground.* Nashville, TN: Rutledge Hill Press, 1998.

Courtaway, Robbi. *Spirits of Saint Louis.* St. Louis, MO: Virginia Publishing Company, 1999.

Cunningham, Laura. *Haunted Memphis.* Charleston, SC: History Press, 2009.

Downer, Deborah L., ed. *Classic American Ghost Stories.* Little Rock, AR: August House, 1990.

Dunphy, John J. *It Happened at the River Bend.* Alton, IL: Second Reading Publications, 2007.

Dwyer, Jeff. *Ghost Hunter's Guide to New Orleans.* Gretna, LA: Pelican Publishing, 2007.

Ewing, James. *It Happened in Tennessee.* Nashville, TN: Rutledge Hill Press, 1986.

Gilbert, Joan. *Missouri Ghosts.* Columbia, MO: Pebble Publishing, 1997.

———. *Missouri Ghosts III.* Hallsville, MO: Mogho Books, 2006.

Goodwin, David. *Ghosts of Jefferson Barracks.* Alton, IL: Whitechapel Productions Press, 2001.

Groom, Winston. *Vicksburg 1863.* New York: Alfred A. Knopf, 2009.

Guiley, Rosemary Ellen. *The Encyclopedia of Ghosts and Spirits.* New York: Facts on File, 2000.

Harrell, Virginia Calohan. *Vicksburg and the River.* Vicksburg, MS: Harrell Publications, 1986.

Hauck, Dennis William. *Haunted Places: The National Directory.* New York: Penguin Books, 1996.

Hein, Ruth D., and Vicky L. Hinsenbrock. *Ghostly Tales of Iowa.* Cambridge, MA: Adventure Publications, 2005.

Hubbard, Sylvia Booth. *Ghosts! Personal Accounts of Modern Mississippi Hauntings.* Brandon, MS: QRP Books, 1992.

Kachuba, John B. *Ghosthunting Illinois.* Cincinnati, OH: Clerisy Press, 2005.

Kempe, Helen Kerr. *The Pelican Guide to Old Homes of Mississippi: Natchez and the South*, vol. 1. Gretna, LA: Pelican Publishing Company, 1989.

Klein, Victor C. *New Orleans Ghosts.* Metarie, LA: Lycanthrope Press, 1993.

———. *New Orleans Ghosts II.* Metarie, LA: Lycanthrope Press, 1999.

Larsen, Christopher. *Ghosts of Southeastern Minnesota.* Atglen, PA: Schiffer Publishing, 2008.

Larson, Captain Ron. *Upper Mississippi River History.* Plymonth, IN: Steamboat Press, 1998.

Lewis, Chad, and Terry Fisk. *The Illinois Road Guide to Haunted Locations.* Eau Claire, WI: Unexplained Research Publishing Company, 2007.

———. *The Wisconsin Road Guide to Haunted Locations.* Eau Claire, WI: Unexplained Research Publishing Company, 2004.

Longo, Jim. *Favorite Haunts: Haunted Odyssey III.* St. Louis, MO: St. Anne's Press, 2000.

———. *Ghosts along the Mississippi: Haunted Odyssey II.* St. Louis, MO: St. Anne's Press, 1993.

Montz, Larry, and Daena Smoller. *ISPR Investigates the Ghosts of New Orleans.* Atglen, PA: Whitford Press, 2000.

Norman, Michael. *The Nearly Departed: Minnesota Ghost Stories and Legends.* St. Paul: Minnesota Historical Press, 2009.

Offutt, James. *The Ghostly Guide to the Show-Me State's Most Spirited Spots.* Kirksville, MO: Truman State University Press, 2007.

Polley, Jane, ed. *American Folklore and Legend.* Pleasantville, NY: Reader's Digest, 1978.

Roberts, Nancy. *Haunted Houses: Tales from 30 American Homes.* Chester, CN: GlobePequot Press, 1988.

Roth, Dave, ed. *Blue and Gray Magazine's Haunted Places of the Civil War.* Columbus, OH: Blue and Gray Enterprises, 1996.

Scott, Beth, and Michael Norman. *Haunted Wisconsin.* Minocqua, WI: Heartland Press, 1988.

Sillery, Barbara. *The Haunting of Louisiana.* Gretna, LA: Pelican Publishing Company, 2001.

Smith, Kalila Katherina. *Journey into Darkness . . . Ghosts and Vampires of New Orleans.* New Orleans, LA: De Simonin Publications, 1998.

Taylor, Troy. *The Big Book of Illinois Ghost Stories.* Mechanicsburg, PA: Stackpole Books, 2009.

———. *The Ghost Hunter's Guidebook: The Essential Handbook for Ghost Research.* Alton, IL: Whitechapel Productions Press, 2001.

———. *Haunted Alton.* Alton, IL: Whitechapel Productions Press, 1999.

———. *Haunted Illinois: Ghosts and Hauntings from Egypt to the Windy City.* Alton, IL: Whitechapel Productions Press, 1999.

———. *Haunted New Orleans.* Alton, IL: Whitechapel Productions Press, 2000.

———. *Haunted St. Louis.* Alton, IL: Whitechapel Productions Press, 2002.

Teel, Gina. *Ghost Stories of Minnesota.* Canada: Lone Pine Publishing International, 2001.

Turnage, Sheila. *Haunted Inns of the Southeast.* Winston-Salem, NC: John F. Blair, 2001.

Vyn, Kathleen. *Haunted Iowa.* Madison, WI: Trails Books, 2008.

Walker, Stephen. *Lemp: The Haunting History.* St. Louis, MO: Lemp Preservation Society, 1988.

Watson, Daryl. *Ghosts of Galena.* Galena, IL: Gear House, 1995.

Windham, Kathryn Tucker. *13 Mississippi Ghosts and Jeffrey.* Tuscaloosa: University of Alabama Press, 1987.

WEB SITES

About.com. "Haunted Bars in New Orleans." http://goneworleans.about.com/od/nightlife/p/hauntedbars.htm.

———. "The LaLaurie House." http://goneworleans.about.com/od/famouslandmarks/a/Lalaurie.htm.

AllStays.com. "The Lemp Mansion." www.allstays.com/Haunted/mo_stlouis_lempmansion.htm.

Altonweb.com. "Alton in the Civil War: Alton Prison." www.altonweb.com/history/civilwar/confed/.

"Ambrose Hall: A new beginning." *The Ambrose Magazine.* April 13, 1975, 10.

Angel, Julie. "Burton Cave Trip." Eiu.edu. www.eiu.edu/-physics/nngrotto/nov10007
.htm.

Arkansas.com. "Holly Grove." www.arkansas.com/city-listings/city_detai.aspx?
city=Holly+Grove.

Arvidson, Lloyd. "The Hamlin Garland Collection." Usc.edu. www.usc.edu/libraries/
archives/arc/findingaids/garland/index.html.

Associatedcontent.com. "An Encounter with the Paranormal in Alton, Illinois." www
.associatedcontent.com/article/2378218/an_encounter_with_the_paranormal_in...

———. "The Ghosts of St. Mary's College in Minnesota." www.associatedcontent.com/
article/699285/the_ghosts_of_st_marys_college_in_ mi.

———. "The Haunting of Griggs Mansion in Ramsey County." www.associatedcontent
.com/article/420382/the_haunting?of?griggs?mansion?in?ra.

———. "See the Ruins of the Alton, Illinois Confederate Prison." www.
associatedcontent.com/article/699999/see_the_ruins_of_the_alton_illiois.html?

At New Orleans. "Lafitte's Blacksmith Shop." www.atneworleans.com/body/
blacksmith.htm.

Blackhawk Hotel. "The Blackhawk Hotel: Our History." www.blackhawk-hotel.com/
history.asp.

Blaschka, Shawn. "Mineral Springs Hotel—Alton, Illinois." WPRS. www.pat-wausau
.org/cases/mineralsprings.html.URAD.htm.

Brown, John Norris. "The Ghost of Graceland." Ghosts and Spirits of Tennessee.
www.johnnorrisbrown.com/paranormal-tn/graceland/index.htm.

Budd, Deena. "The King's Tavern of Natchez." BellaOnline. www.bellaonline.com/
articles/art60216.asp.

———. "Webster Groves, Missouri Haunted House. BellaOnline. www.bellaonline
.com/articles/art60216.

Busbee, James. "The Persistence of Folklore." www.memphisflyer.com/backissues/
issue419/cvr419.htm.

Cabildo Online. "The Cabildo." http:lllsm.crt.state.la.us/cabildo/cab1.htm.

Cinema Treasures. "Orpheum Theater." http://cinematreasures.org/theater/1679/.

Civil War Talk. "The Hauntings of the McRaven House in Vicksburg,
Mississippi." http://civilwartalk.com/forums/hauntings-great-rebellion/
19694-hauntings-mcraven-house-.

Commercial Appeal. "Ghost Hunt: Paranormal Investigator Helps Memphians Get
Their Spectral Fix." http://m.commercialappeal.com/news/2009/oct/24/ghost-hunt.

———. "Victorian Village Home Tour." www.commercialappeal.com/news/2007/
oct/05/home-tour-victorian-village/.

Content for Reprint. "The Mighty Mississippi—How Much River Do You Know?"
www.content4reprint.com/recreation-and-leisure/travel/destinations/
the-mighty-miss.

Crain, Donnie. "Helena: An Historical Gem on the Mississippi River—
    Helena, Arkansas." www.bootsnall.com/articles./02-08/helena-an
    -historical-gem-on-the-mississippi-river.

Creativespirits.net. "McRaven House." www.creativespirits.net/paranormal/
    ghost-definitions/mcraven-house/.

Dark Destinations. "Duff Green Mansion." www.thecabinet.com/darkdestinations/
    location.php?sub_id=dark_destinations&letter.

———. "McRaven House." http://thecabinet.com/darkdestinations/location
    .php?sub_id=dark_destinations&letter=m&1.

DeSoto House Hotel. "History of the DeSoto House Hotel." www.desotohouse.com/
    history.html.

Destination260.com. "First Avenue Minneapolis." www.destination260.com/
    north-america/us/minnesota/first-avenue.

Duffgreenmansion.com. "The Duff Green Mansion: History." www.duffgreenmansion
    .com/.

Eberhart, George. "Haunted Libraries in the U.S.: Florida-Maryland." Encyclopaedia
    Britannica Blog. www.britannica.com/blogs/2007/10/haunted-libraries-in-the
    -us-florida-maryland/http://findarticles.com/p/articles/mi_m3190/is_11_35/
    ai_72119123/.

Edwards, Heather. "Ghosts Linger in Southern Minnesota." http://eastsidereviewnews
    .com/main.asp?SectionID=114&SubSectionID=286&ArticleID=.

Elite Paranormal of Kansas City. "The Rockcliffe Mansion." www.eliteparanormalkc
    .com/viewpage.php?page_id=1.

Facebook.com. "Duff Green Mansion Investigation Reports." http://ru-ru.facebook
    .com/topic.php?uid=14174258484&topic=13133.

Flickr. "Mallory-Neely House—Memphis, TN." www.flickr.com/photos/
    mattartz/2480964191/.

Garden House B&B. "Time-Honored B&B in Downtown Hannibal." www.purpleroofs
    .com/gardenhouse-mo.html.

Garner, Rick, and Dean McKnight. "Ghosts: Field Report of Duff Green Mansion in
    Vicksburg, Mississippi." www.paranormalnews.com/article.asp?articleid=461.

Gatewayno.com. "The Mississippi River." www.gatewayno.com/history/Mississippi
    .html.

Genealogy trails. "Illinois and the 1918 Spanish Flue Epidemic." http://genealogytrails
    .com/ill/flu1918.htm.

Genoawis.com. "History of Genoa, Wisconsin." http://www.genoawis.com/history
    .shtml.

Ghost Hunters of St. Louis. "'Zombie' Road." http://ghosts.itgo.com/investigations/
    zombie/index.htm.

Ghost in My Suitcase. "Duff Green Mansion." www.ghostinmysuitcase.com/places/
    duffgreen/index.htm.

Ghoststudies.com. "The Bottom of the Cup Tearoom." www.ghoststudies.com/
bottomofthecuptearoom.html.

Ghostvillage.com. "A Strange Light in Willer Hall, Quincy University."
www.ghostvillage.com/encounters/2005/10172005.shtml.

Gohlke, Ross. "Earnestine & Hazel's: A dim light in a dark part of town." BluesSpeak.
www.bluespeak.com/feature/96/02/960215.html.

Graveaddiction.com. "O'Flaherty's Irish Channel Pub." www.graveaddiction.com/
oflaherty.html.

Greatriverroad.com. "Visitors Guide to the Lincoln Douglas Square."
www.greatriverroad.com/Cities/Alton/lincoln.htm.

Greenwood, Peggy Thomson. "Beyond the Orphanage." St. Louis Orphanages.
http://genalogyinstlouis.accessgenealogy.com/greenwood.htm.

Harris, Ellen, and Sunny Pervil. "The Ghosts of Whittemore House." St. Louis
Magazine. www.stlmag.com/media/St-Louis-Magazine/November-2005/
The-Ghosts-Of-Whitte.

Hart of the Matter. "Ghost Hollow Road, Part II." www.3.whig.com/whig/blogs/
hartofthematter/?p=651.

Haunted Bluffs of Memphis. "The Haunted Morgue—Unretouched Photos."
www.stevecox.com/haunted/morgue.htm.

HauntedHouses.com. "Ambrose Hall." www.hauntedhouses.com/states/ia/ambrose_
hall.cfm.

———. "Cedar Grove Mansion." www.hauntedhouses.com/states/ms/cedar_grove_
mansion.cfm.

———. "First Avenue Night Club." www.hauntedhouses.com/states/mn/first_avenue
.cfm.

———. "Fitzgerald Theatre." www.hauntedhouses.com/states/mn/fitzgerald_theater
.cfm.

———. "Forepaugh's Restaurant." www.hauntedhouses.com/states/mn/forepaughs_
restaurant.cfm.

———. "Gibbs Farm House Museum." www.hauntedhouses.com/states/mn/gibbs_
farmhouse.cfm.

———. "Grand Opera House." http://www.hauntedhouses.com/states/ia/dubuque_
opera.cfm.

———. "Griggs Mansion." www.hauntedhouses.com/states/mn/griggs_mansion.cfm.

———. "The Haunted Blackhawk Hotel." www.hauntedhouses.com/states/ia/
blackhawk_hotel.cfm.

———. "Hunt/Phelan House." www.hauntedhouses.com/states/in/hunt_phelan_house
.cfm.

———. "Lafitte's Blacksmith Shop." www.hauntedhouses.com/states/la/lafitte_
blacksmith_shop.cfm.

———. "Landmark Center." www.hauntedhouses.com/states/mn/landmark_center.cfm.

———. "Lemp Mansion." www.hauntedhouses.com/states/mo/lemp_mansion.cfm.

———. "Marine Military Hospital." www.hauntedhouses.com/states/tn/marine_
military_hospital.cfm.

———. "Minneapolis City Hall and Hennepin County Courthouse."
www.hauntedhouses.com/states/mn/minneapolis_city_hall.cfm.

———. "Walker House." www.hauntedhouses.com/states/wi/walker_house.cfm.

Haunted New Orleans Tours. "Haunted New Orleans: Ghosts and Spirits."
www.hauntednewneworleanstours.com/hauntedneworleansbars/.

———. "Haunted New Orleans Hotels." http://www.hauntedneworleanstours.com/
hauntedhotels/.

Haunted Tennessee. "Orpheum Theater." www.prairieghosts.com/orpheum.html.

Hauntworld.com. "Real Haunts of Minnesota." http://hauntworld.com/
minnesota_haunted_houses.

Hennepinhistory.org. "Hennepin History Museum." http://hennepinhistory.org/
aboutus.aspx.

History.rays-place.com. "History of Grafton, IL." http://history.rays-place.com/il/
mch-grafton.htm.

Home.comcast.net. "Holly Grove Arkansas History." http://home.comcast
.net/~dfletcher20/hghistory.html.

Hydrite Chemical. "Who Is Hydrite?" www.hydrite.com/Who_is_Hydrite.asp.

Illinois Department of Natural Resources. "Burton Cave Nature Preserve Adams
County." http://dnr.state.il.us/INPC/Directory/Sitefiles/Area4/B.

Illinoisglorydays.com. "Rock Island Villa de Chantal H.S." www.illinoishsglorydays
.com/id288.html.

Infoplease.com. "History." www.infoplease.com/ceo/us/A0859681.html.

Julianolee.com. "Save the Ghosts of the Walker House." www.julianolee.com/285/
save-the-ghosts-of-the-walker-house/.

Kimery, Louis. "The Tennessee Brewery, Memphis TN." www.ikimeryphoto.com/files/
47e406a8752911137843e8c01226b409-1.html.

Kintner, Katie Buller. "Library Life: A Column of Eclectic Rantings." http://associates
.ucr.edu/ckint302.htm.

Legends of America. "Ghosts of Greater St. Louis." www.legendsofamerica.com/
MO-MeramecGhost.html.

———. "The Haunted Lemp Mansion in St. Louis." www.legendsofamerica.com/
MO-LempMansion.html.

The Lemp Mansion Restaurant & Inn. "The Lemp Mansion." www.lempmansion.com/
history.html.

Lifeinlegacy.com. "Life in Legacy—Week of April 17, 2004." www.lifeinlegacy.com/.

Lincolnlofts.net. "Lincoln Lofts: An Elaine Everett Enterprise." www.lincolnlofts.net/
Home_Page.php.

Magnoliamansion.com. "Magnolia Mansion" www.magnoliamansion.com/haunted.htm.

Mcpikemansion.com/history.html. "McPike Mansion—Built in 1869."
http://mcpikemansion.com/history.html.

Memphis.about.com. "Metal Museum." http://memphis.about.com/od/halloween/p/ghosts.htm.

Memphisghost.com. "Earnestine and Hazel's Memphis." www.memphisghost.com/Earnestine_and_Hazels.html.

Memphisheritage.org. "Historic Raleigh Cemetery Needs Help!" www.memphisheritage.org/mhihost/News-RaleighCemetery.html.

Memphistravel.com. "CVB History." www.memphistravel.com/about_us/cvbhistory/default.aspx.

Meyers, Gregory. "Zombie Road: Where Urban Legends Ring True." Paranormaltaskforce.com. www.paranormaltaskforce.com/ZombieUrban.html.

———, and Judith Meyers. "Zombie Road." Haunted America Tours. www.hauntedamericatours.com/ghosthunting/ZombieRoad/index.php.

Mezensky, Catherine. "The McRaven House." Suite101.com. www.suite101.com/article.cfm/civil_war_ghosts/66354.

Midwestweekends.com. "Ghosts of Galena." www.midwestweekends.com/plan_a_trip/history_heritage-historic_houses/ghost_tour.

Miller, Carl H. "The Rise of the Beer Barons." beerhistory.com. www.beerhistory.com/library/holdings/beerbarons.shtml.

Mineral Springs Haunted Tours. "Real Ghostly Stories from Real People." www.mineralspringshauntedtours.com/html/ghost_story.html.

Minnesota Public Radio's Fitzgerald Theater. "About the Fitzgerald: History." http://fitzgeraldtheater.publicradio.org/about/history.shtml.

Mississippi River Field Guide. "Wabasha Caves & Castle Royal." http://fieldguide.fmr.org/site_detail.php?site_id=257.

Mississippi Valley Paranormal. "Grand Opera House, Dubuque, Iowa, September 5, 2009." http://mvparanormal.org/?p=126.

Missourighosts.net. "Ghosts & Haunts in Missouri: Haunted Locations in New Madrid." www.missourighosts.net/newmadrid.html.

———. "Ghosts & Haunts in Missouri: Haunted Locations in St. Louis South of Hwy 64." www.missourighosts.net/stls62.html.

———. "Ghosts & Haunts in Missouri: Hunter Dawson Home Stories." www.missourighosts.net/hunterdawsonhomestories.html.

———. "Ghosts & Haunts in Missouri: Hunter-Dawson Mansion Stories." www.missourighosts.net/hunterdawsonmansionstories2.html.

Missouri State Parks and Historic Sites. "Hunter-Dawson State Historic Site." www.mostateparks.com/hunterdawson.htm.

Morningmystery.com. "Burton Cave." www.morningmystery.com/viewpost_409380.asp.

Nation's Restaurant News. "Adventures in Excavation: The Pontchartrain Uncovers Café's Design Treasures."

Nelson, Tony. "Ghosts in the Coulees?" www.couleenews.com/articles/2005/10/2;7/features/02ghosts.txt.

New Orleans Discount Hotels & Travel Guide." "Pontchartrain Hotel New Orleans."
    www.neworleans-hotels-classify.com/pontchartrain-hotel/.
New Orleans Paranormal & Occult Research Society Ghostly Gallery. "Haunted
    New Orleans." www.neworleansghosts.com/haunted_new_orleans.htm.
Niere, Jeremiah. "A Zombie on Zombie Road." www.paranormaltaskforce.com/
    Zombiestories.html.
Nola.com. "History of the LaLaurie House." www.nola.com/lalaurie/history/
    chronology.html.
———. "The Octaroon Mistress." www.nola.com/haunted/ghosts/?content/octoroon
    .html.
Nottoway.com. "Nottoway Historic Inn." www.nottoway.com/History.html.
Pandemicflu.gov. "The Great Pandemic." http://1918.pandemicflu.gov/your/state/
    illinois.htm.
The Orpheum Theater. "Theater Info." www.orpheum- memphis.com/index
    .cfm?section=theaterinfo.
Paranormal Incorporated. "National Ornamental Metal Museum—Memphis." http://
    paranormalincorporated.blogspot.com/2008/06/national-ornamental-metal-m.
Paranormalknowledge.com. "Andrew Jackson Hotel." http://www.parnormal
    knowledge.com/articles/andrew-jackson-hotel.html.
———. "The Cabildo." www.paranormalknowledge.com/articles/the-cabildo.html.
———. "Le Petit Theatre Du Viewx Carre." www.paranormalknowledge.com/articles/
    le-petit-theatre-du-viewx-carre.html.
———. "O'Flaherty's Irish Chnnel Pub." www.paranormalknowledge.com/articles/
    oflahertys-irish-channel-pub.html.
Paranormaltaskforce.com. "Zombie Road: The Investigations."
    www.paranormaltaskforce.com/Zombiel..html.
Pi Kappa Chi. "Pi Kappa Chi: Fraternity Profile." http://pikappachi.tripod.com/id6.html.
Pilot Light 2000 Historic page. "Historic Cairo: The Magnolia Manor."
    www.pilotlight2009.com/historic/manor.htm.
———. "Historic Cairo: Cairo Public Library." www.pilotlight2000.com/historic/library
    .htm.
The Pontchartrain. "Pontchartrain Hotel Being Converted into Senior Apartments."
    www.thepontchartrain.com/press-1html.
Prodigy.net. "McPike Mansion Alton's Most Haunted House (Illinois)." http://pages
    .prodigy.net/ghostfish/_wsn/page7.html.
Psychics & Mediums Network. "The Psychic Experiences of Elvis Presley's Ghost."
    www.psychics.co.uk/celebrities/elvispresley.html.
Quincy's Tourist Information Center & Great River Road Interpretive Center.
    "Villa Kathrine." www.villakathrine.org/.
Quincy University. "About QU: History." www.quincy.edu/AboutQU/history.php.
Raleighcemetery.com. "History of Raleigh Cemetery." http://raleighcemetery.com/
    history.html.

Ramsey County Historical Society. "Gibbs Museum." www.rchs.com/bggsfm2.htm.

Ray, Becky. Paranormal Activity Investigators. "The Lemp Mansion." www.ghost
    -investigators.com/Stories/view/story.php?story_num=25.

Realhaunts.com. "Real Haunted House." www.realhaunts.com/united- states/
    first-aveclub/.

———. "Saint Mary's College: Heffron Hall." www.realhaunts.com/united-states/
    saint-marys-college-heffron-hall/.

River Town Paranormal Society. "Further Investigation of the Villa Kathrine."
    http://rivertownparanormalsociety.net/blog/?p=10.

Rockcliffe Mansion. "Rockcliffe Mansion: Turn of the Century Mansion Restored to Its
    Original Splendor." www.rockcliffemansion.com/history.shtml.

Ross, Jenna. "These Ghost Hunters Bring Their Tape Recorders." StarTribune.com.
    www.startribune.com/local/south/11593226.html.

Rrmemphis.com. "Misc. Recent Incidents." www.rrmemphis.com/0p040.html.

Ruebel Hotel & Restaurant. "Ruebel Hotel: Our History." www.ruebelhotel.com/.

Saint Louis Symphony Orchestra. "Powell Symphony Hall History." www.slso.org/
    powell//psh.htm.

Sandmel, Ben. "Big River Traditions: Folklife on the Mississippi." Louisiana's Living
    Traditions. www.louisianafolklife.org/LT/Articles_Essays/reole_art_big_river_trad
    .html.

Scenic Byways. "Historic DeSoto Hotel & Green Street Tavern."
    www.quiltingpathways.com/galena/galena-desoto.html.

Shadowlands.com. "Shadowlands Haunted Places Index—Minnesota."
    www.theshadowlands.net/places/minnesota.htm.

Smalltownghosts.com. "Haunted McPike Mansion." http://www.smalltownghosts
    .com/stg1/McPike.html.

Southernmostillinoishistory.net. "Mound City National Cemetery."
    www.southernmostillinoishistory.net/mound+city_national_cemetery.htm.

Spooked TV News. "Zombie Road: The ghosts are true but so is the danger." http://
    spookednews.blogspot.com/2008/11/zombie-road-ghosts-are-true-but-so-is.html.

St. Louis News. "Zombie Road." www.riverfronttimes.com/2007-10-10/news/
    zombie-road/.

St. Louis Paranormal Investigation and Research Interest Team. "Zombie Road—
    7/11/2007." www.spirit-stl.com/zombieroad1.html.

St. Louis University. "Samuel Cupples." www.slu.edu/x28246.xml.

Stollznow, Iaren. "The Lemp Mansion." Haunted America Tours.
    www.hauntedamericatours.com/hauntedhouses/LempMansion/.

Stormfront.org. "Memphis blacks knock on her door & kill beautiful young radio
    personality Rebecca Glahn." www.stormfrontt.org/forum/sitemap/index.php/
    t-127325.html.

Strangeusa.com. "Heffron Hall at St. Mary's University." www.strangeusa.com/
    ViewLocation.aspx?locationid=57743.

Suite101.com. "Ghosts of the LaLaurie House." http://ghosts-hauntings.suite101.com/
    article.cfm/ghosts_of_the_lalaurie_house.
———. "Haunted Heffron Hall—St. Mary's College." http:..ghosts-hauntings.suite101
    .com/article.cfm/haunted_heffron_hall_st_marys_colleges.
Sullivan, Charles L. "The Haunting of McRaven." *Mississippi.* September/October
    1989, 22+.
Taylor, Troy. "The Fitzgerald Theater." Ghosts of the Prairie. www.prairieghosts.com/
    fitz.html.
———. "Forepaugh's Restaurant." Ghosts of the Prairie. www.prairieghosts.com/forep
    .html.
———. "The Franklin House." Ghost Stories from Haunted Alton." www.altonhauntings
    .com/franklin.html.
———. "Ghosts of Quincy." Weird & Haunted Illinois. www.prairieghosts.com/quincy
    .html.
———. "Grand Opera House." www.prairieghosts.com/grandop.html.
———. "The Griggs Mansion." www.prairieghosts.com/griggs.html.
———. "Haunted Wisconsin." www.prairieghosts.comn/hauntwi.html.
———. "The Lemp Mansion." America's Most Haunted Places. www.prairieghosts.com/
    lemp.html.
———. "The Mansion House." Ghost Stories from Haunted Alton. www.altonhauntings
    .com/mansion.html.
———. "The McPike Mansion—Alton's Most Haunted?" Ghosts of the Prairie.
    www.prairieghosts.com/mcpike.html.
———. "Minneapolis City Hall." Ghosts of the Prairie. www.prairieghosts.com/cityhall
    .html.
———. "The Phantom Funeral of Fort de Chartres." Haunted Places.
    www.prairieghosts.com/fort.html.
———. "St. Mary's College." Haunted Minnesota. www.prairieghosts.com/stmaryc
    .html.
———. "Spirits of the Ruebel Hotel." Ghosts of the Prairie. www.prairieghosts.com/
    ruebel.html.
———. "Suicide & Spirits: The Haunting of Alton's First Unitarian Church." Ghost
    Stories from Haunted Alton. www.altonhauntings.com/unitarianchurch.
———. "Villa Kathrine." Weird & Haunted Illinois. www.prairieghosts.com/Villak.html.
———. "Zombie Road." Tales of History & Hauntings. www.prairieghosts.com/zombie_
    road.html.
Tennesseeanytime.org. "Historic Sites—Victorian Village." www.tennesseeanytime
    .org/homework/historicsites/victvill.html.
Theshadowlands.net. "The LaLaurie House: New Orleans, Louisiana."
    http://theshadowlands.net/famous/lalaurie.htm.
Thesouthern.com. "Volunteers Help Keep Magnolia Manor Running." www.the
    southern.com/news/local/article_c3a48998-83c1-5fe6-b158-aef335@25516.ht.

The Tennessee Encyclopedia of History and Culture. "Mallory-Neely House."
    http://tennesseeencyclopedia.net/imagegallery.php?EntryID=M007.
———. "Yellow Fever Epidemics." http://tennesseeencyclopedia.net/imagegallery
    .php?EntryID=Y002.
This Day in History 1878. "First Victim of Memphis Yellow-Fever Epidemic Dies."
    www.history.com/this-day-in-history.do?action=Article&id=50658.
Ticketkingonline.com. "First Avenue Nightclub." www.ticketkingonline.com/tickets/
    first-avenue-nightclub-tickets.htm.
True Hauntings of America. "The Haunting of the Gehm House." http://
    hauntsofamerica.blogspot.com/2007/10/haunting-of-plan-avenue-house.html.
———. "The Haunting of the Grand Opera House." http://hauntsofamerica.blogspot
    .com/2007/09/haunting-of-grand-opera-house.html.
Turner Hall. "Turner Hall, Galena, Illinois: History." www.turnerhall.com/yhistory
    .com.
Uncw.edu. "Who Is Hamlin Garland?" http://uncw.edu/garland/biography.htm.
Unexplained Research. "Legends and Myths of Winona State Spooks of the Past and
    Present." www.unexplainedresearch.com/media/legends_and_myths_of_winona.html.
United States Department of Veterans Affairs. "Mound City National Cemetery."
    www.cem.va.gov/cems/nchp/moundcity.asp.
Unsolved Mysteries. "Loud Ghost, Old Holmbo Residence, La Crosse, Wisconsin-33
    Degree." www.unsolvedmysteries.com/usm348773.html.
Vacationsmadeeasy.com. "Elvis Presley's Heartbreak Hotel—Memphis, TN." www
    .vacationsmadeeasy.com/MemphisTN/lodgin/ElvisPresleysHeartbreakHotel.cfm.
Vacationsmadeeasy.com. "Slaven/Burkle Estate in Memphis, TN." www
    .vacationsmadeeasy.com/MemphisTN/ointsOrfInterest/SlaveHavenBurkleEst.
Wabasha Kellogg. "History of Wabasha." www.wabashamn.org/visitor-resources/
    history-of-wabasha.php.
Walker House. "Walker House Donations." http://walkerhousedonations.homestead
    .com/.
Wapedia. "Wiki: Orpheum Theater (Memphis, Tennessee)." http://wapedia.mobi/en/
    Orpheum_Theatre_(Memphis,_Tennessee).
Waymarking.com. "Magnolia Manor—Cairo, Illinois." www.waymarking.com/
    waymarks/WM88Z8_Magnolia_Manor_Cairo_Illinois.
Wcco.com. "Is Minneapolis City Hall Haunted?" http://wcco.com/topstories/
    Minneapolis.City.Hall.2.362734.html.
Welcome to McRaven Tour Home. "The Most Haunted House in Mississippi."
Westernberb, Kerri. "Anderson House, Minnesota's Oldest Hotel, Closes." StarTribune
    .com. www.startribune.com/lifestyle/travel/41716092.html.
WestSalem. "West Salem History." www.westsalemwi.com/wshist.htm.
The White Noise Forum. "Zombie Road." www.thewhitenoiseforum.com/main/view_
    topic.php?id=673&forum_id=17.

Whittemore House. "Whittemore House: History." http://whittemorehouse
.memberstatements.com/tour/tours.cfm?tourID=57056.

Wikipedia. "Alton, Illinois." http://en.wikipedia.org/wiki/Alton,_Illinois.

———. "Burkle Estate." http://en.wikipedia.org/wiki/Burkle_Estate.

———. "The Cabildo." http://en.wikipedia.org/wiki/The_Cabildo.

———. "Cairo, Illinois." http://en.wikipedia.org/wiki/Cairo,_Illinois.

———. "Davenport, Iowa." http://en.wikipedia.orb/wiki/Davenport,_Iowa.

———. "Delphine LaLaurie." http://en.wikipedia.org/wiki/Delphine.LaLaurie.

———. "First Avenue." http://en.wikipedia.org/wiki/First_Avenue.

———. "Galena, Illinois." http://en.wikipedia.org/wiki/Galena,_Illinois.

———. "Graceland." http:..en.wikipedia.org/wiki/Graceland.

———. "Hamlin Garland." http://en.wikipedia.org/wiki/Hamlin_Garland.

———. "Hannibal, Missouri." http://en.wikipedia.org/wiki/Hannibal,_Missouri.

———. "Helena-West Helena, Arkansas." http://en.wikipedia.org/wiki/
Helena-West_Helena,_Arkansas.

———. "La Crosse, Wisconsin." http://en.wikipedia.org/wiki/La_Crosse,?Wisconsin.

———. "Landmark Center (St. Paul)." http://en.wikipedia.org/wiki/
Landmark_Center_(St._Paul).

———. "Mallory-Neely House." http://en.wikipedia.org/wiki/Mallory-Neely_House.

———. "Mineral Point, Wisconsin." http://en.wikipedia.org/wiki/
Mineral_Point,_Wisconsin.

———. "Minneapolis." http://en.wikipedia.org/wiki/Minneapolis.

———. "Minneapolis Institute of Arts." http://en.wikipeida.org/wiki/
Minneapolis_Institute_of_Arts.

———. "Natchez, Mississippi." http://en.wikipedia.org/wiki/Natchez,_Mississippi.

———. "New Madrid, Missouri." http://wikipedia.org/wiki/
New_Madrid_County_Missouri#History.

———. "New Orleans." http://en.wikipedia.org/wiki/New_Orleans.

———. "Nottoway Plantation." http://wikipedia.org/wiki/Nottoway_Plantation.

———. "Pontchartrain Hotel." http://en.wikipedia.org/wiki/Pontchartrain_Hotel.

———. "Powell Symphony Hall." http://en.wikipedia.org/wiki/Powell_Symphony_Hall.

———. "Prairie du Rocher, Illinois." http://en.wikipedia.org/wiki/
Prairie_du_Rocher,_Illinois.

———. "Quincy, Illinois." http://en.wikipedia.org/wiki/Quincy,_Illinois.

———. Quincy University." http://en.wikipedia.org/wiki/Quincy_University.

———. "Red Wing, Minnesota." http://en.wikipedia.org/wiki/Red_Wing_Minnesota.

———. "St. Louis, Missouri." http://en.wikipedia.org/wiki/St._Louis,_Missouri.

———. "Tennessee Brewery." http://en.wikipedia.org/wiki/Tennessee_Brewery.

———. "Vicksburg, Mississippi." http://en.wikipedia.org/wiki/Vicksburg,_Mississippi.

———. "Victorian Village, Memphis." http://en.wikipedia.org/wiki/
Victorian_Village,_Memphis.

———. "Walker House (Wisconsin)." http://en.wikipedia.org/wiki/
Walker_House_(Wisconsin).

———. "White Castle, Louisiana." http://en.wikipedia.org/wiki/White_Castle,_
Louisiana.

———. "Winona State University." http://en.wikipedia.org/wik/
Winona_State_University.

Williams, Charles and Sarah Bryan Miller. "Powell Symphony Hall." http://videos
.stltoday.com/p/video?id=1563274.

Woods, Amanda. "The Heartbreak Hotel Memphis." Suite101.com. http://tennessee
-travel.suite1- 1.com/article.cfm/the_heartbreak_hotel_memphis.

Woolard, Deidre. "More Nic Cage in New Orleans, Estate of the Day." Luxist.com.
www.luxist.com/2009/04/22/more-nic-cage-in-new-orleans-estate-of-the-day/.

Wundram, Bill. "There's Still Life in the Blackhawk Hotel." Qctimes.com.
www.qctimes.com/news/opinion/editorial/columnists/bill-wundram/
article_8713bad.

Your Ghost Stories. "A Night at the Lemp Mansion." www.yourghostories.com/
real-ghost-story.php?story=75.

INTERVIEWS

Espanjer, Michael. Personal Interview. March 12, 2005.

Marks, Lisa. Personal Interview. April 3, 2010.

Pointer, Patti. Personal Interview. April 2, 2010.

Riley, Brian. Personal Interview. November 16, 2010.

Smollens, Shirley. Personal Interview. July 19, 2009.

TELEVISION PROGRAM

Ghostlab. "Nottoway Plantation and Metro Club." The Discovery Channel. November
5, 2009.

Index